HIDE & SEEK
The Irish Priest in the Vatican
Who Defied the Nazi Command

STEPHEN WALKER

LYONS PRESS
Guilford, Connecticut
An imprint of Globe Pequot Press

Published by arrangement with HarperCollins Publishers LTD

All photographs courtesy of the following: page 1: O'Flaherty family archive except middle © Irish Jesuit Archives; page 2: © Keystone/Getty Images; page 3: O'Flaherty family archive; page 4: top © Keystone/Getty Images, middle © The National Archives UK, bottom left © Keystone/Getty Images, bottom right © Time Life Pictures/Getty Images; page 5: O'Flaherty family archive except bottom © Popperfoto/Getty Images; page 6: top left © The National Archives UK, top right © Hulton-Deutsch Collection/CORBIS, middle © R. Gates/Hulton Archive/Getty Images, bottom O'Flaherty family archive; page 7: top © George Silk/Time Life Pictures/Getty Images, bottom left © The National Archives UK, bottom right © Keystone/Getty Images; page 8: O'Flaherty family archive except top © Action Press/Rex Features.

Lyons Press is an imprint of Globe Pequot Press.

Text design: Sheryl P. Kober
Layout artist: Sue Murray
Project editor: Kristen Mellitt

Library of Congress Cataloging-in-Publication Data is available on file.

ISBN 978-0-7627-8039-6

Printed in the United States of America

10 9 8 7 6 5 4 3 2 1

In memory of my mother
Josephine Walker 1923–2011

TABLE OF CONTENTS

Prologue

AUGUST 14, 1977
AT THE MILITARY HOSPITAL EVERYTHING WAS QUIET. IN THE small hours those tasked with watching the patients had little to do. During the day the building was a different place. Then the corridors and rooms that looked out toward the Coliseum were alive with the sound of people. At night the atmosphere seemed almost reverential, and for those watching the clock until the sun rose, the pace of life was slow.

It was a holiday week in August. From the windows of the complex on the Caelian Hill, night staff could look down on the lights of Rome. The city beneath was asleep, unaware of the drama that was about to unfold.

After midnight, in a room on the third floor, Anneliese, a blonde-haired woman, was spending time with her elderly husband, who was being treated for cancer. The pair were about to embark on the most dramatic hours of their married lives.

For a few moments they stood by the open window. Outside, apart from the sound of an occasional passing car, the night was still. Then the plan began in earnest. Carefully Anneliese maneuvered her frail husband, dressed in his best suit, toward the doorway. He was skeletal, weighing not much more than one hundred pounds.

Gently she shuffled him across the floor, holding his arm as they moved toward the landing. Weeks of planning were now at risk as she made her way down to the ground floor. Holding him close, Anneliese helped her husband negotiate each step. On the ground floor the guard was not around, so they quickly made their way outside and to a rental car that had been parked close to the building. She told him to get into the back of the car and lie down, and when he was inside she covered him with a blanket.

She put her bags in the car alongside some fresh flowers, turned on the car stereo, lit a cigarette, and drove slowly to the main gate. With her passenger well hidden, she approached the security barrier, the sounds of the radio filling the air. Her early-morning departure did little to raise suspicions. The staff were used to seeing her coming and going at all hours, and she had built up a friendly rapport with most of the hospital workers. She had planned everything and as usual had left a bottle of good German wine for one of the guards. She had also told the gate staff what time she would be leaving. If she could make her visit seem normal, she knew her plan had a good chance of succeeding.

In her husband's empty bed a pillow had been placed strategically to fool anyone who might casually glance through the window of his room. A note handwritten in Italian, saying "Please do not disturb me before 10 a.m.," was stuck on his door. The instruction was intended to ward off inquiring nurses and buy much-needed escape time. A friendly guard approached the car, as he often did when he saw Frau Kappler. He stopped to practice his German, smiled, and began talking. Another soldier, keen to while away the boredom of night duty, sauntered over for a chat.

On any other night the visitor would have relished the conversation. Tonight was different. Even though she was in a hurry and nervous, she knew she had to remain calm. However, the guards were in no hurry to wave her on. Had they spotted something? Would they suddenly decide to search the car? Had someone seen her husband escape and tipped them off?

Anneliese desperately wanted to leave quickly and told the guards she was in a hurry because she needed to get some medicine. At last the barrier was opened. She drove away from the hospital along Via Druso and past the ruins of the ancient baths. Rome was quiet. She stopped briefly and asked her husband if he was all right. "Yes, everything is fine," came the muffled reply. There was little traffic and she quickly made for the Grand Hotel. There she met her son. She led him to the back of the car, and for the first time in his life, he saw his stepfather as a free man.

Hours later, when Rome awoke, the city's most notorious prisoner was declared missing. By then Herbert Kappler had been driven out of the country by car. His driver was his German wife, Anneliese, who had married him in prison and had now helped him to freedom. By mid-morning the most wanted man in Italy was heading for a safe house in West Germany. After over thirty years in custody, the former Nazi officer was free. Defying life imprisonment for war crimes, he had masterminded a great escape, from the very city he had terrorized as a Gestapo chief some three decades earlier. The hunter was now the hunted.

CHAPTER I

Appointment to Kill

"I don't want to see him alive again."
—HERBERT KAPPLER PLOTS TO KILL HUGH O'FLAHERTY

ROME, 1944

STANDING ALONE, SIX FEET TWO INCHES TALL, WEIGHING JUST OVER two hundred pounds, and dressed in his distinctive black and red clerical vestments—most other priests wore only black—Monsignor Hugh O'Flaherty was easy to spot. Every day the bespectacled Irishman stood and surveyed the evening scene as Romans went about their daily business. Around him, people made their way to and from work. Some chatted in a leisurely fashion with friends; others, maybe late for appointments, hurried along looking anxious. From his vantage point on the top step that led to St. Peter's Basilica, the monsignor could look out over St. Peter's Square. When the weather was good, it was a perfect place to watch the day end.

Cradling his breviary, O'Flaherty would read and occasionally look up and watch as the Vatican buzzed with life. His daily devotion was an act of faith, but it was also a display of defiance. And across the piazza his behavior was being watched carefully. Beyond the white line that had been painted around the cobbled square

1

to mark the Holy See's neutral territory, Rome's rulers looked on. Through field binoculars, armed German paratroopers studied the priest. They were tasked to watch his every move. Each day the routine continued. O'Flaherty stood and looked out at his observers, who in turn carefully noted all his movements.

This was the monsignor's territory. A Vatican veteran, O'Flaherty had first graced Rome's streets in 1922 and was a well-known figure throughout the city. He was hundreds of miles from his birthplace, but he felt completely at home. St. Peter's Square was his open-air office. Nuns and priests would pass by and say a quick hello; others would pause and stop for a longer chat. To the casual observer these meetings and encounters seemed normal and harmless. In reality they were part of O'Flaherty's operation to gather information and pass messages and money on to those harboring Allied servicemen.

The vantage point was well chosen. From the steps O'Flaherty could see and be seen. He could keep a close eye on German soldiers at the Vatican's boundary, by Bernini's magnificent colonnade. The ever-present Swiss Guards, the Vatican's loyal protectors, could quickly intervene if trouble arose. From his nearby study window, Pope Pius XII could also look down and see the Irishman. It was a perfect spot.

Home to emperors, kings, and cardinals, Rome had witnessed over two thousand years of history. In 1944 it was a dangerous place. The final years of the Second World War were dark days of violence, fear, and hunger. Rome was a racial and political mix: a world of German Nazis, Italian Fascists and Resistance fighters, spies, diplomats, Catholics, and Jews. Into this arena arrived British, American, and French servicemen, escapees from Italian prisoner-of-war camps. The Allied landings in the south of

the country had caused Italians there to surrender uncondition-
ally, and many POWs were simply walking out of the unguarded
camps and making their way through the countryside. It was the
biggest mass escape in history, but without maps or guidance many
didn't know where to go. Encouraged by BBC radio, some set out
for the Vatican on the basis that it was free from Nazi interference. Many were caught quickly by the Germans, rounded up, and
transported to prison camps in Germany. Those who made it to
Rome were hoping to be offered shelter by a secret underground
unit headed by Monsignor O'Flaherty. Even though the Germans
controlled the city, uncovering the Allied escape organization was
proving very difficult for them because the Vatican was beyond
their control. By the spring of 1944 the struggle was becoming
increasingly personal.

One March morning a dark car pulled up at the entrance to St.
Peter's Square and from it emerged three men. Two plain-clothed
members of the Gestapo accompanied a suave, black-booted figure in his late thirties. With blue eyes, fair hair, and a three-inch
dueling scar on his cheek, Obersturmbannführer Herbert Kappler
was the face of the Nazis in Rome. The lieutenant colonel had a
reputation for ruthlessness, and his word was not to be challenged
on the city's streets. An experienced SS officer, he had worked his
way through the ranks after showing an early talent for secret police
work. Handpicked to lead the Gestapo in Rome, Kappler was articulate, well-spoken, and confident. He displayed his loyalty like a
badge of honor, wearing on one finger a steel ring decorated with
the Death's Head and swastikas and inscribed "To Herbert from
his Himmler." In Rome Kappler was head of the Sicherheitsdienst,
or SD, the security service of the SS and the Nazi Party. The SD
was originally set up by Reinhard Heydrich, and by 1944 it had

effectively been merged with the state police and was universally known as the Gestapo.

On this particular morning Kappler hadn't come to check on his subordinates, but had journeyed to the Vatican's boundary to cast an eye over his opponent and make final preparations for a kidnapping. The target was Monsignor O'Flaherty.

The forty-six-year-old priest had become the organizer of the Allied escape operation in Rome by chance rather than by design. In the summer of 1943 a British soldier arrived at the Vatican seeking sanctuary, and Hugh O'Flaherty helped him find refuge in one of the many Vatican buildings, in which he would stay for the duration of the Nazi occupation. It was the start of an initiative that would eventually offer hundreds of men and women shelter and escape from occupied Italy.

A few weeks later three more British soldiers arrived, and they too were given accommodation. By September the original trickle of escapees had turned into a flood. That autumn, St. Peter's Square became the main destination for Allied servicemen seeking safe accommodation in Rome, and their contact there was Hugh O'Flaherty.

It was an open secret—what was happening inside the Vatican—and soon intelligence reports landed on Kappler's desk. The Gestapo chief knew what O'Flaherty's role was, and he suspected that the priest was using rooms in the Vatican and other buildings across Rome to hide the escapees. He gave orders that O'Flaherty be followed and that suspected supporters of what came to be known as the Rome Escape Line be kept under surveillance. Raids were routinely carried out on the homes of Italians sympathetic to the Allies, in the hope of catching escaped soldiers, but Kappler was having little success.

By early 1944 Herbert Kappler and Hugh O'Flaherty were locked in a dangerous game of hide and seek. And the monsignor was winning the battle. Kappler had no doubt that the Irishman was at the center of the escape organization, but he needed to catch him red-handed. However, in addition to plotting to stop the monsignor's activities, he had plenty of other work to do. Kappler and his team spent a great deal of time tracking the movements of members of the Resistance, and the Gestapo were also heavily involved in the interrogation of Rome's Jews and their deportation to concentration camps.

Kappler could claim to his superiors that he was enforcing Nazi rule in Rome and keeping anti-fascist dissent at bay, but he knew he was making little progress with the Allied escape operation. He concluded that the only way to crush the organization was to remove the monsignor, and that meant killing him. Without O'Flaherty he was sure the entire network would crumble.

The daring and controversial move to seize the priest was fraught with difficulties, both political and practical. It would bring Kappler into conflict with the Catholic Church. By March 1944 sixty-eight-year-old Eugenio Pacelli had just completed his fifth year as Pope Pius XII. He was worried about the impact of the war on the Church and the Vatican State. For much of the conflict, the fighting across Europe had seemed distant. However, the arrival of Allied troops in Sicily in July of the previous year, and the air attacks on Rome some months before that, had brought the war to his doorstep.

The German occupation of Rome had created a dilemma for the Pope. Desperate to maintain the independence of the two-thousand-year-old Catholic Church, he was fearful that the Nazis would invade the Vatican itself and prevent its functioning. Within days of capturing Rome, Adolf Hitler had promised that he would respect the Pope's sovereignty and protect the Vatican from the fighting. But Pius XII knew Hitler's guarantee was worthless, because of his other broken promises and because the very presence of German troops in Rome led Allied bombers to regard the Eternal City as a target. The Pope was trying to keep both sides happy in the hope that the Church and its property would survive unscathed. He gained some reassurance from the fact that under international law the Vatican City and all its land and property constituted a neutral state that the Germans were forbidden to enter.

For Kappler this caused some logistical problems, for the kidnapping of O'Flaherty would have to be cleverly orchestrated to take place away from Church property. But the Gestapo commander had a plan. It was crude, but he thought it could work. Two plain-clothed SS men would attend early mass, and afterwards, as the crowds dispersed, they would simply manhandle the monsignor into German territory. As he squinted across St. Peter's Square at O'Flaherty that sunny March morning, Kappler told the two men, "Seize him, hustle him down the steps, and across the line. When you get him into a side street, free him for a moment. I don't want to see him alive again and we certainly don't want any formal trials. He will have been shot while escaping. Understood?" The instructions seemed straightforward enough.

Kappler then got into his car and was driven out of the square, hoping that he had looked at Hugh O'Flaherty for the last time. That night, however, just hours before the kidnapping was about to occur, the plan began to unravel. On this evening, as he often did, the monsignor was working in his office. Ironically, O'Flaherty lived and worked in the Collegium Teutonicum, the German College, as an official of the Holy Office. Although this building was technically apart from the Vatican, it had some protection under international law. Despite its name, the German College was probably the safest place in Rome from which to run an Allied escape operation, as it stood very near the walls of the Vatican and a few hundred yards from the British legation. Church scholars studied at the college, which was under the stewardship of a German rector who was helped by a group of nuns. The place had an international feel to it, and O'Flaherty's neighbors included a German historian and several Hungarian scholars.

When he first arrived in Rome, O'Flaherty became a student at the Propaganda College (so named because it would spread, or propagate, Catholicism), where he became vice rector. He was ordained in 1925 and obtained doctorates in Divinity, Canon Law, and Philosophy. While still in his mid-thirties he was promoted to monsignor. This title, bestowed on a number of priests by the Pope, indicated how the upper echelons of the Church viewed the Irishman's potential.

In the German College, where O'Flaherty would spend most of his career, the accommodations were basic but comfortable. His room had a wardrobe, a few chairs, bookshelves, and a desk always crammed with papers, with his prized typewriter beside them. Nearby stood his golf clubs. A curtain divided off a part of the room, and behind it were a single bed and a washbasin. A radio kept the monsignor in touch with world events.

That evening, as O'Flaherty worked at his desk, there was a knock on the door. Seconds later, in came John May. Of medium build, with bushy eyebrows and a shock of dark hair, he worked as a butler for Sir D'Arcy Osborne, the British minister to the Holy See. May was O'Flaherty's "eyes and ears," a fixer who had contacts throughout the city and an uncanny ability to find supplies officially deemed unobtainable. May's success at sourcing rare items in wartime Rome was legendary, and O'Flaherty once declared that he was a "genius," the "most magnificent scrounger I have ever come across."

When May called on O'Flaherty, he looked every inch the English manservant, dressed formally in a white shirt, gray tie, black jacket, and dark, striped trousers. In his broad cockney accent May came straight to the point, telling the monsignor what he had just discovered from a contact who had access to Kappler's plans. Having revealed details of the kidnapping operation, he insisted that the monsignor should avoid the next morning's early mass and disappear from view for a few days. O'Flaherty, who had been a boxer in his younger days, dismissed his visitor's concern and responded characteristically: "So long as they don't use guns I can tackle any two or three of them with ease. Though a scrap would be a bit undignified on the very steps of St. Peter's itself, would it not?"

The next day May arrived at mass early, keen to make sure the kidnapping attempt was foiled. As expected, two SS men sat in the congregation and tried to blend in, unaware that their hosts had prepared a welcome for them. Even though the would-be kidnappers were dressed in plain clothes, they stood out from other churchgoers. Throughout mass May kept his eyes on them at all times. When the service ended, the worshippers rose and slowly made their way toward the exits. As the crowd moved toward the daylight that streamed in from the square, several Vatican gendarmes suddenly appeared at the shoulders of the SS men. Outnumbered, the unwelcome visitors were then ushered outside into the morning air, past their intended victim, who was standing close to the door. The monsignor simply watched as the two men were bundled into a side street and disappeared from view.

It was over. O'Flaherty had outfoxed his rival.

Soon afterwards Kappler was informed that the kidnapping had not succeeded. For a man so used to getting things his own way, the failure to remove O'Flaherty from the scene was a rare setback. Kappler controlled the city from the former offices of the German embassy's cultural section. Number 20 Via Tasso housed the Gestapo headquarters as well as a prison and interrogation center, and all over Rome the address spelled police brutality and torture. Here partisans, Jews, communists, gypsies, and those who harbored Allied soldiers were interrogated and physically abused. Few came out of Via Tasso unscathed. The battle against the escape organization would continue, and Kappler knew he would need to adopt new tactics.

CHAPTER 2

Destination Italy

"Catholicity makes us pure-minded, charitable, truthful, and generous."

—HUGH O'FLAHERTY

SEPTEMBER 1943

IN THE FOUR YEARS DURING WHICH HERBERT KAPPLER HAD LIVED in Rome, he had come to love the city. He felt at home, so comfortable in fact that he encouraged his parents to move there from Germany. Well-read and politically literate, he knew much about his hosts, having studied Italian history. But he was a loner, with few friends, and was trapped in an unhappy marriage. Hoping to divorce his wife, he meanwhile embarked on a series of extramarital affairs. During his time in Rome he would have a string of mistresses, among them a Dutch woman who worked alongside him as an intelligence agent.

Outside work Kappler's interests included growing roses, walking his dogs, and photography. He also enjoyed good food and had a penchant for collecting Etruscan vases. He loved to spend time with his adopted son Wolfgang, who was a product of the Lebensborn program, a Nazi social experiment where children were procreated by Germans deemed to be of pure Aryan stock. The project had the blessing of Reichsführer-SS Heinrich Himmler, who encouraged his officers to have children with true Aryan women.

Born into a middle-class family in Stuttgart in September 1907, as a young man Kappler showed little interest in a career in the police or the military. After secondary school he wanted to learn a trade, so he studied to be an electrician and obtained jobs with various firms. By his mid-twenties he had decided that his future lay elsewhere. In the early 1930s Germany was undergoing enormous social and political change. The Nazi Party was on the rise, and Kappler was becoming increasingly attracted to its ideals.

In August 1931 he joined the Sturmabteilung, or SA, a paramilitary group that had a key role in the Nazi Party and played an important part in Hitler's rise to power in the 1920s and 1930s. However, when Hitler seized control of Germany in January 1933, banning political opposition and turning the country into a one-party state, the Schutzstaffel, or SS, came to prominence and would be placed under the control of Heinrich Himmler. SS members generally came from middle-class backgrounds whereas the SA had a more working-class membership. In December 1932 Herbert Kappler made the move to the SS.

As the world around Kappler was changing, so too was his personal life. In September 1934 he married twenty-seven-year-old Leonore Janns, a native of Heilbronn, and they took an apartment in Stuttgart.

With German rearmament in full swing, Kappler was called up to complete military training three times between the summer of 1935 and the autumn of 1936. By now he had secured his first promotion, to SS-Scharführer (sergeant), and worked in Stuttgart's main Gestapo office. His potential was spotted by his superiors, among them Reinhard Heydrich, who, as head of the Gestapo from April 1934, was already a key figure in the Nazi regime. This connection in particular would help Kappler later in his career.

Another promotion followed for the ambitious Kappler, and as an SS-Oberscharführer (staff sergeant), he was later selected to attend the Sicherheitspolizei, or Security Police, leadership school in Berlin, becoming the first non-Prussian to graduate from the institution. Now he was a Criminal Commissioner and clearly destined for higher things. He was fast-tracked, and shortly before the Second World War broke out, he was posted to Innsbruck, which, after the Anschluss (the annexation of Austria), was within Hitler's Reich. Kappler's work in Austria caught the attention of senior military figures in Berlin, and he had soon established a reputation as a hard-working, loyal Nazi who acted swiftly against opponents. Not surprisingly, his stay in Austria was brief.

In the autumn of 1939, as Britain and France went to war with Germany, Kappler's travels continued and he found himself in Rome, working as a police attaché at the German embassy. He had been selected to join a new wave of staff who would work out of German diplomatic missions. Kappler replaced Dr. Theodor Helmerking, whose time in Rome had been regarded by senior figures in German intelligence as disappointing because he was not interested in the work. By contrast, Kappler was viewed as both ambitious and clever, and his superiors in Berlin were convinced his arrival in Rome would mark a noticeable change. His job was to advise the German ambassador to Italy, work with the local Fascist police force, and organize intelligence and espionage operations in the city.

Across the city, the man who would become Kappler's wartime adversary was also settling into a new job. Hugh O'Flaherty had been away from Rome for a few years, posted to Haiti and Czechoslovakia, but by 1938 he was once again working in the Vatican. His title was Scrittore, or Writer, in the Holy Office, his task being to examine the Church's teachings and important doctrinal matters. He was delighted with his new role.

O'Flaherty's journey to Rome had begun in the rugged countryside of rural Ireland. Born in Cork in February 1898, he spent the early years of his life in Killarney, in County Kerry, where his father was a policeman with the Royal Irish Constabulary. The eldest of four children, Hugh, like his brothers, Jim and Neil, went to the town's Monastery School, which was run by the Presentation Brothers, a traditional Catholic body with the twin values of faith and discipline at its core.

The school's religious ethos was to have a lasting and life-changing effect on the young Hugh. From an early age he made no secret of his wish to become a priest. However, his path to taking holy orders was not a straightforward one. At the young age of fifteen, he secured a junior teaching post and taught for three years. Originally Hugh had thought the teaching profession would satisfy him, but he clearly wanted to do something else with his life. In his heart he always knew he wanted to be a priest, and so, despite the fact that he was older than most other applicants, he applied to Mungret College.

The former agricultural school enjoyed an idyllic setting, on farmland surrounded by woods south of the River Shannon, some three miles from the city of Limerick. Formally known as the Apostolic School of the Sacred Heart, the college was run by the Jesuit Order. There were two schools on the site: a secondary school for young boys and an apostolic boarding college for older students. O'Flaherty joined the older boys, who, once their studies were complete, were expected to travel abroad to spread God's word as missionaries. Even though Hugh had no Latin and was by now twenty, two years older than the upper age limit, he was offered a place.

In the late summer of 1918, as the Great War entered its final months, Hugh O'Flaherty stood at the grand columned entrance of Mungret College clutching his bags and books. His new home was an impressive sight. The handsome stone building housed a chapel, dormitories, and classrooms with views onto fields where cattle grazed. Within days he was out exploring the rolling countryside. Nature walks were part of college life, and every month the boys went out to enjoy the area's beauty spots.

The new entrant clearly relished his studies and soon established a reputation as a creative thinker. The young O'Flaherty wrote an award-winning essay entitled "The Best Means of Spreading Irish Culture," speaking with admiration of those who had died for the ideal of a Gaelic Ireland. He argued that there were two "beacon lights" that offered the way forward, "Catholicity and Nationality." To him it was already clear that "Catholicity makes us pure-minded, charitable, truthful, and generous."

At the same time, the growth of modern music and dance exercised the young student's mind. He proclaimed that much of it was "degenerating" and "demoralizing," and it should be banned because the dances were the "unchristian productions of African savages."

As in many Jesuit schools, the regime at Mungret was strict. Boys who stepped out of line received corporal punishment. Those found guilty of an offense were issued with a docket and told to report to a priest, who would administer the appropriate number of slaps. In this structured and morally strict environment, O'Flaherty blossomed personally and academically. He studied philosophy, ecclesiastical history, theology, and scripture and was often at the top of his class. He also became proficient in Latin.

The seminarian was also a fervent advocate of the Irish language. He maintained that it should be spoken as much as possible and argued that his fellow students should spend a few weeks of their holidays in an Irish-speaking district. The priests who taught them worked hard to promote the use of Ireland's native tongue. One teacher wrote in the college journal that the boys should study Irish "to render you immune against the worst forms of Anglicization."

Hugh and his classmates were also encouraged to discuss current affairs, and O'Flaherty enjoyed the college's debates. On one occasion, in the packed sports hall in front of teachers and students, Hugh's team was assigned to speak for a motion that called for the prohibition of alcohol. O'Flaherty's arguments helped to win the debate.

The trainee priest had some knowledge of abstinence. He was a teetotaller, having made a pledge to refrain from drinking or smoking when his brother Jim had fallen seriously ill with pneumonia. Should his brother regain his health, he vowed, he would never drink or smoke. Jim recovered and Hugh kept his promise.

O'Flaherty's rhetorical skills were not confined to the discussion of social issues. In another debate he argued against the motion "The USA stands for the world's peace." The seminarian declared, "The American government is run by Freemasons and wealthy speculators and it is to their interest to have the European countries at war." It was an interesting argument for a man who, some twenty-five years later during the Second World War, would find himself saving the lives of American servicemen.

Away from studying and debating, Mungret set great store by sport. The boys were encouraged to play cricket, rugby, and soccer, but emphasis was placed on Gaelic sports too. However, it was golf that became O'Flaherty's passion, and he would enjoy it for the rest of his life.

Since the college's central purpose was to prepare young men for a life working overseas as priests, O'Flaherty and his friends spent much time wondering where in the world they would be sent. The much-admired map in the college's study room was heavily smudged with the fingerprints of students speculating about their future. But matters closer to home were also occupying the thoughts of many in the dormitories of Mungret. Ireland was in turmoil as Britain's rule was being challenged in a guerrilla war waged by the Irish Republican Army. As violence raged across the country, it became impossible for the college authorities to shield their charges from the events of the outside world.

One morning in December 1920, with the Christmas holidays about to begin, the dining hall was filled with an air of happiness. However, within minutes all that would change. On cue, as he did every day, a college prefect who was circling the tables began to hand out the morning post. He passed O'Flaherty and gave him a letter. The mature student paused, opened the envelope, read the note inside, and then shared the dreadful news. "Chris Lucy has been shot," he told his friends. Lucy, a former Mungret boy, had joined the 1st Battalion of the IRA in County Cork and had been killed some weeks earlier. The boys listened in silence. Then their shock turned to anger.

This was the fourth time in recent months that they had heard how one of their friends had been killed by British forces. Raised teenage voices now echoed across the refectory. "One day we will sink the whole British Navy," one voice yelled defiantly. It was Hugh O'Flaherty who made this vow, for his political views were by now well formed.

Not long before he left Mungret, the young O'Flaherty's dislike of Ireland's rulers was reinforced by an encounter with them first hand. In Limerick in March 1921, British soldiers shot dead the city's mayor and former mayor. O'Flaherty and two classmates, Martin and Leo, visited the men's grieving families to pay their condolences. The three of them left the college grounds and walked into Limerick, unaware that every visit to the homes of the dead men was being monitored by British troops. To the watching eyes the three young seminarians were seen as IRA sympathizers. After they had met the families, O'Flaherty and his two friends set off for Mungret. As they passed the police barracks in William Street, they were rapidly surrounded by members of the "Black and Tans," a British unit of temporary police constables, so called because of the colors of their fatigues. Constantly on the lookout for IRA units, they had a fearsome reputation and had been responsible for the deaths of hundreds of civilians. "We will take a look at you in the Barracks," one of the constables told the students, who were then arrested and ordered inside the building.

The three young men insisted that they were students and explained that their visit had been simply pastoral. Convinced they were being misled, the "Tans" continued their questioning. But luck was on the side of the students, because as they were being taken into the barracks a passerby spotted that they were from Mungret. The dean of the college was alerted, he contacted the police station to substantiate his students' story, and they were released. For the young O'Flaherty the episode was another reminder of why he opposed British rule in Ireland. In the college journal he wrote of the affair, in the understated manner that would become his trademark during his days in Rome. He recorded that some boys had "gone off to Limerick for the day" and added coyly that "some had exciting experiences, arrests, escapes, etc." As 1921 drew to a close and Ireland faced an uncertain future, Hugh O'Flaherty's life became a little clearer. The young student heard that he was to be sent to Rome to continue his theological studies.

CHAPTER 3

Rome Is Home

"I don't think there is anything to choose between Britain and Germany."

—HUGH O'FLAHERTY

ON A FAIRWAY AT ROME GOLF CLUB, THE JAPANESE AMBASSADOR could only watch with amazement and a little envy as his opponent's ball arced high and long and then landed close to the green. The tee-off was textbook. It was perfect, a wonderful drive that set up the second shot beautifully. It was 1928 and this was the diplomat's farewell game, a last chance to enjoy eighteen holes in the company of friends before returning to Tokyo. And it was not going according to plan. He was playing a man who had a lifetime of practice that had begun on the greens of Killarney. It was a rather one-sided contest. The monsignor was in fine form and clearly relishing the day a little more than his playing partner.

At the picturesque club, sited on grassland outside Rome, Hugh O'Flaherty's golfing skills were often the topic of conversation. To some the gifted player seemed unconventional. He didn't dress like a golfer, sometimes wearing gray pants and a favorite orange sweater, and his unusual grip was frequently the butt of jokes. "Why don't you hold the club like any other human being?"

one player teased him, remarking that the monsignor seemed to grip the golf club rather like the stick used in hurling, a sport favored by O'Flaherty's countrymen.

The priest was very capable of taking the banter and shot back a detailed reply. "For the correct grip in hurling, the left hand is held below the right. I am holding my golf club just the opposite, my right hand is below the left," he explained with a smile to all those present.

The technicalities were probably lost on his opponents, but his ability to play and win the game wasn't. His continued success on the greens meant that he had to concede a couple of shots to less able players. Par for the course was seventy-one, and O'Flaherty regularly came close to that.

His fellow players also wondered how a busy priest weighed down with church duties had time to play golf. For O'Flaherty it was an opportunity to relax and forget the cares and worries of the job. He told a friend that there was "nothing like golf for knocking all the troubles of this poor world out of your mind."

Even though he loved the game, there were times when the distance he had to travel and the price of playing seemed too high. In a letter home he wrote, "The links are far from the city and, besides, to be a member one must know how to rob a bank and keep what is robbed." Despite his reservations about spending hours driving, chipping, and putting, there were other benefits to his favorite pastime. The club had a very influential membership and O'Flaherty began meeting many leading members of Roman society—including royalty, aristocrats, diplomats, and politicians—who would later prove useful to his escape network.

Those who regularly played the course included Count Galeazzo Ciano, who was married to Mussolini's daughter, Edda. Ciano was the Italian foreign minister, and O'Flaherty is credited with teaching him the finer points of the game. Another regular player at the club was the former king of Spain, Alfonso.

It was on the golf course that the monsignor was introduced to Sir D'Arcy Osborne. Like O'Flaherty, the British diplomat loved nothing more than taking the Italian air with his clubs on his back. The game was part of Osborne's life, so much so that he often used golfing references in his correspondence. Exasperated by the intransigence of a position taken by the powerful of the Vatican, he once wrote that trying to get them to change their mind was like "trying to sink a long putt using a live eel as a putter."

With a direct line to the Papacy, Osborne was one of the most influential people in Rome. He was the image of the English gentleman: well mannered, charming, and courteous. A bachelor, he was tall and slim and always immaculately dressed. As a career diplomat he was highly regarded in London, and as a cousin of the Duke of Leeds, he was well connected and counted the Duke and Duchess of York as friends.

Osborne had a deep affection for Italy, a country he had first visited at the turn of the century, when he had been won over by the people and the scenery. He joined the diplomatic service, and after postings in Washington, Lisbon, and The Hague, he became Britain's minister to the Holy See in 1936. He spoke Italian and French and loved art, expensive shoes, and fine wine. Like all those who occupied the position of ambassador to the Vatican, he was a Protestant, in case there was a conflict of loyalties. Given O'Flaherty's Irish nationalist background and Osborne's British establishment credentials, the pair were an unlikely match. Yet over time they became good friends and would meet both in the clubhouse and at the Vatican.

In the early weeks of the Second World War, Osborne's knowledge and diplomatic skills were much in demand. There was a fevered debate about when Italy would enter the conflict and much concern in Vatican circles over how this would affect its protected status. As Britain's representative to the Vatican, Osborne's views were sought by the leaders of the Catholic Church and he was used to test ideas and opinions.

In the spring of 1939 a new resident was holding court in the Vatican's Apostolic Palace. On March 2 Cardinal Eugenio Pacelli became Pope on his sixty-third birthday. In one of the shortest conclaves in the Church's history, he was elected by sixty-two cardinals. The first Roman-born Pope in over two hundred years, Pacelli took the name of Pius XII, in honor of his predecessor, Pius XI.

The new Pontiff had had little time to settle into office when, on March 15, the Germans entered Prague. Over the next few months papal envoys would become involved in shuttle diplomacy with Mussolini, Hitler, and the Polish and French governments in a bid to avert war. The discussions did not succeed. On September 1, 1939, Hitler invaded Poland, and two days later Britain and France declared war on Germany.

In his office in Rome Kappler had begun to gather information from all over the city on both anti-fascists and undercover agents he could employ. Because he wanted to recruit informers within the Vatican, he was watching the new regime of Pius XII with particular interest. But, before he could make much progress, he was instructed to return to Germany.

Two incidents had occurred, just hours apart, that would focus attention on Hitler's leadership, events that required the skills of Herbert Kappler. These two investigations would not only enhance the police attaché's reputation but also bring him into direct contact with the Führer. When Kappler arrived in Berlin, there was only one story occupying the minds of the Nazi leadership. Days earlier, in a Munich beer hall, Hitler had acknowledged the adoring crowds as he stood in front of a swastika-draped stage. Hundreds of supporters had come to hear the Führer speak at an annual get-together for the Nazi Party's old guard. At 9:07 p.m. he finished his speech, earlier than planned, and left the building. Hitler had planned to fly back to Berlin, but poor weather made this impossible and he was taken to the railway station instead.

The decision to change his travel plans saved Hitler's life. At 9:20 p.m. a bomb, hidden in a pillar close to where he had been speaking, exploded. The ceiling and balcony collapsed, killing eight people and injuring many others.

As Hitler made his way back to Berlin, German police held in custody a thirty-six-year-old carpenter from Württemberg who had been arrested as he tried to leave the country and enter Switzerland. Georg Elser had traveled by train from Munich and had been spotted trying to cross over at the border town of Konstanz. A trade unionist and an opponent of Nazism, he had first gone to Munich a year earlier to observe the Führer deliver his annual speech at the Burgerbräukeller. Over the next twelve months the carpenter planned his attack for the following year's event at the beer hall. He became a regular diner there, and over time he built a bomb that he would eventually place in a pillar near the podium. As anticipated, on the evening of November 8, Hitler was to deliver a speech in the Burgerbräukeller, and Elser planted his device and timed it to go off at around 9:20 p.m.

Shocked at how close someone had come to killing the Führer, the Nazi high command handed the investigation over to the Gestapo. When Kappler arrived in Berlin, he was assigned to be part of the team interrogating Elser, who initially had refused to say anything. The police attaché had been in this position many times before: In Austria he had interrogated anti-Nazi dissidents and in Rome he had begun the same work. Now, as he sat opposite Elser, his main job was to break the man's silence.

Elser was bombarded with questions. How did he prepare the bomb? When did he go to Munich? But perhaps what Kappler and his Gestapo colleagues were most interesting in knowing was who had helped the carpenter. They began to track down anyone who knew Elser and had been in contact with him in recent months. Investigators caught up with Else Stephan, Elser's girlfriend, who was questioned personally by Himmler and then taken to Hitler himself. Of the latter encounter she later said, "Behind a table sat a man in a field-gray uniform. He didn't look up when one of the SS men reported: 'My Führer! This is the woman!' Good Lord, it really was Hitler. Hitler put down a folder he had been reading and looked at me. He didn't say anything. I felt most embarrassed. I wanted to salute but I just couldn't raise my arm."

Hitler looked at his visitor for a while before speaking. Then he said, "So you are Elser's woman. Well, tell me about it." Else Stephan told Hitler her story just as she had done with Himmler, who was in charge of the investigation. Eventually, after Elser was beaten, investigators secured a confession. Postcards from the Burgerbräukeller had been found in his coat, and one of the waitresses recognized him as a regular customer.

Elser was then tortured by the Gestapo, who initially found it difficult to accept that the carpenter had acted alone. Hitler himself was convinced that he had been helped by British Secret Service agents. Under questioning Elser insisted that he had carried out the operation without any help. Himmler personally took part in a number of the interrogations and on one occasion told the suspect, "I'll have you burned alive, you swine. Limb by limb quite slowly . . . do you understand?"

Kappler would maintain in an interview some years later that he had treated Elser properly during the interrogations. "I always spoke to Elser very calmly. He opened up to me without reservation. And I also had the impression that he was telling us the truth on all points—and this was corroborated when his statements were checked."

Elser made a confession that ran to hundreds of pages. He was imprisoned at the Sachsenhausen and Dachau concentration camps, remaining at the second until the final weeks of the war, when he was taken from his cell and killed. The American forces were nearby, but with the war about to end, the German high command clearly had some old scores to settle.

Back in 1939, hours after Elser's arrest, Kappler would find himself examining another "plot" to topple Hitler. This one, bizarre and complicated, did involve Britain's Secret Service, and at the highest level. The plan began one winter's morning and involved two British intelligence agents and one Dutch agent.

Before dawn Sigismund Payne Best was awake. A man in his fifties, he headed Britain's highly secretive Section Z in the Netherlands. He got up and, as he shaved, mentally reviewed what lay ahead for him over the next few hours. He was nervous. He had reservations but knew he had little choice. He kissed his wife goodbye, told her he might be late, then hurried to his office. There he glanced at the morning paper. A stop-press item about the attempt on Hitler's life in a beer hall caught his eye. It reported how the Führer had escaped but others had been killed. Best then headed to meet some colleagues, all the while wondering if the incident in

Munich he had just read about had anything to do with a group of German officers he had recently become acquainted with.

Payne Best called at a house to pick up two colleagues. Richard Stevens, a less experienced British intelligence officer likewise based in The Hague, was an agent with whom he had recently begun working. The other man was Dirk Klop, who had been seconded from the Dutch intelligence service. As the three men chatted about the day ahead, Stevens produced loaded Browning automatic pistols, which they each pocketed. Then, as storm clouds gathered, they made their way to the border with Germany.

In the cold November air they arrived at Café Backus, a restaurant near the Dutch town of Venlo, close to the border with Germany. The men were familiar with the red-brick building, which had a veranda out front and, at the back, a large garden with children's swings.

The venue for the meeting had been carefully chosen. It was in the Netherlands, but stood in a stretch of land between the German and Dutch customs posts. Best, Stevens, and Klop had come to the border to continue discussions with high-ranking Nazi officers who wanted to overthrow Hitler. In previous meetings the trio had been told that there was support for Hitler's removal and the restoration of democracy, which would lead to an Anglo-German front against the Soviet Union. In London senior military officials and politicians including the prime minister were being kept informed about the discussions. The story had one problem. It was not true. The British and Dutch intelligence officers had been duped as part of a sting organized by the German intelligence service.

Best and Stevens had been dealing with an officer named Major Schämmel, who claimed to be a member of an anti-Hitler plot. Schämmel was in fact Walter Schellenberg, a rising star in the world of German military intelligence who would later become the head of the SS foreign-intelligence section.

When the three agents arrived at the café, the scene was peaceful. A little girl was playing ball with a dog in the middle of the road; nearby, a German customs officer was watching for traffic. However, this time something seemed different. When they had been at the café before, the barrier to the German side had been closed; they now noticed that it had been raised. Best sensed danger. As they drove into the car park, their contact, Schämmel, spotted them and waved at them from the veranda. At that moment a large car came from the German side of the border and drew up behind the visitors. Within seconds shots were fired in the air, and the two Britons, Dirk Klop, and their driver were surrounded by German soldiers and ordered to surrender.

Stevens turned to his colleague and said simply, "Our number is up, Best." They would be the last words the pair would exchange for five years.

Within hours they were in Berlin, and Herbert Kappler had more interviews to conduct. The so-called Venlo incident was a coup for German military intelligence and a source of embarrassment for the British government. The Germans not only had captured senior British intelligence figures but their removal from clandestine activities was also a crucial blow to British espionage efforts across Europe. Kappler remained in Berlin to help in the interrogation of Best and Stevens. The pair were questioned at length and were later imprisoned at Sachsenhausen and Dachau, where Best reportedly came into contact with Hitler's would-be assassin Georg Elser.

The Elser affair kept the issue of Hitler's leadership in the headlines. Stories about plots and coups against the Nazi leader continued to surface. When Kappler returned to Rome to resume his duties as police attaché there, Hitler's future was a subject that was dominating the chatter among the city's diplomatic circles.

In January 1940 Sir D'Arcy Osborne was called to meet Pope Pius for a private audience. The pair discussed the war and considered a series of scenarios. The Pope claimed he knew the names of German generals who had said that Hitler was planning an offensive through the Netherlands in the weeks ahead. He said this need not happen if the generals could be guaranteed a peace deal by the Allies that would see Hitler deposed, and in return Poland and Czechoslovakia would be free of German rule. The Pope was nervous and asked Osborne to keep the contents of the discussion secret, telling him, "If anything should become known, the lives of the unnamed German generals would be forfeit."

Osborne refused the Holy Father's request and reported the contents of the encounter to officials in London. In his official report the minister to the Holy See wrote that he thought the discussions had been vague and reminded him of the Venlo incident. His words carried extra weight because the arrest of the three intelligence officers at Venlo was still an embarrassment to many in London.

The following month Osborne again met with the Pope, who told him that, according to information he had been given by prominent German generals, Hitler was planning to invade Belgium. As he had done before, the Pope talked about a potential uprising against the Führer in Germany. He suggested that there could be a civil war in Germany and that a new anti-Hitler government might have to start as a military dictatorship. Again the Pope wanted to know what—if the Führer was overthrown and a new regime put in place—would be the basis of negotiations with the Allies.

The Pope insisted that these details be kept to a small number of people. He agreed, however, that Osborne could mention them in a letter to Lord Halifax, the foreign secretary, in the hope that this would have a limited readership. The Pope's obsession with secrecy was understandable. Everyone was being watched. Every visitor was recorded, every meeting noted. Osborne's daily habits were routinely logged and the details were stored at the headquarters of the Italian secret police. The Vatican was also in the sights of the German police attaché, who was now recruiting informers across the city to spy on the occupants of the Holy See. Although Italy had yet to officially declare hostilities against the Allies, in Rome the intelligence war was well underway. Caught up in this battle, the Pope knew that a diplomatic process had to be maintained, and at the same time he was determined that nothing threaten the status of the Catholic Church. To protect the Church's interests, he kept lines of communication open with both the Allies and the Germans.

Under the Lateran Treaty of 1929, the Vatican was guaranteed independence. This accord between the Holy See and the Italian state established diplomatic conventions as well as agreements on physical access. Italy recognized the 108-acre site, which included the Vatican and St. Peter's, as an independent sovereign state. The agreement also covered 50 acres outside the Vatican walls and gave protected status to a number of extraterritorial buildings, including three basilicas and Castel Gandolfo, the Pope's country retreat. The accord made the Vatican City the smallest state in the world. In response the Holy See recognized Rome as the capital of the Italian state and pledged to remain neutral in international conflicts. The Pope was not allowed to interfere in Italian politics. While he felt entitled to speak out in general terms about the war, he was worried that his private discussions with Sir D'Arcy Osborne would become public and his role could be misinterpreted.

By the early summer of 1940, some of the Pope's predictions had come true, and although the overthrow of Hitler by his generals did not happen as expected, the Germans had arrived in the Low Countries that May. A month later, despite a plea from Britain's prime minister, Winston Churchill, Benito Mussolini declared war on the Allies. The move would have an immediate personal effect on Sir D'Arcy Osborne. Could he continue to stay in Rome as a British representative while Italy was now at war with Britain? The Vatican solved the predicament and informed the Italian government that it could offer lodgings for diplomats within the Vatican City. As a neutral state, the Vatican could allow ambassadors and other diplomats to reside on its territory.

Back in London, Osborne's bosses were worried that, although a move into the Vatican would enhance his personal safety, it might make communication between London and Rome more difficult. They offered him the use of a secret radio transmitter. Aware of the dangers of being caught and how such activity could compromise his new hosts, he declined the offer. Three days after Mussolini's declaration of war, Osborne took down the British coat of arms at his office, gathered up his belongings and furniture, and moved to a pilgrims' hostel on the south side of St. Peter's, inside the Vatican. He was to be housed temporarily in an annex of the Santa Marta Hospice known as the Palazzina. There he was given four rooms. He took with him his typist, Miss Tindall; his butler, John May; and his cairn terrier, Jeremy. Osborne was now in a new environment, a tiny enclave shut off from the immediate dangers of war, a place where he clearly felt safe.

His temporary home was eventually transformed, and at vast expense, a new kitchen and bathroom were installed. Osborne made himself comfortable, putting up paintings, portraits of the royal family, and maps of western Europe to plot the progress of the war. For the next four years this would be the headquarters of the British Vatican envoy. Sir D'Arcy Osborne and Hugh O'Flaherty were now neighbors. Theirs was a relationship that would be crucial to the operation of the Allied Escape Line.

Osborne's new address placed him high on the watch list of the Italian secret police. They put him under surveillance, wanting to know if he was spying for British intelligence or passing on messages to anti-fascists in Italy. The British envoy knew he was being watched; he wrote at the time: "I believe that daily reports are sent out on our doings. They must be damned dull reading."

As it did for Osborne, the war would have a profound effect on O'Flaherty's daily life. While hostilities continued across Europe, the monsignor's official job in the Holy Office started to change. By 1941 tens of thousands of Allied servicemen were being held in prisoner of war camps across Italy. The Vatican believed it was important that the POWs' welfare was routinely checked to ensure they were being held in accordance with international conventions. Pope Pius wanted two of his officials to visit the camps regularly. He appointed Monsignor Borgoncini Duca as his Papal Nuncio, and needing an English speaker to communicate with British prisoners, he asked Monsignor O'Flaherty to act as Duca's secretary and interpreter. The Pope's decision changed O'Flaherty's life.

Despite his ingrained hostility toward the British, the monsignor would develop empathy for the prisoners and would become more sympathetic to the Allied cause.

Duca and O'Flaherty began to travel the country together, but they took very different approaches to the job. Duca was more relaxed and seemed unhurried; when he traveled by car he usually managed to see only one prison camp a day. O'Flaherty used his time differently. He accompanied the Papal Nuncio to the camps, but in the intervals between visits he would return to Rome on the overnight train. Once back in the capital he would pass on messages from prisoners to Vatican Radio to ensure that their relatives knew they were safe. The monsignor also speeded up the delivery of Red Cross parcels and clothing and helped in the collection of thousands of books for the prisoners.

O'Flaherty's work clearly improved the morale of the POWs, but he did more than supply them with creature comforts. He became their champion—a significant move for a man who in his youth had little good to say about those who wore the uniform of the British Army. The monsignor began to lodge complaints about the way the men were being treated, and his protestations led to the removal of the commanders at the hospitals at Modena and Piacenza. He also visited South African and Australian prisoners at a camp near Brindisi. There he distributed musical instruments including mandolins and guitars. Much to the annoyance of the prison's management, the trip boosted the morale of the inmates and lowered that of their captors.

By now the monsignor was seen by the Italian military's high command as a troublemaker. Pressure was exerted on the Vatican to remove him; eventually O'Flaherty resigned his position. Officially the Italian authorities claimed that the monsignor's neutrality had been compromised. They said he had told a prisoner that the war was going well. It was a feeble excuse. Unofficially they wanted him out of the way because he was exposing the mistreatment of prisoners.

His visits to the prison camps made O'Flaherty increasingly aware that more needed to be done to help those who were suffering during the war. He may not have realized it at the time, but it seems likely that his meetings with Allied POWs helped to crystallize his thinking. When hostilities had first begun across Europe, he had viewed the conflict as an independent neutral observer, deliberately refraining from taking sides. He had always felt that both the Allies and the Germans were guilty of propaganda and he didn't know what to believe. He had even once remarked, "I don't think there is anything to choose between Britain and Germany."

Now, as the war came ever closer to the streets of Rome, Hugh O'Flaherty discovered where his loyalties lay.

CHAPTER 4

Secrets and Spies

"I take my hat off to him."

—SIR D'ARCY OSBORNE ON
BRITISH ESCAPEE ALBERT PENNY

AUTUMN 1942

GRIPPING THE HANDLEBARS OF HIS BICYCLE, ALBERT PENNY nonchalantly pedaled his way into St. Peter's Square. Dressed in workman's overalls, he blended in with the crowd and managed to evade the gaze of the normally observant Swiss Guards. As escape bids went, it was a first-class display of chutzpah. Days earlier the young British seaman had walked out of a POW camp at Viterbo, obtained some clothes, and under his own steam made his way to Rome. In the shadow of the Basilica, he confidently rode around the fountains, slipped into the gardens of the Vatican, and soon found himself outside the Santa Marta Hospice. It was an extraordinary stroke of luck.

Suddenly he was approached by Anton Call, who was most surprised to have discovered a British serviceman on the run. Call, with eight years' experience in the Vatican gendarmerie under his belt, had a vague recollection that the Vatican's special international status might help in this situation. Instead of returning the sailor to the Italian police, he contacted Sir D'Arcy Osborne, who was just yards away on the top floor of Santa Marta.

The British envoy admired Penny's courage, later declaring, "I take my hat off to him." He officially petitioned the Vatican authorities to allow the escapee to stay, arguing that this was permissible because the Vatican was a neutral state. Permission was given, and Penny lived in Osborne's apartment while his fate was decided. Eventually he was exchanged for an Italian prisoner. The episode clearly struck a chord with Osborne and his neighbor Hugh O'Flaherty. Now for the first time they had an escaped Allied serviceman to deal with.

By the end of 1942 the monsignor had ended his work as an official Red Cross visitor to the Allied POW camps, but he still wanted to help Allied servicemen. O'Flaherty and Osborne probably did not realize it then, but the Penny episode was about to be repeated on their doorstep dozens of times. The seaman had not intentionally decided to become a trailblazer, but with his daring escapade on a bicycle, he would become a forerunner for the many hundreds of servicemen who would later make a beeline for the Vatican.

The incident was not without repercussions and the biggest loser was Anton Call, the sympathetic policeman who had discovered Penny and handed him over to Sir D'Arcy Osborne rather than taking him to his superiors. The Italian authorities blamed Call for the affair. The policeman was arrested on a trumped-up charge, expelled from the Vatican, and put in prison, although he was later released and given a minor role with the carabinieri. Osborne was furious about Call's treatment and would record his thoughts privately: "It all makes me, against my will, very anti-Vatican and anti-Italian."

By the autumn of 1942, watching the activities of the Vatican had become one of Herbert Kappler's top priorities. In October the head of the Gestapo, Heinrich Himmler, paid a three-day visit to Rome. He was temporarily running the Reichssicherheitshauptamt (RSHA), the Reich Security Main Office, because its head, Reinhard Heydrich, had died in June after being mortally wounded by Czech resistance fighters. It was in this capacity that Himmler was most interested in the continued presence of foreign diplomats in the Vatican. He was convinced they were spying for their respective countries and he wanted the Vatican to expel them. It was made clear to Kappler who should be targeted.

In Himmler's sights were two diplomats in particular: the British minister to the Holy See, Sir D'Arcy Osborne, and the U.S. chargé d'affaires to the Holy See, Harold Tittmann. After the bombing of Pearl Harbor in December 1941 and the Americans' entry into the war, Tittmann was asked by his bosses in Washington to move into the Vatican. The American diplomat lived under the same terms as Osborne and, like his British counterpart, resided in the Santa Marta Hospice.

German surveillance of the Vatican took many forms. Some of it was done by simply watching and listening. Diplomats such as Osborne and Tittmann also assumed that, as well as being observed, their mail and phone conversations were monitored. Osborne began to resent it. He once complained that it was like being "a prisoner in a concentration camp."

Much of the minutiae of the targets' daily life was recorded. In the case of Osborne and O'Flaherty, details of their visitors, their lunch partners, and anyone they met on walks around the Vatican were all catalogued. Kappler had first become interested in O'Flaherty's activities when the monsignor visited Allied POW camps, and he knew the monsignor was a close friend of Osborne. At this stage O'Flaherty and Osborne had not begun to operate the Escape Line, and Kappler's suspicions about them simply revolved around suggestions that they were passing on intelligence to the Allies. Kappler desperately wanted evidence that the two men were spying, for this would put pressure on the Vatican authorities to act against them. Ambitious and keen to show his superiors in Berlin that he was effective, he knew this evidence needed to be good.

Kappler's most reliable information about the personalities in the Holy See came from a twenty-eight-year-old translator named Alexander Kurtna, who worked in the Vatican. Kurtna had first been recruited by Kappler in 1939, and the police attaché regarded him as his best source. In recent months Kappler had been able to inundate his bosses in Berlin with intelligence reports peppered with Kurtna's observations.

Kurtna's personal journey to becoming an agent in Rome was a fascinating one. He was born in 1914 in Tsarist Estonia, where his father was a civil servant and his mother a teacher. After spending time in the Estonian Army, he decided to become a Catholic priest. He converted from Russian Orthodox and attended a Polish seminary run by the Jesuits. He was then awarded a scholarship and went to Rome to study at the Pontifical Russian College, which educated priests who were to be sent on missions to the Soviet Union.

But life in the holy orders was clearly not for Kurtna. Although he was academically gifted and fluent in several languages, including Russian and German, the Jesuits decided that the young Estonian was not suited for the priesthood. He left the Pontifical Russian College and managed to get work as a translator with the Congregation for the Eastern Churches, a Vatican department that looked after priests based in eastern Europe.

Kurtna's new job required him to translate letters and reports and brought him into contact with a small circle of priests, monsignors, and Vatican officials. He became acquainted with Cardinal Eugène Tisserant and Monsignor Giovanni Montini.

Before long Kurtna took on outside work, putting his language skills to greater use. Keen to develop his contacts, he began to make connections with Rome's German community. He met Dr. Ferdinand Bock, the director of the German Historical Institute, which officially supported a series of research projects and unofficially was a cover for a German spying network. Bock and the young translator got on well, and the academic agreed to fund Kurtna to carry out research. It is clear Bock had other reasons to support a young student with good connections within the Vatican.

Kurtna's skills were now in demand. His frequent trips to Russian-occupied Estonia and his relationship with the Vatican had also been spotted by Soviet intelligence officers. The Russians were particularly interested in Kurtna's relationship with Cardinal Eugène Tisserant, the director of the Congregation for the Eastern Churches, the group that Kurtna translated for. The cardinal was believed to be trying to smuggle priests into eastern Europe to promote Catholicism. Kurtna was asked to watch events in the Vatican and report back to a Russian diplomat based at the embassy in Rome. Kurtna agreed. The former seminarian was now living an exciting life and playing a dangerous game, and it was about to become even more complicated.

As it happened, Dr. Bock was a friend of one of the most important people in Rome: Herbert Kappler. It was a friendship that would ultimately benefit Kurtna. Within days he found himself sitting opposite Kappler in his office at the German embassy. As they talked, the SS commander was impressed by the Estonian's contacts and experience, and a deal was struck. Kurtna was quickly put to use by the police attaché and tasked with preparing reports on Vatican–German relations and in particular the activities of the Catholic Church in Poland and the Baltic states. Using his contacts in the Vatican and through his role as a translator, Kurtna was able to discover much confidential information on the Church's work in German-occupied areas of eastern Europe.

Kappler's relationship with the young man was complex and problematic. He knew that Kurtna was a double agent and understood that whatever information the Estonian discovered about the Vatican would go straight back to Moscow. He also knew that Kurtna could report German activities as well, which meant Kappler could get the translator to feed his Soviet handlers misleading information. Even though the entire situation was difficult, Kappler clearly felt it was a risk worth taking. The former seminarian offered the police attaché an insight into the Vatican, which to date no one else had been able to match.

In his reports to Berlin, Kappler did not hide Kurtna's Soviet links, and while he did not identify his source, he put the Russian connection to good use, informing his boss that he had established links with the Soviet intelligence service.

Kappler's dossiers were passed to the foreign ministry of the RSHA, based in Berlin. The RSHA was one of twelve SS administrations and had been set up in 1939 to bring together the Nazi Party and other similar government groups. It had a foreign-intelligence division, Amt VI, and Reinhard Heydrich, its overall head until his assassination in June 1942, had made the gathering of such intelligence a priority.

Heydrich also had a track record of targeting the Vatican. In an instruction to staff in 1940, he had encouraged his agents in the field to exploit intelligence opportunities surrounding bishops and priests and to step up surveillance relating to theological students in Rome. In particular, Heydrich was keen to learn more about Cardinal Eugène Tisserant, one of Kurtna's main contacts. In the wake of the German advance across eastern Europe, he was sure that the French-born cardinal wanted to spread the Catholic faith to Russia and other Baltic states. The RSHA firmly believed that the Vatican's ultimate goal was to convert thousands of people so that Germany would eventually be surrounded by Catholic countries.

The ambitious Kappler, keen to keep his boss Heydrich happy, used Kurtna's information to the full. His star agent's discoveries formed the basis for a series of his reports, and the police attaché felt that he was making great progress in infiltrating the Vatican and keeping tabs on its leading personalities. But the progress didn't last long. Kurtna was unmasked by Italian military intelligence through old-fashioned detective work. Having staked out an apartment in Rome, they raided it and discovered hidden behind a radiator a transmitter that was being used to communicate with Moscow. The Italians then began intercepting radio messages from Russia. One transmission had directed the contact to go to another apartment in the city to deliver a message to the occupants. The messenger was told that when he went to the apartment he would meet a couple, a blonde woman and a man dressed as a priest. The man who would have the appearance of a priest was, in fact, Kurtna; the woman was his wife, Anna Hablitz from Leningrad, whom he had just married. Members of Italy's military intelligence arrested Hablitz outside her apartment and then waited at the railway station for her husband, who was returning from Estonia. Kurtna's arrest and incarceration in the summer of 1942 brought to an end Kappler's drip-feed of quality information on his targets within the

Vatican. The Estonian had been his most important source inside the Vatican, so it was an enormous blow to the police attaché.

Other contacts continued to pass on details of Church matters to Kappler, but their intelligence could not match that of the Estonian. Two German nationals provided occasional pieces of information: an academic called Engelfried and a woman, Frau Kühn-Steinhausen, who worked in the Vatican's archives.

Kurtna's detention by the Italians meant Kappler had to rely on a disparate and often bizarre group of potential informers who were motivated by politics, personal circumstances, and very often money. One such individual was Charles Bewley, who had served as the Irish ambassador to Germany and the Vatican. Bewley had an impressive background. A close examination of his curriculum vitae shows why he was of interest to German intelligence. A member of a Dublin family well known in business circles, he had been brought up as a Quaker but became a Catholic while a student at Oxford. He had a successful academic career in England and was the only Irishman apart from Oscar Wilde to win the Newdigate Prize for English verse. He returned to Dublin to practice law and became involved in politics, supporting Sinn Fein during its early years. Fervently anti-English and holding pro-Nazi views, he had gained experience dealing with German officials during his years in Berlin.

When Bewley was appointed as Ireland's envoy to the Vatican, one journalist prophetically wrote, "As a student of affairs he is well aware that the first representative of the Irish government will need to walk very warily if he is to avoid pitfalls." When Bewley left the Irish diplomatic service, he retired to Italy and kept up his German and Vatican contacts. Kappler was informed by his bosses in Berlin that Bewley was an Amt VI agent and was paid monthly. The

Irishman was a regular on the social scene and used such occasions to garner information that he included in the reports he sent to Berlin.

For Kappler it may also have seemed an ideal way to target Hugh O'Flaherty. On paper it would have seemed logical that, as an Irishman with what appeared to be good contacts in the Vatican, Bewley was well placed to uncover details about the activities of his fellow countryman in Rome. However, there was a major problem with Bewley's "intelligence": It was mainly gossip that he had picked up from parties or from Vatican contacts, which meant that he was unable to answer specific questions Kappler put to him.

At one stage German intelligence chiefs thought it would be possible to use Bewley's Irish connections to good effect. Kappler was told to ask the former ambassador to make contact with Irish theology students who were in the Vatican, in the hope of gaining some intelligence. Bewley was unable to provide a list of the students' names, and in the end the idea was abandoned.

By now the war had entered its most frightening stage. The Nazis had begun to put in place the Final Solution, an unprecedented plan for the genocide of all the Jews of Europe. Deportations from Germany began, and death camps were established in remote areas of German-controlled Poland. By the summer of 1942 a million Jews within Nazi-controlled Europe had died. German military intelligence chiefs were anxious to know how Pope Pius XII would respond to the mass deportations of Jews. If he condemned the Nazi regime's actions, how would this change its relationship with the Vatican? Berlin decided to put extra effort into intelligence gathering in Rome, and Kappler was now helped with extra staff, including Helmut Loos, who became his special assistant and had specific responsibility for organizing intelligence on the Holy See.

The arrival of Loos aided Kappler's efforts to penetrate the Vatican, for his new assistant had an exemplary track record. He had worked as a Vatican specialist for Amt VI, the RSHA's foreign-intelligence section, and had experience running agents. In Rome he quickly made contact with a series of people who had been recruited by Amt VI. They included people such as aspiring journalists, translators, and publishers. Even so, the quality of information Loos was offered varied greatly. Some of it was of genuine interest, but like the material offered by Charles Bewley, much of it was merely gossip and rumor. For Kappler and his assistant it was crucial to learn how to differentiate fact from fiction. Their intelligence-gathering operation received a boost when Berlin approved the installation of a radio transmitter on the roof at Via Tasso. It meant Kappler could send reports back to Germany in an instant. Previously he had used the German embassy's radio transmitter, which was considered safer than the telephone. As Kappler and Loos's fight against the Vatican entered a new phase, dramatic events were about to change the course of the war.

In the early hours of July 10, 1943, British, American, and Commonwealth troops landed on the coast of Sicily. The arrival of a 160,000-strong force raised hopes among the people of Italy that Mussolini's men would surrender soon and that it would speed up an Allied march on Rome. The Italian capital was now in the sights of British and American commanders, but, worryingly for those in the Vatican, the Allies were looking at the city from the air and not the ground.

CHAPTER 5

The End of Mussolini

"At this moment you are the most hated man in the country."
—KING VICTOR EMMANUEL III
OF ITALY TO BENITO MUSSOLINI

JULY 19, 1943

POPE PIUS XII SPENT MOST OF THE DAY GAZING AT THE SKY through binoculars as wave after wave of Allied bombs pounded his beloved city. From a window in the Vatican's Apostolic Palace, he watched as three hundred bombers blitzed the southeastern part of the capital. The attack killed nearly fifteen hundred people and injured many thousands more. As the bishop of Rome, he had long feared and indeed predicted this moment. So grave were the Pope's fears that back in June 1940, on the day that Italy entered the war, he had lobbied Sir D'Arcy Osborne to ask the British not to bomb Rome. The British government agreed to do its best to avoid damaging the Vatican City, but they could not guarantee that their bombers would avoid the surrounding area.

Weeks before this first air raid on the city, Osborne had met the Pope and the prospect of an aerial bombardment was raised again. This time the Pope was reported to be "worried sick." He had every reason to be concerned. When the bombs came they tore through university buildings and houses and struck the medieval basilica and the railway yards in San Lorenzo. The church there was held sacred as the burial place of Pope Pio Nono (Pius IX). The explosions also shook the earth at Campo Verano cemetery, where Pius XII's brother and parents were buried. Late that afternoon, as the smoke still hung in the air and the light faded, the Pope did something he had not done since the summer of 1940. He called for a car and decided to leave the confines of the Vatican.

Shortly before 5:30 p.m. a black Mercedes, decked out in the papal colors, left the Vatican City and took the Pope and one of his deputies, Monsignor Montini, across the city. They arrived at San Lorenzo to view the damage and meet the victims. Dressed in his skullcap and flowing white cassock, the Pope embraced the crowd that surrounded the car. Held back by policemen and troops, the people shouted "Long live the Pope." Amid the rubble, and close to the bodies that had been pulled from the buildings, he knelt and prayed. He said the De Profundis, and for two hours he talked with the survivors and walked among them. As the Pope talked, Monsignor Montini handed out cash to the homeless and the bereaved. When the two men returned to the car, Pope Pius's clothes were marked with blood.

Back in the Vatican the Pope took stock of what he had witnessed and heard. The city that he regarded as his own was in shock, bewildered and angry. The day marked a turning point in the war. The Eternal City was wounded and Romans were paralyzed with fear. Many wondered when more Allied air attacks would happen, and others were frightened that the Fascist police would use the opportunity to launch more raids on those who opposed them politically. Their predictions proved correct.

The police believed an illegal radio was transmitting within the city; it was eventually traced to the home of one of Rome's ancient families. Princess Nina Pallavicini, a widow who was opposed to Mussolini, lived in the Palazzo Pallavicini-Rospigliosi, near the Quirinale. Within hours after the Allied bombs ripped through the city, a raiding party came looking for the princess and the radio. Fortune favored the young woman and she heard the visitors arrive. She quickly pried open a window at the rear of the house, jumped to the ground, and ran for her life. She hurried through the streets to the Vatican, where she asked to see her friend Hugh O'Flaherty. The monsignor took her in and hid her in the German College. The princess was the first person to be offered long-term sanctuary by O'Flaherty and would become one of the most useful members of the Escape Line. She would spend the remainder of the war making false documents for Allied escapees and would often escort them around Rome.

Princess Nina was soon joined by another fugitive keen to escape the clutches of the authorities. Private Gino Rosati, a member of the Royal West Kent Regiment, listened to the sounds of the bombing of Rome in his cell in Regina Coeli prison, where the Italian authorities held many Allied prisoners. Born in England to Italian parents, Rosati had joined the British Army and seen action in North Africa at El Alamein in September 1942. He had been wounded and was transferred to Naples before being taken to Rome. Ironically his name may have aided the British soldier's escape. In the Italian capital he was placed in the political prisoners' section because the authorities were convinced he was an Italian citizen. Wearing British Army battle dress, he had managed to slip past the guards and get outside the prison complex. He encountered a friendly Italian soldier who generously showed him the way to St. Peter's Square.

He was taken into the barracks of the Vatican gendarmerie, where he was interrogated by an officer and then handed over to Sir D'Arcy Osborne. It was essential to establish, through close questioning, the bona fides of escaped prisoners who sought sanctuary in Vatican territory. In Rosati's case his name may have initially raised suspicions that he was a spy. But Osborne, ever conscious that he could become the victim of an Italian or German police trap, satisfied himself that the young soldier was genuinely on the run and allowed him to stay in the British legation.

As a servant of the Church, O'Flaherty knew he had to keep his activities clandestine and could not publicly do anything that might undermine the neutrality of the Vatican. As the British government's representative to the Vatican State, Osborne also knew he had to tread a fine diplomatic line. He was an official guest of the Pope, so his work with escaped prisoners had to remain hidden, and it made practical sense to remain distant from the everyday running of the group. Nevertheless, one evening he told O'Flaherty he could offer some assistance. "I will help you personally with funds as far as I am able, but I cannot use official funds, even if I could get enough, and I must not be seen to be doing anything to compromise the tacit conditions under which I am here in the Vatican State."

Osborne's financial support was accepted gladly. But the diplomat went further by volunteering the services of his butler. John May became the unofficial liaison officer between the monsignor and the minister. Fluent in Italian, with a wealth of contacts across Rome, May was an ideal choice. In the months ahead it was his job to source supplies for escapees and to identify those Swiss Guards who were ready to turn a blind eye to the escape operation, which was still in its infancy. May and O'Flaherty started to work in tandem, and soon many more escapees would arrive on their doorstep.

Kappler's men continued to closely watch Hugh O'Flaherty and Sir D'Arcy Osborne, still convinced that they were passing information on to the Allies. But Kappler's surveillance of the Vatican temporarily took a backseat when he became involved in one of the most dramatic twists of the war. For some time Italians had voiced criticism of Mussolini's regime. Across the country people were hungry, and in the south many were close to starvation. There was little support for Mussolini's regime, and within days of the Allied bombing of Rome, his colleagues turned on him when the Fascist Grand Council met and voted 19 to 8 to have him removed as leader. The next day King Victor Emmanuel had to act. He sent a message to Mussolini and called him to a meeting at the royal residence.

Rome was bathed in sunshine as the Fascist leader made his way to Villa Savoia. At five in the afternoon his driver swung the car through the iron gates leading into the royal grounds and stopped in front of the steps of the house. Their host was waiting near the entrance, dressed in the uniform of the Marshal of Italy. The two men shook hands and walked slowly inside.

In the familiar surroundings of the drawing room, they began to talk, first about the weather and then about the Grand Council's vote. Mussolini dismissed the vote, saying it had no legal standing and that he remained confident of his position.

Then the king struck. Turning to his guest, he said, "At this moment you are the most hated man in the country. I am your only remaining friend. That is why I tell you that you need have no fears for your safety. I will see you are protected."

Mussolini grew pale and listened in silence. When at last he spoke again, he intoned quietly, "Then it is over." He said the words several times. The meeting ended, the two men shook hands, and outside Mussolini was placed in a waiting ambulance, which quickly left the royal estate. The twenty-one-year Mussolini era had ended. King Emmanuel was now in charge.

Mussolini was replaced by Marshal Pietro Badoglio, formerly governor general of Libya. Now in his seventies, Badoglio had enjoyed a long career as a soldier and had led the Italians to a military victory in Ethiopia. Yet he was an odd choice. He had no political experience. He had a reputation for being a ditherer. And Badoglio was also an alcoholic. However, within hours he had established a temporary administration made up of generals and civil servants. Badoglio may have performed this task with a touch of schadenfreude, since Mussolini had sacked him in 1940.

As the former Fascist leader was experiencing his first evening in protective custody, the king announced on the radio to the Italian nation that he had accepted Mussolini's resignation. Badoglio also went on the airwaves, to proclaim that the war against the Allies would continue and the alliance with Germany would continue.

Hitler was sitting in the conference room in his "Wolf's Lair" when he heard the news. The building, tucked away in dense evergreen forest in East Prussia, was an inner sanctum where the Führer met members of his high command. When he learned what had happened in Rome, he was furious. The coup had caught him unawares, and while he knew there was anti-Mussolini feeling across Italy, he had not believed it would be acted upon. Moreover, he distrusted Pietro Badoglio, fearing correctly that he was preparing to negotiate a peace deal with the Allies. Hitler suspected that the Americans and the British were in some way involved in the Mussolini coup. In addition he judged that further Allied landings on the Italian mainland could prompt an Italian surrender and that therefore it was essential to organize a countercoup in Rome and seize the city. Hitler was in a race against time.

He spoke on the telephone to senior commanders, held meetings, and read briefing papers, then started to put together a plan that he would christen "Operation Oak." On paper it looked straightforward, but in practice it would prove very different. The mission consisted of three stages: Mussolini would be found; he would be restored to power; the German-Italian alliance would be strengthened. First, the whereabouts of the former Fascist leader had to be determined. Twenty-four hours after the kidnapping, Hitler handpicked the man to lead Operation Oak. Otto Skorzeny, a young Austrian commando captain, six feet four inches tall and well built, was his choice.

Skorzeny set up his headquarters in the ancient town of Frascati, a picturesque suburb of Rome about ten miles from the capital. Known for its vineyards, it was also home to the general headquarters for German troops in Italy and housed the offices of Marshal Albert Kesselring, the supreme commander of the Southern Front, in charge of military operations in the Mediterranean region and North Africa. For the next six weeks it would also be the command center of Skorzeny's secret mission.

Skorzeny needed local help and called on the services of Herbert Kappler and Eugen Dollmann. Like Kappler, Dollmann was an SS man and had lived in Rome for a number of years. However, the two were rivals and did not get along. Dollmann, a colonel, was highly rated by Himmler and was his personal representative in Rome. Kappler may well have been envious of Dollmann, who was better educated and also was the favorite of General Karl Wolff, the commander of the SS in Italy.

When Skorzeny told Himmler he needed help in Rome, Kappler and Dollmann were volunteered. The two SS men were summoned from Rome to Skorzeny's headquarters in Frascati for dinner.

After they had eaten, Skorzeny explained to his guests what his plans were. Privately both Kappler and Dollmann thought the mission was flawed. They saw Fascism in Italy as finished and believed there was little point in bringing Mussolini back into power. However, they kept their thoughts to themselves. When Skorzeny met them both at Kappler's office some days later, Dollmann had considered being honest with the commando captain. "Once again it would have been heroic of me if I had told the State Security Bureau's agent flatly what I thought of his plans for Rome, but I naturally refrained from doing so," he would later record in his diary.

Like his colleague, Kappler kept quiet, but eventually he made an attempt to change Skorzeny's mind. He flew to meet Heinrich Himmler and expressed his reservations. He said that the operation planned by Skorzeny was pointless and advised Himmler that Mussolini would only be able to return to power by "the strength of German bayonets." It was a pointless trip. As Reichsführer-SS, Himmler was Skorzeny's boss and one of the most important men in the Third Reich. He was also committed to the plan.

So Operation Oak began in earnest, with a reluctant Kappler an important part of it. With his small staff Kappler could not offer manpower to Skorzeny's operation. But he could provide good local knowledge and a wide range of contacts. Skorzeny provided forged banknotes, and with these Kappler was able to tempt his spies to sell information about Mussolini's movements. For the next few weeks, seeking out the former Fascist leader would become the police attaché's priority.

CHAPTER 6

Operation Escape

"God will protect us all."
—HENRIETTA CHEVALIER TO HUGH O'FLAHERTY

ONE EVENING IN 1943, AS THE DAY'S LIGHT WAS FADING, HUGH O'Flaherty left the Vatican and made his way to the other side of Rome. At Piazza Salerno he walked around a corner then went through an archway between a grocer's and a butcher shop. Slowly he climbed three flights of steps. He read the numbers on the doors and, finding the correct address, rang the bell.

He was quickly ushered in. Once inside the apartment in Via Imperia, he towered over Henrietta Chevalier, who stood just five feet four inches tall. The attractive middle-aged woman had neat hair and wore earrings and a necklace. A widow from Malta living on a small pension, she had lost her husband just before the start of the war. Her English was perfect, though she spoke with a trace of a Maltese accent. She had six daughters and two sons, and one of her boys worked at the Swiss embassy, while the other was being held in an Italian prison camp. Although her home was small, she had agreed to house two escaped French soldiers. O'Flaherty was delighted that she was willing to help, but he needed to impress on her the dangers of taking in escaped prisoners.

"You do not have to do it," he told her, adding that those found harboring prisoners of war could be executed. He said he would take the men away if she had any concerns about their staying in her home. If Henrietta was scared, she certainly did not show it. In fact she seemed quite relaxed about the priest's warning. "What are you worrying about, Monsignor?" she replied. "God will protect us all."

A quick glance around the apartment showed the monsignor how important Henrietta's faith was to her. Fittingly, a tapestry of Our Lady of Pompeii, who traditionally helped those in need, hung in one of the two bedrooms. On a table sat a small statue of St. Paul. Prayer was an important part of Henrietta's daily life. She firmly believed she and her family would be safe and told her visitor she was happy to help for as long as possible. O'Flaherty's newfound Maltese friend would stick to that promise.

From that night on, the Chevaliers' tiny apartment would never be the same again. Their military guests would sleep on mattresses and Henrietta and her children would share the beds. Space would be at a premium and soon there would be a daily line for the bathroom. The changed circumstances would have to be kept secret. The apartment was now out of bounds to all but family members. The Chevaliers' friends couldn't come to see them and the girls could not invite visitors. But it wasn't all bad news. For the younger daughters the new male houseguests were a novelty and brought a sense of fun. Within days apartment number nine would echo to the strains of endless gramophone records, and Henrietta's young girls would have a choice of dancing partners.

Back in his room in the German College, Hugh O'Flaherty was happy in the knowledge that he had secured shelter and a willing host for the two escapees.

By September 1943 the Germans were edging closer to taking over Rome. In the same month, O'Flaherty had three new arrivals to welcome. Henry Byrnes was a captain in the Royal Canadian Army Corps. He arrived in style at the Holy See. A prisoner of war, he was being marched to the Castro Pretorio barracks in Rome when he and two colleagues gave the soldiers guarding them the slip. Byrnes, John Munroe Sym, a major in the Seaforth Highlanders, and Roy Elliot, a sub-lieutenant in the Royal Navy, met an Italian doctor. Fortunately Luigi Meri de Vita was a friendly soul, well disposed toward escaped Allied servicemen. He put the three escapees in his car and drove them across Rome to the Vatican. After managing to get into the Holy See, the three men quickly found their way to Hugh O'Flaherty's door.

The monsignor immediately put Byrnes and Elliot to work. The pair began to compile a list of Allied servicemen they knew were in hiding across Italy. Once the paperwork was complete, Byrnes passed the details on to Father Owen Sneddon, a contemporary of the monsignor who was now assisting the Escape Line. Sneddon, a New Zealander, worked as a broadcaster for the English-language Vatican Radio service. The station was part of the Vatican's communication network, and although the Pope technically controlled it, it was run day to day by the Jesuit Father Filippo Soccorsi. The station was an important tool for the Escape Line, but broadcasters had to be careful because the Germans monitored the output and each broadcast was translated.

Once Father Sneddon was ready, he peppered his broadcasts with the names supplied by Byrnes and Elliot. The details were picked up by the War Office in London, which informed the men's families that their loved ones were alive. It was an old trick that O'Flaherty had first perfected when he was an official visitor to the

POW camps. When the monsignor returned to Rome from seeing prisoners, he would pass on their personal details to Father Sneddon. It was a simple way to let people know that their relative was alive, and this method went undetected by the Germans.

The Vatican reflected the outside world, and the atmosphere in the Holy See was nervous and apprehensive. Osborne and O'Flaherty wondered what their lives would be like in a post-Mussolini world. Rumors filled the void of uncertainty. There was much talk about an Italian surrender followed by a German invasion of Rome. One fear that wouldn't go away was a suggestion that the Germans would capture the Vatican and seize the Pope and take him abroad.

There was good reason for this worry. Days after Mussolini's kidnapping, in the Wolf's Lair an angry Hitler berated the Pope and the Holy See: "Do you think the Vatican impresses me? I couldn't care less. We will clear out that gang of swine."

Hitler was considering kidnapping the Pope, arresting the king and Marshal Badoglio, and occupying the Vatican City. The threat to seize Pope Pius XII was believed to be so likely that, in early August, the Vatican's secretary of state, Cardinal Maglione, summoned all the cardinals in Rome to a special meeting. He explained that the Germans had plans to seize Rome and then take control of the Vatican buildings and remove the Pope. The threat was regarded as so plausible that the commander of the Pope's Swiss Guards was ordered not to offer any resistance when the German troops tried to gain access to the Vatican.

Staff inside the Holy See started to take precautions should the Germans seize the site. Sensitive Church documents were hidden across the Vatican and some diplomatic papers were burned. Sir D'Arcy Osborne, now beginning to worry that his personal diary would be seized if the Nazis took over, had to think carefully about what he was committing to paper. He made some entries designed to fool prying eyes and others that were light on detail. At one stage he wrote: "I wish I could put down all the facts and rumors these days, but I can't. It is a pity for the sake of the diary."

The Germans were continuing to watch the Vatican intently, and the behavior of Badoglio's administration was under constant scrutiny. After German code-breakers listened to a conversation between President Franklin Roosevelt and British Prime Minister Winston Churchill, in which the two leaders discussed an armistice, the Nazis knew that an Italian surrender was coming. The Nazis had also discovered that secret talks were under way between the Allies and the Italians and were able to dismiss Badoglio's official response that he was fully supportive of the Nazi war effort. Because they suspected that it was only a matter of time before the Italians surrendered, the restoration of Benito Mussolini as leader was becoming urgent, though the Germans had to first find him.

The events in Rome and the questions surrounding Italy's future in the war had initially overshadowed the efforts to find Mussolini, but now senior Nazis were becoming restless. They put pressure on Kappler, making it clear that he must locate the former dictator within days.

Kappler's network of informers, who were being partially funded by Skorzeny's fake banknotes, had so far failed to deliver solid intelligence on Mussolini's whereabouts. Rumors abounded as to his precise location. Every time a story surfaced or there was an alleged sighting of the man, Kappler and his team had to investigate it. One rumor suggested that he was being held in a hospital in Rome awaiting an operation; Kappler discovered this to be untrue. Another story held that Mussolini hadn't left the royal residence at

Villa Savoia, but that also proved a false trail. Each alleged sighting of Il Duce contradicted the last one.

Trying to stay one step ahead of the Germans, the Badoglio administration began to move Mussolini around. Through a contact in the Italian police, Kappler had learned that the country's most famous prisoner had first been taken by ambulance from Villa Savoia to the Podgora barracks in Via Quintino Sella, a thirty-minute high-speed drive from the royal residence. Kappler was also able to establish which part of the building Mussolini had been held in. He now knew that he had slept in a camp bed, in a small office that overlooked the parade ground where the cadets marched.

Fascinating though this information was, for Kappler it was all too late. Mussolini's captors had already moved their precious charge to another location. He had been driven from Rome to the port of Gaeta, where he was put aboard a vessel named the Persefone and taken to the island of Ponza, twenty-five miles to the north. Ponza, which was around five miles long, had a history as a penal colony.

Kappler's efforts to find Mussolini did not go unnoticed. The Führer himself was keeping an eye on Kappler's attempts to track down the former dictator. The previous month, August 1943, Hitler had called the police attaché in to see him. Having completed four years in Rome, Kappler thought he was about to be moved elsewhere in the Third Reich, but Hitler had other ideas. For the young SS man the meeting went better than he had expected. Hitler praised him and made it clear that his work in Rome was very important. He told him that he valued his contacts and that he was needed in the hunt for Mussolini and for future work organizing surveillance in the city. Ironically the very mission that Kappler had doubts about, the rescue of Mussolini, had secured his future in Rome.

Day by day Kappler's office worked to piece together Mussolini's secret journey from Villa Savoia. The police attaché's staff tried a variety of methods. Pro-Nazi officers in the Italian Army and police force were constantly badgered for tidbits of information. Staff also monitored the airwaves for any unusual reports or coded messages.

Finally they made a breakthrough. One of Kappler's agents, who had been listening to Italian communication networks, came across an intriguing phrase. He heard the words, "Security preparations around the Gran Sasso complete." The message had been sent by an officer named Gueli, one of Mussolini's captors, and was meant for a superior.

At nine o'clock in the evening on September 5, Kappler sent a cable to senior officers in Berlin informing them that it was extremely likely that Mussolini was in the vicinity of the Gran Sasso mountain. He also noted that he had sent out a fresh reconnaissance party, which should report back shortly.

Kappler's team would quickly discover that the former dictator was indeed where they suspected, in the Apennine Mountains in the Abruzzo region of eastern Italy. He had most recently been taken by boat from the island of Ponza to a villa on Maddalena, an island off Sardinia, and from there was flown to the winter resort of Campo Imperatore, near the Gran Sasso. The Italians had chosen Mussolini's final hiding place wisely. They put him in a room in the Hotel Campo Imperatore, some seven thousand feet above sea level.

As a hiding place the secluded location was ideal, because it was close to the highest peak in the Apennines and could be reached only by a ten-minute ride in a cable car. Although he was surrounded by hotel staff and policemen, Mussolini was the only official guest at the hotel. In conversations with his captors, Gueli and Faiola, he referred to his new surroundings as the "highest prison in the world." As he played cards, read, and listened to the radio, Mussolini was unaware that his German allies, after six weeks of searching, were just one step away from rescuing him. Kappler, although a reluctant participant in the manhunt, had proved his worth.

As the rescue plans were finalized, the Allies and the Italians struck in different ways. Allied bombers took to the skies over Italy. This time one of their targets was the major headquarters for German troops at Frascati. In a lunchtime attack four hundred tons of explosives fell on the town, killing and injuring many hundreds of residents and German soldiers. The German military complex was hit, and Otto Skorzeny's quarters were wrecked. Field Marshal Kesselring climbed from the wreckage unharmed. He sensed the bombing was only part of a planned series of events.

Kesselring was right. The attack was a forerunner to an Allied landing in Salerno, but there was more bad news to come for the Germans. That evening, as smoke still hung over large parts of Italy, Marshal Badoglio announced on the radio that Italy had surrendered. The Italian leader said that he had requested an armistice from the Allied commander, General Eisenhower, who had accepted it. Badoglio's radio address took the Germans by surprise. They had known it was coming, but not when. The timing, rather like that of Mussolini's kidnapping in July, had caught them short.

Colonel Eugen Dollmann, who had been assisting Kappler in the search for Mussolini, was tasked with finding out what was happening on the streets of Rome. There was great confusion in the city, and the rumors were many and varied. These ranged from reports that Allied troops were arriving to seize Rome to stories that German troops were about to take control.

At the German embassy there was an altogether different atmosphere. Staff there, convinced that they were about to be ordered to leave the city, had begun to burn documents. However, amid all the chatter and speculation, Dollmann had secured one critical piece of hard information. When he reported back to Kesselring at the Frascati headquarters, the commander-in-chief of the Southern Front was intrigued. Dollmann had discovered that before the armistice announcement an American general, Maxwell Taylor, had been smuggled into Rome for secret discussions with Badoglio. Taylor, second-in-command of the U.S. 82nd Airborne Division, had been on a reconnaissance mission to examine the possibility of an airdrop of paratroopers close to Rome.

The discussions between Taylor and Badoglio had turned into farce when the Italian leader changed his mind about an airdrop and then asked for the armistice announcement to be postponed. Angered by the Italian dithering, Eisenhower agreed to abandon the airdrop but refused to accept a cancellation of the announcement. Kesselring didn't know this detail but assumed General Taylor's presence in Rome meant that an Allied airborne invasion of Rome was imminent. He told Dollmann that if Allied paratroopers landed, the goal of securing Rome was lost.

Kesselring knew he had to act fast. He first attempted to block all the entry points into Rome. When the king and Badoglio heard of the Germans' intentions, they too acted quickly. In darkness, clutching a few of their possessions, the royal family, along with Badoglio and his ministers, fled the city.

No orders were left with the army and no one was given military command. As dawn broke on September 9, Rome was at the mercy of the Germans.

Over the course of the day, gunfire could be heard across the city as pockets of Italians, made up of soldiers and civilians, began to resist the German troops who were edging their way toward the center of Rome. The resistance was patchy and uncoordinated. Some of the Italians were bedraggled and appeared to be hungry, and many had no ammunition. The Germans had the upper hand militarily and tactically. On September 10 the battle for Rome entered its final phase.

With the city under siege, Hugh O'Flaherty and Sir D'Arcy Osborne could only watch and wait as they stayed put in the Vatican. They could see and hear the sounds of battle outside the Vatican's walls, but for the moment they were like prisoners of war themselves.

The Pope was now seriously worried that the Germans would first take Rome and then move into the Vatican. He told his staff to keep their suitcases packed and then asked Cardinal Maglione to contact the German ambassador to the Vatican, Baron Ernst von Weizsäcker, for some clarification. Maglione asked him if the Germans would respect the neutrality and extra-territorial status of the Holy See's property. As gun battles continued across the city, Weizsäcker contacted his masters in Berlin. The Pope had to bide his time.

By now German "Tiger" tanks were moving through the streets, and the last lines of resistance were being overcome. The initial unease felt in the Vatican had now turned to panic. Everyone in the Holy See was on full alert. In an unprecedented move, St. Peter's Basilica was closed off and the gates to the Vatican City were shut. The Swiss Guards, who normally patrolled with ornamental pikes, were issued firearms.

The Pope had good reason to seal off the Vatican City: He wished to keep the whole site immune from the chaos that was engulfing Rome. Across the city was fear and uncertainty. Burglaries, assaults, rape, and murder had spread to all districts as Romans—good and bad—took matters into their own hands. But Friday night was their last evening of unrestrained lawlessness. By the following evening the city was swarming with SS men, infantrymen, and German troops of all descriptions. The battle was over, and as darkness fell Rome had new rulers.

Field Marshal Kesselring declared martial law, and his ten-point proclamation was pasted on walls throughout the city. His decree stated that Rome was under his command and all crimes would be judged according to German laws of war. He also made it clear that snipers, strikers, and saboteurs would be executed. All private correspondence was prohibited and all phone calls would be monitored.

That night, at the Wolf's Lair, Hitler recorded a special broadcast that was transmitted shortly afterwards on Radio Rome. His delight at having captured the Italian capital was obvious, though it was punctuated with a series of warnings, and he declared that Italy would suffer for deposing its once-favorite son. Clearly Mussolini was on the Führer's mind. Hours later the mission to rescue him from the heights of the Gran Sasso began.

The Nazi high command had also become worried that the intelligence work and planning organized before the Italian surrender would go to waste. Even during the battle for Rome, Himmler had sent a message to Captain Skorzeny and General Kurt Student, the commander of Germany's airborne forces, reminding them that Mussolini's rescue was still a top priority. Both men concluded there were three ways to carry out the rescue. They could arrive at the Gran Sasso by parachute, perform a landing by glider, or launch a ground attack.

On the afternoon of Sunday, September 12, a group of gliders carrying German paratroopers made their way to the remote mountain resort. Mussolini was sitting by the window in his room and saw Skorzeny's glider crash-land outside the hotel. The young captain climbed out and ran toward the building. He overpowered a radio operator and bundled a number of carabinieri out of the way. He climbed the stairs and on the second floor turned right. Moments later he found himself face to face with the man he had been hunting for six weeks, Benito Mussolini.

Skorzeny spoke first. "Duce, the Führer has sent me to set you free."

"I knew my friend Adolf Hitler would not abandon me," Mussolini replied.

By now the other paratroopers had secured the building and the cable car. The underground passage that linked the hotel and the resort's station was also in German hands. The kidnapping had taken its toll on Mussolini: He looked tired and ill and a little unkempt. Wearing a felt hat and an overcoat that was too big for him, Mussolini walked out of the hotel, where his every movement was tracked by a German newsreel cameraman who had come along to record the rescue. He made his way to one of the gliders and then, tucked behind the cockpit, sat beside Skorzeny.

The take-off from the mountaintop nearly ended in disaster. The glider shot down into a chasm, but the pilot was able to pull out of the nosedive. An hour later they landed safely and then Mussolini and Skorzeny were put on another plane. Aboard the Heinkel 111, they were flown for an overnight stay in Austria. Back in Rome Herbert Kappler was anxiously waiting for news, and when it came he quickly passed it on to officials in Berlin. Shortly after six o'clock he cabled a message informing them that the rescue of

Mussolini had been carried out successfully and that a meeting had been arranged with senior officers in Vienna.

The next day Skorzeny and Mussolini were due to fly to Munich, where the former dictator would meet up with his wife.

Before he retired to bed that night, Skorzeny received a telephone call. It was Hitler, who told the young captain, "Today you have carried out a mission that will go down in history and I have given you the Knight's Cross and promoted you to Sturmbannführer."

The Führer was thrilled that Mussolini had been freed, and he was clearly in the mood to congratulate those who had helped in the rescue mission. After Skorzeny was honored, there were others to be recognized. Herbert Kappler was also on the list, and he was given the Iron Cross for his work. However, for him there was another reward to come. He was promoted to Obersturmbannführer, the highest rank of his career. Five weeks earlier he had been ordered to stay in Rome by the Führer and told to concentrate on police intelligence work. Now, with the city in German hands, Lieutenant Colonel Kappler had an even bigger job to do.

CHAPTER 7

Occupation

"We Germans regard you only as Jews, and thus our enemy."
—HERBERT KAPPLER

HUNGRY AND POORLY DRESSED, A GROUP OF FOURTEEN ALLIED servicemen arrived at the entrance of the Holy See looking for shelter and food. They were taking an enormous risk by traveling in such a large group and looking out of place. But they were lucky, for a friendly priest from St. Monica's monastery offered them respite and made contact with Anton Call, a carabiniere who was on close terms with Monsignor O'Flaherty and Sir D'Arcy Osborne and had helped to hide Albert Penny, the British seaman who had arrived at the Vatican on a bicycle.

Call advised the new arrivals to approach the Vatican in twos and threes. He said once they got inside they should declare they were prisoners of war and ask to be handed over to Osborne's butler, John May. The next day Call discovered that the servicemen were in a local barracks. The plan had failed. The escapees had managed to fool the Swiss Guards but not the gendarmes, who handed them to the carabinieri in St. Peter's Square. All fourteen men were taken to the Vittorio Emmanuele barracks.

That night Call visited O'Flaherty. The police officer gave the priest details of the new detainees and O'Flaherty gave him 3,000 lire to buy food for the escapees. Within hours the men were well fed and well dressed. Because the Germans did not visit the police barracks, O'Flaherty considered it a safe place to leave the servicemen. But the men's freedom was short-lived, for in late October the Germans unexpectedly arrived at the barracks. Two of the group managed to escape, but the remaining twelve were rounded up. For O'Flaherty the episode was a clear reminder that the escape operation needed more space and resources.

For Herbert Kappler the discovery of the escapees justified his policy of keeping the Vatican under surveillance and confirmed that he was right to keep a close watch on O'Flaherty. In his developing battle with the monsignor, it was an enjoyable early triumph. Even so, for every escapee Kappler's men caught, many more evaded detection.

O'Flaherty was now taking huge personal risks. On one occasion he met three escaped South African servicemen in Rome, and while he was taking them to the apartment he had found for them, they were stopped by three SS men. Luckily the Germans were lost and just wanted directions. Another time he escorted two more South Africans from a railway station to their safe house. He visited hospitals where escapees were being treated and regularly secured their release to pro-Allied families in the city.

It was an open secret that O'Flaherty was the man behind the escape operation. By late October 1943 around one thousand servicemen had been placed in safety in homes across Rome and in farms and buildings outside the city. Kappler wanted to catch the monsignor red-handed but knew he could only arrest him away from Vatican territory.

By now the monsignor and his friend and collaborator John May realized that the two of them could not handle the escape operation on their own. "Look, Monsignor, this thing is too big for one man, you can't handle it alone . . . and it's hardly begun!" May said. O'Flaherty agreed that another senior figure was needed to share the workload of recruiting host families, raising money, and visiting suitable accommodations for the escapees. Count Sarsfield Salazar of the Swiss legation was approached. Salazar had been interned when Italy declared war but had later been released. He had originally joined the staff of the American embassy and gained experience dealing with prisoners of war when he visited intern-ment camps as an official inspector. And now, as a diplomat for a neutral country, he had the ideal background. Salazar agreed to join May and O'Flaherty.

The trio's first priority was to secure more accommodations, so O'Flaherty went house hunting, crisscrossing the city by tram and on foot looking for suitable houses and apartments. After living in Rome for nearly two decades, he knew the city intimately and soon found an apartment in Via Firenze and another, about a mile away, in Via Chelini.

But, in addition to safe houses, the Escape Line needed cash to pay for food and clothes for the escapees. The issue of money was discussed at nighttime meetings between Osborne, O'Flaherty, and May. The British minister agreed to seek financial assistance from the Foreign Office in London, and over the next nine months, large sums of money were made available. Eventually Foreign Office officials would secure a loan through the Vatican Bank of three million lire. It was a risky strategy for them because they knew a paper trail leading to Osborne could jeopardize his position in Rome. One senior British civil servant summed up the arguments and concluded that it was best to make funds available. He wrote: "It is worth taking a good many risks, including that of compromising his position in the Vatican, to send money to British prisoners, wherever they may be in Italy." Money would also come from other sources, including a Jesuit account and from the American government through its chargé d'affaires, Harold Tittmann.

One day, while sitting in his room in the Vatican, O'Flaherty answered the phone and heard the unmistakable voice of Prince Filippo Doria Pamphili. A member of one of Rome's oldest families, the prince could trace his ancestors back to Admiral Andrea Doria, known as the liberator of Genoa. He was a friend of the monsignor and sympathetic toward his Escape Line. An opponent of Fascism, he had refused to accept Mussolini's rule and had declined to fly the Italian flag from his palace to mark the Fascist leader's anniversary—a move that had particularly angered Mussolini because the prince's residence was across the street from where crowds used to gather to hear Il Duce speak. Pamphili was first imprisoned and then banished to southern Italy, though in recent months had been allowed to return to Rome. He had become friendly with O'Flaherty before the war, and the monsignor had often been to parties at his home. Having secretly become involved in anti-fascist groups that helped refugees, the prince was now telephoning O'Flaherty to say he wanted to see him.

The journey from the Vatican to the Palazzo Doria in Via del Corso didn't take long. There the two men adjourned to the prince's impressive picture gallery, where they were surrounded by Renaissance and baroque paintings, some of the city's finest works of art. Ever conscious of watching eyes and listening ears, the prince told O'Flaherty, "Even in my own palazzo I am not safe from spies now." He then explained that he wanted to help the escape organization and handed over 150,000 lire, which at the time was equal to some $8,000.

O'Flaherty was being watched by Kappler's men, who noted his trip to the prince's residence.

As autumn arrived, Kappler was adjusting to his new life as the chief of the Gestapo in Rome. Now he had the entire city under his control. One day specific orders came from Berlin. Kappler's secretary put the call through to her boss, who listened intently. First the caller congratulated him on his promotion and then there were words of praise for his deputy, Erich Priebke, who, like Kappler, had been awarded the Iron Cross for his work in finding Mussolini. Kappler had made sure that his work tracking down the former dictator had not gone unnoticed by his superiors in Berlin. He had sent one cable reminding them that Mussolini was discovered "exclusively from intelligence sources controlled by me."

After the caller offered his good wishes to the Obersturmbann-führer came the instructions, relayed in stark terms from Heinrich Himmler's office. The deportation of Rome's Jews was to be Kappler's first task following his promotion. This command, he was told during the phone call, would be followed by a radio message that would confirm the order: Kappler was to begin the "Final Solution" in the city. He had been in his new post only a few days, but he was already once again at odds with his bosses in Berlin. Just as he had initially opposed the plan to rescue Mussolini, he also found this latest plan objectionable. He didn't agree with the order he had just received. He felt he knew Rome well, certainly better than those sitting behind desks in Germany. He believed any attempt to deport the city's Jews would do little to engender sympathy among a local population already angered by the German occupation. Then there were the practicalities of a mass roundup. How could widespread deportations be organized? Days earlier Kappler had been instructed in a message from Berlin to secure the routes in and out of the Vatican. He had questioned whether he had the manpower for such measures and replied that "instructions to this effect can only be carried out if additional forces are brought up."

Kappler was sure he did not have enough men for the task, and what staff he did have lacked any experience in these matters. It was a bad plan, but he knew he had to do more than simply object to it. If he was to successfully oppose this latest order from Berlin, he needed allies. He traveled the short distance to Frascati to meet Field Marshal Kesselring, who had dealt with Jews on a previous occasion in Tunisia. Rather than carry out mass deportations, Kesselring had formed the Tunisian Jews into work gangs, and Jewish leaders who had been arrested were released after payment of a fine. When Kappler told him how many men he would need to organize deportations across Rome, the field marshal was alarmed. Kesselring said he could not afford to have men tied up in such matters because they were needed to defend Rome. Kappler had found his ally. The new head of the Gestapo in Rome then started to put together his own plan.

Kappler summoned the city's Jewish leaders. On the last Sunday of September, he ordered two of Rome's leading Jewish representatives to attend a meeting with him. Shortly after six in the evening, Ugo Foa and Dante Almansi stood outside Kappler's office in Villa Wolkonsky. They had not been told why the head of the Gestapo wanted to see them. At first their host was polite and the conversation was pleasant, but Kappler's mood soon changed and he told his two visitors, "We Germans regard you only as Jews, and thus our enemy." He then chillingly warned them that unless the Jewish community handed over 50 kilograms, or more than 110 pounds, of gold within the next thirty-six hours, two hundred Jews would be deported to Germany. If the gold was handed over, no one would be harmed.

Kappler's plan had no official sanction, and he was operating alone in the hope that his actions would delay the deportations.

Angry and worried, Foa and Almansi left their meeting with Kappler knowing they needed advice and help. Foa, a former magistrate, and Almansi, president of the Union of Jewish Communities, were both well connected in Rome. They spoke with contacts in the city's Fascist police, but there was little the Italian police could do to change Kappler's mind. The two Jewish leaders knew they had to act.

Word of the Gestapo chief's ultimatum quickly spread among the city's twelve thousand–strong Jewish community. Foa and Almansi felt they could raise the amount demanded, but they were concerned that they could not do it within Kappler's deadline. They set to work immediately. In an office close to the Tiber River, beside the central synagogue, donations were left. As darkness fell, a line had formed to hand over rings, chains, pendants, and bracelets. Even gold fillings were removed from teeth, and slowly the amount collected edged toward 50 kilograms. Twice Foa and Almansi appealed to Kappler to give them more time, and twice he agreed.

The Vatican had also been informed of the demand Kappler had placed on the Jewish community. Aware of the difficulties in reaching Kappler's figure, Pope Pius XII offered to lend them gold if there was a shortfall. The Holy See said the loan could be arranged for any amount and could be repaid in installments, without interest. However, the Vatican's loan was not needed. By early afternoon on Tuesday, September 28, Kappler's target was finally reached.

Packed into ten boxes, the gold was taken under police guard across the city to Villa Wolkonsky, where Kappler had issued the demand nearly two days earlier. The Obersturmbannführer declined to see Foa and Almansi. The two Jewish leaders were then told to take the gold to Via Tasso, a short distance away. There they were greeted by a young SS captain who in error under-weighed the amount and then, after much delay, correctly measured the gold. The correct amount had been delivered and the two men prepared to leave. As a parting gesture of defiance, Foa declared that he would personally go to Germany at some stage to retrieve the gold. As darkness fell, Foa and Almansi returned to their families and friends. Rome's Jewish community felt a sense of relief. Across Europe Jews were being rounded up and transported to death camps. Yet to date it seemed that Italy was exempt, and the Jews of Rome believed that the payment of gold would prevent any deportations from their own city. It was a false hope.

Within hours SS men were at their door, raiding the offices of Rome's Jewish community, the very community that had dug deep and pulled together the gold. The SS took money and documents, including the details of Jews who had donated gold. Two weeks later they returned and took away old manuscripts and rare books.

Kappler still hoped he could win the argument that the deportation of the Jews should be abandoned. He had all the rings, bracelets, and other gold items put into one box and sent to Berlin. The package was marked for the attention of Obergruppenführer Ernst Kaltenbrunner, who was Himmler's deputy in the Reich security empire. Kappler attached a cover letter. In his note he explained why he was against the planned deportation of Jews. Such a move, he wrote, would deprive him of the chance to exploit the Jewish community for intelligence purposes. He added that Field Marshal

Kesselring had approved plans to use Roman Jews in labor gangs across the city.

When Kaltenbrunner opened the box, he was indifferent to the gold and unconvinced by Kappler's reasons for abandoning the deportation of Jews. The gold was of little consequence and would remain in Kaltenbrunner's office, untouched, until the war ended.

Kappler's arguments he tackled head-on. He contacted Kappler and instructed him that the deportation must be his top priority. Kappler must "proceed with the evacuation of the Jews without further delay." Kaltenbrunner's tone was equally direct as he told Kappler that "it is precisely the immediate and thorough eradication of the Jews in Italy which is the special interest of the present internal political situation and the general security in Italy." He dismissed any suggestion that the operation should be delayed and added that "the longer the delay, the more the Jews who are doubtless reckoning on evacuation measures have an opportunity by moving to the houses of pro-Jewish families."

By now Kappler's opposition to the deportations was causing much anxiety in the corridors of power in Berlin. If the Final Solution was to be enacted in Rome, the Nazi leaders knew they had to put their own man in charge. In the first week of October, an SS captain and a detachment of Waffen SS men were dispatched to Rome to hasten the roundup of Jews. If Kappler was uncomfortable receiving questionable orders on the telephone, he probably felt even more uneasy hearing them in person in his own office.

At Villa Wolkonsky the newly arrived Captain Dannecker sat opposite Kappler. Even though Kappler outranked him, he knew his guest had to be taken seriously. Theodor Dannecker was a troubleshooter, sent from Berlin with Himmler's blessing. He had a track record of carrying out Jewish deportations, and twelve months earlier had organized roundups of Jews in Paris.

Dannecker told Kappler that he required manpower of at least one motorized battalion and wanted the operation to be kept entirely secret. He also needed the names and addresses of Rome's Jews. Kappler was running out of excuses and time. Realizing he had lost the argument, he handed over the list.

On Saturday, October 16, as rain fell on the streets of Rome, lines of SS officers and military policemen made their way to the city's Jewish ghetto. This time the Nazi policemen had not come for gold, money, or documents. This time they wanted men, women, and children. Kappler's attempt to delay the deportations had failed. Armed with submachine guns, the SS police and Waffen SS ordered around twelve hundred people out of their homes. Frightened, wet, and cold, and clinging to what small possessions they could carry, the captives were placed into open army trucks.

Most of them were still in their nightclothes. As the children cried and screamed and the adults openly prayed, they were driven to the Italian Military College, close to the Tiber River. It was a carbon copy of the raids Dannecker had led in Paris. By midafternoon the operation was over. Nearly nine hundred of those arrested were women and children. At the military college the prisoners were examined and interviewed, and around 230 non-Jews were released.

News of the deportations reached the Vatican very quickly. As the German raids began, Princess Enza Pignatelli Aragona Cortes, a young aristocrat well known on the Rome social scene and involved in charity work, was awakened by a phone call from a friend. The caller lived near the Jewish ghetto and informed her of the German raids. The princess decided she must inform the Pope.

She had known Pius XII for some time and had been received by him in the Holy See. The princess left her home and traveled to the Jewish ghetto to witness what was happening. She then went directly to the Vatican and, although she had no appointment to see the Pontiff, was quickly granted an audience. In the Pope's study the princess informed him of what was happening and told him he must act to stop the deportations. The Pope seemed genuinely surprised to hear the news. He said he had believed the Jews would remain untouched after the payment of gold. Then he made a phone call and, as he saw the princess out, promised that he would do all he could to help.

Cardinal Luigi Maglione, the Vatican's secretary of state and one of the Pope's aides, summoned the German ambassador to the Vatican. Maglione asked Ambassador Ernst von Weizsäcker to use his influence and intervene to stop the deportations, saying, "It is painful for the Holy Father, painful beyond words, that right here in Rome, under the eyes of the Common Father, so many people are made to suffer because of their particular descent." The ambassador considered Maglione's comments and asked, "What would the Holy See do if these things continued?" It was the key question and clearly referred to the morning raids. The cardinal replied, "The Holy See would not wish to be put in a situation where it was necessary to utter a word of disapproval."

Weizsäcker responded with a series of compliments about the Vatican. He praised the Catholic Church for steering a neutral course in the war and then suggested it would be wise if the Holy See refrained from making a protest, telling the cardinal, "I am thinking of the consequences that a step by the Holy See would provoke." He added that these measures came from "the highest level" and stressed that their conversation must be regarded as confidential. In response Maglione asked Weizsäcker to intervene by appealing to his "sentiments of humanity."

The meeting was cordial and diplomatic. Even so, Weizsäcker's reference to the "highest level" was seen as a threat by an already nervous Vatican. The Pope did not want a showdown with Rome's new rulers. There were too many uncertainties. If he protested too strongly about the deportations, would the relationship he had established with the Germans change for the worse? Would Berlin continue to respect the independence of the Vatican State? Such questions were considered against a backdrop of persistent rumors that the Germans would invade the Holy See and seize the Pope. Just as he had done since the start of the war in 1939, Pius XII knew he had a diplomatic game to play.

That night Kappler worked late to complete a report on the day's events for Himmler. Just before midnight he finalized his dispatch and had it transmitted to the office of the Reichsführer-SS in Berlin. Kappler reported that the "action against the Jews started and finished today in accordance with a plan worked out as well as possible by the office." Even though there were insufficient numbers of German police, he stated that 1,259 people had been arrested, but that those of mixed blood and foreigners had been released, leaving just over 1,000 still in custody. Kappler also noted that the operation had gone ahead without any opposition and that the use of firearms had not proved necessary.

Two days later all the prisoners were taken to a railway station and squeezed into trucks and transported to Auschwitz. Within a week eight hundred would be dead.

On the day the Jews left Rome's Tiburtina Station on their one-way journey to Auschwitz, Sir D'Arcy Osborne met the Pope. There was only one topic of conversation. The British minister told the Pope that he had "underestimated his own moral authority" and talked of "the reluctant respect in which he was held by the Nazis because of the Catholic population of Germany." Osborne was gently pushing the Pontiff to be more forceful. He asked him to consider that an occasion could arise that might involve his taking a "strong line." They discussed the security situation in Rome and the behavior of the German army and police. The Pope said he had no complaints about either organization and told Osborne that he would never leave Rome unless he was removed by force.

As one thousand of Rome's Jews met their deaths, many of their friends and neighbors were beginning new lives in hiding places across the city. During and after the raids most Jews left their homes, fearful that there would be more deportations. Some sought sanctuary in the homes of friends while others found it in Catholic parish churches and convents. Some fled the city completely to hide in the countryside. For the next nine months Rome's Jews would constantly be looking over their shoulders.

The deportations angered Hugh O'Flaherty, who, when he heard what had happened, commented that "these gentle people [are] being treated like beasts." He is said to have told one colleague that the sooner the Germans were defeated the better. This marked a personal turning point in the priest's view of the war. He had moved from being neutral at the beginning of the conflict, to being sympathetic to the Allies, to now actively wanting the defeat of the Germans.

The arrests of Jews also had significance for O'Flaherty's growing escape organization, as it made it easier for him to elicit help from ordinary Romans who had previously been indifferent to the Germans. In addition the raids seemed to have secured him some leeway with Vatican leaders, for they were now prepared to let him carry on with his activities unhindered even though his work called into question the Church's neutrality.

Soon Jews were searching out the monsignor, who was happy to offer shelter to those who felt themselves to be in danger. Some he offered accommodation in buildings owned by the Church, others he helped to leave Italy. One day a couple approached him on the steps of St. Peter's. They were German Jews living in Rome who feared they would be rounded up and deported. They offered the priest a gold chain and asked him to use it to secure the safety of their seven-year-old son. O'Flaherty said he had a better plan. Most likely relying on the creative skills of his friend Princess Nina Pallavicini, by now part of the escape operation, he had false identity papers drawn up for the couple. They continued to live in the city using their bogus documents while their son was given sanctuary by O'Flaherty. The three were reunited after the war.

In the days following the deportation of the Jews, Rome was filled with fear and panic that the raids would continue. The city was holding its breath to see what the new rulers would do next. German uniforms were evident in all parts of the city and Kappler's men set about marking their territory. A white line was painted around the Vatican State to show where the neutral territory of the Holy See ended and German rule began. Its presence was also a direct challenge to O'Flaherty, who could see the boundary when he stood reading his breviary on the steps of St. Peter's. It was Kappler's way of making it clear who was in charge, and it presented a stark warning. Once you cross this line, he was saying, you play by my rules.

CHAPTER 8

Target O'Flaherty

"I am afraid Colonel Kappler is a very angry man."
—PRINCE FILIPPO DORIA PAMPHILI

IN THE MORNING SUNSHINE, ON A PIAZZA OFF VIA DEL CORSO, Herbert Kappler stepped out of his car and looked up at the sixteenth-century building in front of him. He was outside the home of the anti-fascist aristocrat Prince Filippo Doria Pamphili. An outspoken critic of Mussolini who was known to have helped Jewish refugees, the prince was a target of German surveillance. An anglophile, he was in fact half English and had been educated at Cambridge University. Prince Filippo's anti-fascist stance was well known, and Kappler now had fresh information that the nobleman was funding O'Flaherty's escape operation.

As he stood outside the Palazzo Doria, the Obersturmbann-führer had every reason to be excited. His contacts had informed him that the wealthy prince was meeting the monsignor inside the house. This was too good an opportunity to miss. Armed SS men had already been stationed throughout the area, and on Kappler's cue his officers sealed off the approaches. Standing in the street, Kappler took in the house for a few seconds before his men went to the front door and demanded entry. O'Flaherty was inside, having entered minutes before, and was enjoying the prince's hospitality when the Germans arrived.

The two friends were discussing money when the prince's secretary spotted the SS men. Sensing that his home was surrounded, the prince advised the monsignor to hand himself over to the Germans. O'Flaherty knew that, away from the neutrality of the Vatican, he was no longer safe from arrest. But he wasn't going to make Kappler's job easy and simply surrender. He took the donation of 300,000 lire that the prince had just made, said his good-byes, and rushed down the stairs. Passing through the hallway, he asked the prince's staff to delay opening the front door, then took the narrow steps leading down into the cellar. In the darkness he heard a rumbling. He looked closer and saw coal pouring down into the cellar. The prince was having his winter fuel delivered.

O'Flaherty peered out into the yard and saw two coalmen standing by a parked lorry. In an instant the idea hit him. He removed his robes and put them in a coal sack he found nearby. Wearing just a shirt and trousers, he smeared his face with coal dust, put the sack on his back, and made his way to the open trapdoor, which led onto the courtyard. As one of the delivery men approached, O'Flaherty quietly and quickly took him into his confidence. He explained that he was a priest being pursued by the Germans, and the man agreed to say nothing. Then, coolly and slowly, carrying what appeared to be a full sack, the monsignor began to walk across the courtyard in full view of the watching SS men. They waved him through and he walked around the corner. Minutes later, when it was safe to do so, he dumped the sack and put his robes back on.

Looking more like his normal self, the monsignor made his way back across the Tiber to St. Peter's. It was a journey he had done hundreds of times. As O'Flaherty traveled across Rome, Kappler's team searched every room of the Palazzo Doria. There was no sign of the cleric, and Kappler could not understand how the priest had evaded them. After a two-hour search he gave up and withdrew his men. That afternoon normality slowly returned to the prince's home. Several hours later, as he wondered what had become of his friend, the phone rang. It was a welcome voice, saying, "I'm back home." O'Flaherty was safe in his room in the Vatican. The prince told the monsignor about the raid and Kappler's resultant frustration. "I am afraid Colonel Kappler is a very angry man. He spent two hours here, and he did say that if I happened to see you I was to say one of these days he will be entertaining you in Via Tasso!"

The failed kidnapping attempt made the monsignor reconsider his safety and prompted his decision to end the personal visits to the Palazzo Doria. Every time he crossed the boundary of the Vatican, he was vulnerable to kidnapping, so he had to find other ways to keep in touch with what was happening beyond the boundaries of the Holy See. He continued to stand in his customary position on the steps at St. Peter's, where messages would often be delivered to him. He and Prince Filippo started to communicate by letter and used nuns and priests to transport notes and cash. It was a straightforward system. O'Flaherty would write a note that a cleric would deliver by hand to the prince. The messenger would wait at the Palazzo Doria for a reply and then bring back to the Vatican an envelope, in most cases containing a donation for the Escape Line.

This system worked well until O'Flaherty was tipped off about a raid on Prince Filippo's home. The priest knew he had little time to act. In his office he kept forged identity cards that were given to those who went into hiding. He found three that would be suitable for the prince, his wife, and their daughter and wrote a note to the prince informing him of the impending raid, enclosing the identity cards. A young priest was then dispatched to the Palazzo Doria under strict instructions to give the envelope only to a family member. On receiving the warning the prince and his wife and daughter went into hiding.

Embarrassed at the failure to capture O'Flaherty, Kappler tried a new tactic. In the Gestapo's custody was a deliveryman who had been arrested as he brought supplies from the countryside to a market in Rome. Kappler's men had been watching him and had noticed that he was being used to ferry money back to rural families who were hiding escaped prisoners. They knew he was part of the escape operation and threatened to have him shot, but then they offered him a deal: If the man helped the Gestapo trap O'Flaherty, his life would be spared. The deliveryman agreed. Released to carry out the plan, he made contact with the monsignor at the Vatican within hours and told him he had some information about an escapee. The priest asked the man to meet him at his usual spot on the steps at St. Peter's in the morning. The Germans' plan was to use the man as bait to lure O'Flaherty over the white line that demarcated Vatican territory and then kidnap him.

When O'Flaherty told May about the planned meeting, the Englishman felt the story didn't seem right. Suspecting the hand of the Germans, he said he would discreetly observe the meeting in case anything went wrong. The next morning O'Flaherty, breviary in hand, stood as he always did on the steps leading to St. Peter's Basilica, watching as clergy and civilians went about their business. Nearby, May waited with three Swiss Guards, poised to intervene if the monsignor needed help.

As people spilled out into the square after mass, the attempt to capture O'Flaherty began. A dark Gestapo car with its engine running was parked on the German side of the white line. Within minutes May had spotted the delivery worker. The man came into the square and glanced back at the German car. Moments later he looked up at O'Flaherty and then walked on. He passed by the priest again, and this time May was convinced something was not right. By now the deliveryman had three stark options: One was to go ahead with the plan; the second was to abandon it, retrace his steps, and face the anger of the Germans; the third was to seek sanctuary in the Vatican. He chose the last. He glanced at the monsignor for a final time and then made a dramatic exit by running down a narrow street near the Holy Office.

O'Flaherty had probably not taken in the situation as quickly as May, who was convinced that the delivery worker was being used by the Germans. The butler went off to find the man and offered him accommodation for the night. With the help of a friend, O'Flaherty again had managed to stay one step ahead of the Germans. Meanwhile Kappler was left feeling frustrated that another kidnapping attempt had failed.

By mid-October the weather was deteriorating and the first snowfall had arrived in the Apennine Mountains. Cold and injured, an Irish Guardsman named Lieutenant Colin Lesslie was hiding in a remote hillside cottage after escaping from custody just before the Italian surrender. He made his way into the mountains and made contact with Cedo Ristic, a Yugoslav army officer who worked for the International Red Cross. Ristic found a civilian suit for the soldier and provided the escapee with a train ticket for Rome. Lesslie spent his first few hours in Rome going from church to church before meeting up again as arranged with Ristic, who found him a place to stay for a week. Eventually word of Lesslie reached O'Flaherty, who went to meet the escapee in his hiding place. "Our first Irish Guardsman," the monsignor proclaimed on seeing the British officer. "Now let us see what we can do for you." He spent the next few minutes gently quizzing Lesslie on his background. When O'Flaherty was satisfied that he was genuine, he told Lesslie that the two of them needed to make a little journey after nightfall.

Several hours later O'Flaherty returned with a shirt, trousers, and clerical robes, and within minutes Lesslie looked every inch a monsignor. O'Flaherty was dressed a little more humbly, as an ordinary priest. The two men then left the building and traveled by car to the perimeter of the Holy See, where O'Flaherty told his companion they were about to take a short walk and that Lesslie should leave the talking to him. After gliding past the Swiss Guards, the pair made their way into the Vatican grounds. O'Flaherty was satisfied that this latest escapee was bona fide, but he wanted the British and American diplomats to meet him.

At the British legation in the Santa Marta Hospice, Sir D'Arcy Osborne seemed relaxed as he nursed a large scotch and soda and chatted with the Escape Line's latest arrival. The British envoy and his American counterpart, Harold Tittmann, began to quiz Lesslie on the conditions of Allied prisoners in northern Italy. The conversation went on for a while until O'Flaherty, sensing his guest was getting hungry, brought matters to a close.

The real monsignor and the impostor then retired to O'Flaherty's quarters in the German College. Dinner was served by a German nun, who placed the two meals on O'Flaherty's desk. The two men chatted and then Lesslie spotted the monsignor's golf clubs in the corner of the room. Lesslie was a golfer too, and for the next hour or so, the two of them had fun practicing chip shots into the wastepaper basket. That night O'Flaherty slept in his iron-framed bed and Lesslie had the sofa.

After breakfast the next morning, Lesslie was taken to hide in one of O'Flaherty's apartments. He was housed with a Yugo-slav communist, but the pairing didn't work out, as Lesslie thought the man's behavior compromised security. Lesslie was moved to another apartment, but eventually O'Flaherty decided he would be safer closer to the Vatican.

O'Flaherty had access to the North American College, which, as a Vatican building, was safe from German raids. On the col-lege's grounds stood an old granary and there the monsignor housed escaped prisoners and refugees of different nationalities, including Americans, Frenchmen, and a Yugoslav. O'Flaherty put Lesslie in charge of the escapees, telling him, "In places like this we need a bit of discipline and who better to enforce it than an Irish Guards officer."

His success with Lesslie encouraged O'Flaherty to disguise other escaped servicemen as priests and smuggle them into the Vatican. One of those who took up residence in the North Ameri-can College was U.S. Army Major Raymond Downey, who nor-mally flew B26 Marauders and had been commanding officer of the 37th Bomb Squadron. Downey had been on a bombing mis-sion to blow up a railway bridge four miles north of Todi. After he was hit and crash-landed, he slept rough in the countryside before finding his way to Rome while in search of shelter. He was taken to O'Flaherty, who provided him with clerical vestments. Dressed as a priest, Downey was able to hide in the North American College.

Writing in his diary, Downey described the moment he was taken into the building. "The men here are a most unusual group. We have six or eight young Americans (of Italian descent), all but one of whom received his degree in medicine in June '42. They were supposed to sail on a repatriation ship in July but the boat was held up at the last moment and they had to remain in Rome. In constant danger of being picked up and thrown in a camp by either the Fascists or Germans they were lucky enough to end up here."

To maintain their disguise Downey and his colleagues had to wear their clerical robes when out walking. However, their days as fugitives were spent mainly hidden away, where they would read, write, and play bridge and table tennis. Their surroundings were pleasant; they could shower when they wanted; and they ate well, even though food was in short supply in certain parts of the country. In fact, eating figured prominently in the escapees' lives, as Downey's unpublished diary suggests: "Had afternoon tea with an odd assortment of bread, cake, sandwiches and other junk—all good. Then started shortening my cassock with needle and thread I chiseled from Monsignor O'Flaherty. Got about a quarter finished when the grapevine came through that there was more cake in the other room."

The escapees loved nothing more than receiving a letter from home. O'Flaherty set up a simple network so that families could communicate with their loved ones. Letters were often sent by relatives to the Red Cross in Rome, where a widow by the name of Bruccoleri worked. She was a good friend of the monsignor, and when she spotted a letter that was addressed to one of the Rome escapees, she would put it aside. Her teenage daughter, Josette, would then put it in her schoolbag and take it to O'Flaherty, who would ensure its safe delivery.

In November 1943 there was another arrival at the Vatican who would change the Allied escape operation. Like Downey, another major had been eking out an existence in the Italian countryside. Sam Derry of the Royal Artillery had been living in caves and sleeping in haystacks and, along with other British soldiers, had become reliant on food from local Italian farmers. The major had been a prisoner of war at Chieti camp, and while being transported by train he had dramatically jumped to freedom.

Derry came across groups of other Allied escapees and within days found himself in command of around fifty British soldiers. One hundred and twenty miles behind enemy lines with a group of tired, hungry, and poorly clothed men, the major knew he had to act. Knowing how close he was to Rome, he decided to contact the Vatican. He met a local priest. "Father," he asked, "is it possible for you to get a message into the Vatican?" The priest gave him an odd look but replied that it was possible, then asked whom he wanted to contact. "Anybody English in the Vatican," Derry replied, handing the priest a note saying that a group of Allied prisoners was in dire need of clothes and money. He had signed the request, "S.I. Derry, Major."

Derry was taking a big risk and he knew it. Initially he had felt that sending a plea for help to the Vatican was the best thing to do, but as he waited for a reply, he wondered if he had made a blunder and had compromised the whole group's safety. Over the next few days Derry had moments of anxiety when he half expected to see a group of Germans arrive and arrest them.

Having arrived safely at the Vatican, the note was passed to O'Flaherty, who showed it to Osborne. The envoy agreed that money should be sent and 3,000 lire was duly dispatched. Osborne was intrigued by Derry's request and clearly felt that a soldier of his rank could be of great use to the Escape Line. "Let us see what happens to the money and then perhaps you can bring him to Rome and we can have a talk with him," he told O'Flaherty.

On O'Flaherty's instructions the priest who delivered the money to Derry asked for a receipt. The major obliged with the requested paperwork and cheekily asked for more cash. When O'Flaherty read Derry's second request, he was clearly amused by his audacity, telling May, who was visiting him, "This is the boy for us, John. He's got a bit of drive. Send him 4,000 lire and bring him here."

Derry distributed the first payment of 3,000 lire among his men. He instructed his fellow escapees to buy second-hand clothes and to pay small amounts to the local farming families who had provided the soldiers with food and shelter. Four days later the priest appeared with more money, and this time he had an order from the Vatican. Derry must come to Rome.

One cold November morning, just after dawn, a small land-owner named Pietro Fabri collected Derry, and in a cart weighed down with cabbages, the two men began the slow and rather bumpy journey to Rome. As they drew near the city, Derry was in awe of the domes and towers and was particularly transfixed by the sight of St. Peter's.

On the outskirts of the capital, just short of the German roadblocks, the cart stopped and Derry hid under the cabbages. Soon, at an apartment in the city, Fabri handed over his passenger. There Derry met Aldo Zambardi, whose job was to take him to O'Flaherty. Zambardi greeted him in Italian and then said, in perfect English, "I have been sent here to meet you. Did the money from the Vatican arrive all right?" Yes, Derry told the Italian, who said he was going to take him to the Vatican on the tram.

Derry's attire, which he hadn't changed for some time, caused Zambardi some concern. The major was wearing cut-down desert boots, ink-stained army fatigues, and a tattered shirt. A pair of ill-fitting trousers and an undersize coat were produced, along with a cloth cap. In his new outfit Derry boarded the tram with Zambardi. He was under strict instructions to pretend to be asleep and under no circumstances to speak. It was a hard journey for the major to feign sleep because he was excited to take in the splendor of Rome's sights, but he knew he must do nothing to arouse suspicion. After getting off the tram the two men walked to St. Peter's Square.

Among the German soldiers and the civilians, Derry spotted a tall figure in priest's robes standing with his hands folded and his head bowed. O'Flaherty appeared to be praying, but Derry sensed he had noticed their arrival. Zambardi went toward the priest, who quietly instructed the two men to follow him a short distance behind. They walked behind the monsignor, passing through the colonnade and into a small street. Then they entered a small square and went through a door, above which Derry noticed the bold inscription. His Latin was rusty but he knew what "Collegium Teutonicum" meant, and as an escaped British POW, he felt a little uneasy to be entering the German College.

O'Flaherty led the two men into a small office. He and Zambardi spoke briefly in Italian and then the monsignor turned to Derry and said, "Now my boy, we will go up to my room but we are leaving Aldo now, so you had better give him his coat back." Derry returned the overcoat, thanked Zambardi for his help, and followed O'Flaherty to his room. Over cookies the two men chatted about the war and escaped prisoners. At first Derry was reluctant to divulge too much information, but he soon relaxed and they began swapping stories. Derry had a dozen questions for his host, but they would have to wait. O'Flaherty brought their talk to an end, saying there would be time to discuss things later. In the meantime would his guest like a bath? Since Derry had not had a proper bath in over eighteen months, it was too good an opportunity to refuse. The two men were of similar build, so O'Flaherty offered the major some clothes and showed him the bathroom. "Take your time and come back to my room when you are ready—and don't get lost on the way," he said.

Later, when Derry returned to O'Flaherty's room, the monsignor was not there, so Derry took the opportunity to look around. He was puzzled. He had entered the building without being challenged, yet Rome was under German rule. He was in some kind of religious college but didn't know if he was in the Vatican. If he was in the Vatican, why hadn't the Vatican guards stopped him? He was either a guest of the Vatican or else a prisoner in some kind of elaborate German plot. As he thought about which scenario was more likely, the door opened and in stepped a dark-haired man carrying a briefcase. "Major Derry, I believe?" the man asked in an unmistakable London accent. John May then opened his briefcase and offered Derry a bottle of spirits and several packets of cigarettes. "I thought you would be glad of these to celebrate your arrival," he told Derry. Moments later O'Flaherty returned and the three men chatted for a few minutes, before the monsignor excused himself and left.

Derry was baffled by all the comings and goings. May told him who O'Flaherty was and what his role was in the Holy Office. He explained that he himself was butler to Sir D'Arcy Osborne, the British minister to the Holy See. It was all beginning to make sense, although it still sounded a bit far-fetched. Derry almost had to pinch himself. He was inside the Vatican, in a German college, as the official guest of an Irish priest and an English butler.

Over dinner with Osborne everything would become clearer. But before that there was the small matter of a disguise for Derry. Even though it was a short walk from O'Flaherty's room to Osborne's residence, the escapee needed to be wearing appropriate clothes. Once dressed in a long black cloak, silver-buckled shoes, and a vivid scarlet sash, the major was a very passable monsignor. He walked beside O'Flaherty, who was dressed identically. The two men then left the Holy Office, passed the Vatican gendarmerie, and entered the Santa Marta Hospice. They took the elevator to the top floor, where they were greeted by May and an Italian footman. Moments later Derry found himself sitting in the drawing room cradling a White Lady cocktail. For him the next few hours were like paradise. His aperitif was followed by a grapefruit, steak with mushrooms and tomatoes, a delicious dessert, and cheese. For a man who had been living on handouts from farmers, this was supreme luxury.

Over cigarettes and coffee Osborne came straight to the point. He told Derry about the escape operation run by O'Flaherty, May, and Count Salazar, and he explained how it worked. By now it was getting late, and the monsignor bade everyone goodnight and told Derry he would pick him up the following day.

Derry and Osborne continued to talk until late into the night. In O'Flaherty's absence the envoy explained how the monsignor now needed to stand back from the escape operation. It was well known that the Irishman had been running the organization and the Germans had already tried to kidnap him, so it was now very risky for the monsignor to continue. Osborne then said that they wanted to find somebody to coordinate the work. Looking Derry straight in the face, he asked, "Now that you know what it is all about, are you prepared to take command?" Derry paused. After life in the prison camp and being on the run, he was ready for a new challenge. "Of course, sir," he replied. Osborne told Derry that he would have to rely on O'Flaherty in the early stages, while he got to know the operation, but he was convinced the pair of them would work well together.

Before Derry could begin his new role, he had one final job to do. He had to return to his own group of escaped prisoners, who were still in the countryside near Salone, to put a new officer in charge and to distribute more money for food and clothing. He was taken there by Pietro Fabri, who had brought him into Rome in his cart.

Even as the British major spoke to his men, back in England, in Derry's hometown of Newark, in Nottinghamshire, a police officer from the local force was calling on his father. The explicit purpose of Inspector Morley's visit was to inform Mr. Derry that his son, who had been reported missing, was alive and well. His other motive was to gain private details that could be used by Sir D'Arcy Osborne to confirm Major Derry's identity.

When he returned to Rome, Derry had no reason to know that his father had been visited. He had even less reason to know that Osborne had sent a coded message to the Foreign Office asking for investigators to carry out a check on his background. Scotland Yard had been informed, who in turn had requested the help of Newark police. When the major went to see Osborne, he thought he was going for a routine chat, but he soon found himself being interrogated. Derry's answers satisfied the envoy. The escape operation had its new man at last. Sam Derry was issued with false papers and given a new identity. He became Patrick Derry, an Irish writer employed by the Vatican. In late November 1943 he assumed military responsibility for the Escape Line.

CHAPTER 9

Closing the Net

"The fact that the Vatican has never been raided does not mean it never will be."

—SIR D'ARCY OSBORNE

AT EXACTLY SEVEN O'CLOCK THE VISITORS NOISILY ARRIVED AT THE door of Henrietta Chevalier's apartment. When she heard the thud of rifle butts, she was in her kitchen sewing. Rising from her chair, she walked to the door. She didn't want to let them in, but she was in no position to refuse her visitors entry. The armed German officer and four soldiers brushed past her and began to look around the apartment. The officer demanded identification papers from her son Paul. He handed them over and watched as the German scanned them and then passed them back. "How many of you live here?" demanded the officer. Henrietta gestured toward the table, "Six, as you can see."

As one of O'Flaherty's trusted hosts, Henrietta had quickly mastered the art of deception. The table had conveniently been laid out for six diners, and other precautions had been taken to clear the apartment of any evidence that would attract the Germans' attention. The mattresses the escapees slept on had been put away and there was no trace of their clothes or personal possessions.

One by one each soldier entered the tiny kitchen. Very little of what they found proved of interest. Henrietta watched as they went through some boxes and papers. In one corner of the living room, a soldier browsed through the family's record collection. Henrietta's daughter Gemma stood watching and tried to contain her fear. In the pile of discs was an English one that would instantly arouse suspicions and start a raft of inevitable questions. Thankfully the German's search was cursory and he didn't spot it. By now he and his colleagues seemed restless and frustrated. They had more searches to carry out and hoped they would have better luck elsewhere. The officer sent his men outside, then said goodbye to Henrietta and closed the door. The Chevaliers could relax for the time being.

Hours earlier Paul, who worked at the Swiss legation, had learned that the area was to be searched by the Germans. At 6:50 p.m. one of Henrietta's neighbors, who knew she hosted escaped Allied prisoners, gave her warning. By the time the Germans crashed into her front door, ten minutes later, Henrietta's four "lodgers" were gone. Earlier, each of the escapees had been sent out for a long walk with one of the four Chevalier daughters. They returned to the apartment in pairs, as they had left, so as not to cause suspicion.

The German raid had been ordered by Herbert Kappler, who wanted to find a radio transmitter that he believed was being used in one of the buildings close to the Chevaliers' apartment. Kappler's control of Rome was some three months old. His empire had expanded greatly since the early days of the occupation: Once his unit had consisted of just two Gestapo officers, but there were now seventy-four. At Via Tasso, where Kappler was based, an interrogation center had been built alongside the twenty-cell prison, which housed partisans, anti-fascists, and anyone the Nazis wanted off the streets.

The city was now under curfew, and Kappler's men were working alongside a special unit of the Italian police nicknamed the "Koch gang." Their leader, twenty-five-year-old Pietro Koch, had created a ruthless band of officers who spent much time crisscrossing Rome on the lookout for Jews, communists, and known anti-fascists.

By December 1943 the Resistance's underground war against the Nazis was being stepped up. Over three days they mounted a series of attacks. A German officer was shot dead as he walked out of one of the city's hotels. Gun attacks took place at a restaurant frequented by German troops, and eight soldiers died when a bomb was thrown at them by a Resistance fighter, who escaped on a bicycle. In another attack the Hotel Flora, used by the German high command, was bombed. The Germans' response was swift. The curfew now started at 7 p.m. instead of 11:30 p.m. and the use of bicycles after 5 p.m. was prohibited. Then Pietro Koch's special police squad was called into action, and using Gestapo and Fascist agents, they raided three Vatican institutions.

In heavy rain one winter's evening, Koch's men, supported by members of the SS, stormed the Lombard Seminary. The contingent included Kappler's colleague, SS Captain Erich Priebke, and several other SS men. The building displayed a notice stating that it was a Vatican property and searches were prohibited. The declaration was signed by Major General Rainer Stahel, the German military commander of Rome, but the Vatican's warning sign was ignored by Koch and Kappler's men.

They began to search the premises and quickly removed the rector from the chapel where he was conducting evening prayers. As he was being led out, others were able to escape. Some Jewish men were able to make their way to safety in an adjoining building. A number of the seminary's illegal residents ran into the cellar and entered a secret room designed for such a contingency. Several fugitives found improvised hiding places. One man played dead by lying in an open coffin while others managed to hide themselves in the skirts of nuns who were attending mass.

The next place to receive the Koch treatment was the Institute for Oriental Studies, where there were some twenty Jews and anti-fascists. Like those who were staying illegally in the seminary, they had a prearranged escape drill. When the search began, a number of fugitives found their way to the Russicum, a Jesuit-run school that trained priests for missionary work in the Soviet Union. The search went on until the next morning; during the raid Koch's men stole anything of value. Shortly after seven o'clock they left with a total of eighteen prisoners, including Jews, anti-fascists, and the trade union leader Giovanni Roveda, who was also a high-ranking member of the Communist Party. Within hours of the raid ending, many of those who had been hiding in the cellars and secret rooms decided it was time to move. Fearful that Kappler's and Koch's men would come back, men, women, and children moved out. They would never return.

The raids on the three Vatican properties caused consternation in the Holy See. It prompted two major questions: Should Vatican properties be used to harbor fugitives? And were the Germans now planning a takeover of the Vatican City? Those within the Catholic Church who were uneasy about offering shelter to refugees used the raids to support their arguments. One official wrote that those still hiding in extra-territorial buildings should be told they are "not at all secure." He added: "those who find themselves in other ecclesiastical buildings should be urged to change lodging." That report was written by an unidentified official who worked for Cardinal Maglione.

The day before the nighttime raids, the cardinal's office had received information from an Italian colonel that the SS police force in Rome was about to be strengthened from four hundred men to two thousand. According to the informant, once those numbers were achieved the Germans planned to conduct a huge search in which every building in Rome would be raided. What concerned the Vatican was that Church properties, including convents and monasteries, would not be exempt from searches. The Italian officer also told the Vatican that Kappler had not ruled out the idea of attacking and taking over the Vatican City. This revelation heightened fears in the Holy See.

The Italian colonel's report gained credence in Church circles when it was followed by the raids on Vatican properties. Many in the Holy See began to ask what would be next. Pope Pius XII had been given guarantees by Hitler that he would respect the Church's sovereignty, but it seemed that this personal assurance was now in doubt.

The Vatican was now caught up in a world of rumor and counter-rumor. Months earlier a radio station purporting to be German, but in fact part of a clandestine British propaganda operation, had broadcast a story that the Pope was to be removed from Rome and taken to Liechtenstein. When Cardinal Maglione heard that Kappler was intending to move against the Vatican, he met with Baron Ernst von Weizsäcker. Maglione pressed the German ambassador for some answers, and in turn Weizsäcker questioned Kappler, who denied knowing about such a plan. Nevertheless, it is clear that action against the Pope had been considered at the highest level of the Third Reich.

In July 1943, at the Wolf's Lair, Hitler had famously lost his temper and, referring to the Vatican, had vowed to "clear out that gang of swine." The plan never materialized, but in September Hitler summoned the commander of the SS in Italy to his East Prussian headquarters. He told General Wolff he wanted to occupy the Vatican and transfer the Pope to either Germany or Liechtenstein. Wolff asked for time, saying that across Italy his units were stretched thin. Hitler wanted regular reports from him, and over the next six weeks Wolff routinely filed dispatches on the security situation. Finally, in December, he told Hitler that the occupation of the Vatican and the removal of the Pope would draw a negative reaction throughout Italy as well as among Catholics in neutral states. He urged the Führer to abandon the kidnapping plan, and it was never carried out.

Records show that the suggestion about the Pope leaving the Vatican for Liechtenstein surfaced in a message sent by an officer by the name of Sandberger to Berlin in October 1943. He stated that "if a skilful person were to make the suggestion to the Pope that he should move to Liechtenstein it is conceivable that he would agree." The note infuriated Kappler, who sent a cable contradicting Sandberger. He was furious, calling Sandberger's idea "a gross misunderstanding." Kappler wondered if it was meant as "a joke" and insisted that such a suggestion was irresponsible, stating that the Pope would never consent to leave the Vatican.

The Vatican was naturally unaware of the intricacies of the debate surrounding the future of the Pope, but undoubtedly officials felt the strain created by the Germans' arrival in Rome. As the first Christmas of the Nazi occupation approached, there was still great anxiety and fear behind the walls of the Holy See. Understandably, O'Flaherty and Derry shared those concerns.

They had Allied prisoners hidden both in the Vatican and all over Rome, and the Germans had threatened to shoot those harboring Allied escapees.

Mindful of a possible escalation of German raids, Derry's first job was to step up security. He felt that both the escapees and those running the organization did not take security seriously enough. It was, he feared, their Achilles' heel. He left the Vatican and went on a tour of the safe houses and hiding places where escapees lived. He insisted that every fugitive memorize an evacuation drill in case their property was raided. Conscious that the ever-watchful Germans would like to place spies within the ranks of the Allied escapees, Derry also introduced a clearing system for new arrivals. He would interview them first, and they would be placed with local Italian families only when he was satisfied they were genuine.

By now some two thousand escapees were housed in about forty sites across Rome. The organization had grown dramatically since O'Flaherty, May, and Salazar had started it. Byrnes and Elliot had provided invaluable administrative support, working hard on their list of escapees. This was sensitive information and Osborne warned Derry, "You must still be very careful about what you put in writing; the fact that the Vatican has never been raided does not mean it never will be."

The growing organization also needed more financial backing. While Osborne had never had a day-to-day role in the operation, he had effectively become its banker. Money was needed for clothes, meat, and bread, and those who looked after prisoners were given 120 lire a day. Osborne received funds from the British government. One million lire was made available, and over four weeks, 69,000 lire was distributed to pay for the living costs of the escapees. Harold Tittmann, the American envoy, was also contributing money to pay for the upkeep of, mainly, American airmen who had escaped from their downed planes.

It was Derry's job to make sure such money was spent wisely and accounted for. He knew that after the war some official would expect to see how the cash had been used, so he bought a rudimentary ledger and began to record each transaction. However, he soon realized it would be better for security reasons if certain names were protected, so he devised a code system. Each member of the escape organization was given a cover name to be used in all communications. Monsignor O'Flaherty was predictably christened "Golf," Sir D'Arcy Osborne became "Mount," Henrietta Chevalier was "Mrs. M.," Count Sarsfield Salazar was "Emma," and Derry was "Patrick," in line with his alias. Many other names were devised for priests and supporters who hid escapees. It was an attempt to give the operation an extra layer of protection and to keep Kappler's men at bay. In phone conversations, all of which were assumed to be bugged, and in documentation, code names were used. Coded language was another necessary precaution. To confuse listening Germans, escaped prisoners were referred to as "dispatches" or "parcels," and occasionally O'Flaherty would say he had a package or some "golf clubs" to deliver.

By now the organization, which had grown beyond anyone's expectations, had an empire of escapees on its hands, and there was much corresponding paperwork. The documentation sometimes caused headaches for O'Flaherty and Derry. Because large sums of money were being spent on supplies, and deliveries needed to be tracked, it was essential to keep proper records. At the same time the monsignor and the major were worried that if the paperwork was discovered, the safety of many hundreds of people would be compromised. So each evening Captain Byrnes, who was in charge of looking after receipts and other invoices, followed a bizarre procedure. He took the dockets and details of expenditure, placed them in cookie tins, and hid these in the Vatican gardens. Derry, O'Flaherty, and Osborne still believed the German threat to raid the Vatican was real, so the cookie-tin routine was regarded as a necessary daily precaution.

As the year drew to a close, Derry had become an integral part of the Escape Line. He and O'Flaherty complemented each other. The monsignor was impulsive, whereas Derry was rather more circumspect and often analyzed situations before making a decision. This difference was illustrated by their approach to new arrivals and potential members of the escape operation. Where Derry was always initially inquisitive and cautious about those seeking help, O'Flaherty welcomed every new escapee with open arms.

It was the monsignor's nature to see the good in everyone, and he was always prepared to take people at face value. Indeed he often appeared to be in a hurry to dispense help. It was his Christian faith that taught him to try to assist as many people as possible without delay. But this openness bothered Derry, who was convinced that the organization was vulnerable to penetration by German or Italian spies. He was convinced that this was a weakness that Kappler could easily exploit.

On December 8, as he stood outside O'Flaherty's room, Derry was certain that the fatal moment had arrived. He knew Kappler had come close in the past to breaking the escape organization, and he wondered if this time the German had gotten lucky.

Within seconds of opening his door to him, the monsignor told Derry that there was a new arrival. Derry turned to see a small-framed man with a dark complexion who had just arrived.

The sight of Joe Pollak made his heart sink. Derry had met him before at Chieti prison camp. Pollak had a curious history. He was Jewish and had been a medical student in Czechoslovakia. When the war began, he went to Palestine and then joined Britain's Royal Pioneer Corps before being transferred to the Royal Army Medical Corps. He served in Greece, then was taken prisoner and transferred to Chieti prison, where he served as an interpreter and an assistant in the camp hospital. Derry was convinced Pollak's story about being brought to Italy from Greece didn't add up, and he suspected that the Czech was working as a Nazi spy.

As he tried not to show any concern, Derry told the new arrival, "It's a hell of a surprise to see you here." Pollak then began to explain to him how he had escaped. Derry was determined to stay calm and not reveal any information about his work with O'Flaherty. He questioned his former prison colleague, and Pollak told him he was in Rome with six other male escapees and two Italian girls. Trying to stall him and play for more time, Derry then asked him for the names of his co-escapees. As Pollak started to list them—"Well, there's Lieutenant Furman, Lieutenant Simpson . . ."—the names changed Derry's mood instantly, making him feel a lot happier. They were Derry's old pals, comrades who had been with him in Chieti. Both Bill Simpson and John Furman he regarded as savvy individuals who would have sniffed Pollak out if he wasn't on the level.

Derry was heartened by what he had heard, yet he was still uneasy about Pollak and wanted to know if Simpson and Furman could vouch for their Czech friend. Derry was understandably nervous. Just weeks into his new role as military commander of the British Escape Line, he was worried that he was about to jeopardize the entire operation. So he asked Pollak to come back the next day and bring Furman with him. Pollak agreed, and the next morning he and Furman turned up at the Vatican to be greeted by a delighted Derry.

After handshakes and backslaps Derry took the two men to O'Flaherty's room in the German College. There he ushered Furman inside but asked Pollak to go into a room along the corridor. He offered Furman a drink, and the two old friends started to swap news. Then Derry explained why he had asked Pollak to go elsewhere, and he outlined his misgivings to Furman. For the next few minutes Derry quizzed the lieutenant about Pollak's background and behavior. It soon became clear to Derry that any suggestion that the man was working as a spy was simply unfounded. Furman gave his Czech colleague a glowing testimony and Derry's fears were allayed.

The major brought Pollak back to the monsignor's room and told him, "I owe you an apology." He added that Pollak had done a great job and that he had been wrong to doubt him. Derry then took both men into his confidence about the Escape Line and offered them jobs, which they were happy to accept. His caution over Pollak had proved unnecessary, but his worry that O'Flaherty's trusting manner could expose the organization to sabotage still gnawed at him. The growth of the escape operation meant that continually more people knew of its existence and that with every new arrival the chances of its being uncovered by the Germans increased. O'Flaherty's reputation had now spread beyond Rome, and he would often receive appeals for help from unexpected quarters.

One day the monsignor received a message from an Italian called Peter Tumiati, who wanted to meet him, pass on some information, and hand over a cash donation for the organization.

Derry was tasked to meet the visitor at the normal rendezvous point at the colonnade in St. Peter's Square. Tumiati had been imprisoned by the Fascists and was now working as an agent for British military intelligence.

Derry, as instructed, went to meet Tumiati, who introduced himself and told the major he had traveled up from the Allied lines at Bari, in the far south of Italy. He handed over 20,000 lire and then asked if there was anything else he could do to help. Tumiati's donation and request placed Derry in a dilemma. He didn't know whether to believe him. O'Flaherty clearly trusted the Italian, and when Derry asked the monsignor about Tumiati's background, the response was short but straightforward. His colleague simply confirmed that he knew Tumiati.

This did little to dispel Derry's fears. Who was this man Tumiati? Was he genuine? Was this an attempt by Kappler to penetrate the escape organization? Derry knew he had to test Tumiati, so he asked him to get some maps for him. It was a simple request, one which Tumiati carried out with ease. Derry then decided to send Tumiati back to Bari with a list of all the Allied prisoners who were on the run. The idea was that this information would then work its way back to the men's families at home. The move had risks attached to it, but he felt that even if the material fell into German hands they would not discover anything they did not already know. He still didn't trust Tumiati completely but felt this idea was the best option.

Derry discussed the plan with O'Flaherty and May. The issue of Tumiati's safety was raised. If the Italian was stopped by the Germans and discovered with the information, he would most certainly be shot. How could they give Tumiati information without putting his life in danger? May then weighed in with a suggestion. "Microfilm the lot. I can arrange it," he said. They agreed, and hours later May turned up with a tiny microfilm that contained the details of a couple of thousand soldiers, sailors, and airmen. Derry stared at the lists carefully prepared by Captain Byrnes in microscopic writing. "Where do we go from here?" he asked May.

Osborne's butler was one step ahead of Derry. He whisked away the tiny microfilm and returned later with a batch of bread loaves. He had placed the microfilm into some dough and baked it without destroying it. Tumiati now had a cover, and he was pleased with May's ruse. As he prepared to leave for Bari, Derry teased him by reminding him not to eat the wrong loaf. Weeks later it became clear that Tumiati had returned safely and had passed on the details. He had agreed to get a key phrase broadcast on a BBC radio bulletin, which would confirm his safe return. Later, as Derry listened in, he heard the crucial words and knew that the British government had received Tumiati's list.

Now the authorities in London knew the full extent of O'Flaherty and Derry's work. By December 1943 many Allied servicemen were preparing to face their first Christmas in hiding, and O'Flaherty was determined to make their holiday as festive and enjoyable as possible. Two days before Christmas he, Henrietta Chevalier, and several priests were crammed into the monsignor's little room. For hours they wrapped hundreds of tiny parcels and decorated them with silk ribbons. They were small presents for each man in hiding and attached was an English Christmas card.

Derry had other ways to instill a bit of Christmas cheer. He sanctioned the purchase of additional food, cigarettes, and wine. Furman and Simpson, by now key members of the organization, thought up an ingenious way to deliver some turkeys to the safe houses. The two men carried the birds around Rome hidden inside suitcases.

Keeping with tradition, O'Flaherty began his Christmas with mass on the ground floor of the chapel of the German College. Christmas dinner was served, as normal, by the nuns, and he and Derry dined together. On December 26, the British Boxing Day, or St. Stephen's Day as the Irish called it, O'Flaherty's guests included Dr. Thomas Kiernan, the Irish envoy to the Vatican, and his wife, Delia. Mrs. Kiernan was a well-known ballad singer and had toured Ireland and Britain before she and her husband had moved to Italy. In Rome she had thrown herself into the role of diplomat's wife. The Kiernans were regulars on the social scene and were often invited to parties attended by the occupying Germans.

To the Nazis the couple came across as a charming couple who maintained Ireland's official policy of neutrality. But Delia had a secret: She was one of O'Flaherty's strongest supporters. The monsignor would often ask her to provide food and assist him with escapees. It was dangerous work because she wasn't just putting her own life and her husband's in danger, but she was seriously compromising the entire Irish diplomatic mission, which would be shut down if her actions were discovered. Delia believed the risks were worth taking, however: "For a time I had wrestled with my conscience and prayed for guidance about what I should do to help Father O'Flaherty. A voice inside me said charity was something God intended for all humanity, in war and peace. And I remembered the words of St Paul: now abideth faith, hope and charity, these three, but the greatest of these is charity." Her response to the monsignor was typical. So many people that O'Flaherty came in contact with were impressed by his quiet requests for help—requests they found hard to turn down.

Over Christmas, in the monsignor's small room, the Kiernans were joined by a number of priests who had dropped by to join in the festivities. As always, Delia was called upon to sing, and she performed "The Spinning Wheel," one of her best-known songs. Father Buckley, who was better known by his code name "Spike," entertained everyone with his rendition of "Mother Machree." It was a happy occasion and provided a welcome relief to the stresses of warfare. Across the city, in her little apartment in Via Imperia, Henrietta Chevalier was doing her utmost to make sure her extra houseguests were being looked after and that an array of turkey, brandy, cake, and fruit was on hand.

These joyful gatherings provided a welcome break from the ongoing battle between Kappler and O'Flaherty, but were short-lived. For the Obersturmbannführer had been plotting, and before the year ended he was involved in one of the Nazis' most ambitious plans to date to penetrate the Vatican.

On December 28, the Holy See took possession of a property in Via Alessandro Brisse, in the Monteverde Nuovo area of Rome. The building was to house the new Georgian College, which would be home to clerical students who had traveled from Georgia, in the Soviet Union, to study in Rome. The project had the blessing of Pope Pius XII and the Vatican's Congregation for Eastern Churches, which remained keen to support any effort that would develop Catholicism in that part of the world. The initiative was also seen as a way of reinforcing the historical link between the Popes of Rome and Georgian Catholics. The plan was to build a chapel, a library, and study rooms like those in other Catholic institutions across Rome. The cost of establishing the new complex was of critical importance, and officially it was being funded by an anonymous benefactor. The Pope and other senior Vatican figures had been informed that the mystery donor was prepared to pay for the building and then wished to transfer its ownership to the Vatican.

In the second week of December, the proposal was discussed by the Pope and Cardinal Tisserant of the Congregation for Eastern Churches, and they agreed to the plans. Not known by the Pontiff and other senior churchmen in the Holy See, the unnamed donor was not some well-meaning wealthy Catholic but in fact the German intelligence service, which was providing over one million lire to pay for the building. The intention was to construct a college from which German agents could secretly use to spy on the Vatican.

At the heart of the clandestine operation was one of Kappler's informers. Basilius Sadathierascvili, a colorful Georgian, had begun living in Rome before the war. He had worked in a variety of jobs, including journalism and dealing in works of art of questionable quality, and more recently had worked as an interpreter for the German military authorities in the city. This contact most likely led him to Kappler, to whom he began to pass on information.

The idea of the Georgian College had been hatched and put into operation by intelligence staff in Berlin at the headquarters of the Reich Security Main Office and involved members of Amt VI, the RSHA's foreign-intelligence section. The plan was bold and, if successful, would achieve German intelligence leaders' long-held ambition of infiltrating the Vatican. For Kappler this latest attempt to penetrate the secret world of the Holy See sounded very familiar. In 1942 he had hoped Alexander Kurtna would provide key intelligence as he worked closely with the Congregation for Eastern Churches, but the Estonian, who was working for both the Germans and the Russians, had been arrested by the Italians. Now, using another informer, Kappler was effectively retracing his steps.

Using money that was most likely counterfeit, Kappler paid Sadathierascvili 50,000 lire, after which the Georgian was sent to Berlin to meet senior German intelligence officers, who briefed him about the operation. The plan was to make Sadathierascvili the lay administrator of the college. He would be put in charge of the building work and would construct two secret rooms, which would be set aside for his own use. One room would house a radio transmitter and the other would be used for German agents. The rooms were to have their own entrance and would be built with the assistance of Lieutenant Stephen Untewenger, an SS signals officer who worked in Kappler's office. The building was to be ready within months.

By October Kappler was clearly becoming frustrated with both his battle against the Vatican and his war against the Resistance. On the evening of the 26th, he cabled to Berlin that "the Vatican has apparently for a long time been assisting many Jews to escape." He also highlighted the battle to win the hearts and minds of Romans and bemoaned the fact that "our propaganda is inadequate. We consider it urgently necessary for pro-German Italians to enlighten the population."

In November there would be a new arrival at Kappler's office whose background and experience would be ideally suited to tracking the activities of those who worked in the Vatican. Georg Elling had served with the German military during the First World War and had been ordained as a priest. Since then, however, he had left the priesthood and turned his back on the Catholic Church.

Elling had become attracted to the ideas of Hitler in the 1930s and subsequently joined the Nazis, working in the party's intelligence wing. Elling's attachment to Kappler's office was only temporary. He would shortly move to a post in the German embassy in the Holy See, where he would pose as the cultural attaché and use the position to control agents and collect information on Vatican staff. Fluent in English and Italian, he was given the title of "research auxiliary" and passed himself off as a freelance historian studying the life of St. Francis of Assisi. His appointment to the German embassy had been sanctioned by high-ranking members of the RSHA but had initially been opposed by the German ambassador to the Holy See, who felt there was no need for another person in the embassy, arguing that the building was already "overstaffed."

Weizsäcker lost the argument, however, and Elling arrived in Rome and was based initially in Kappler's headquarters in Via Tasso. At first the Gestapo officers were supportive of their new colleague, helping him find his footing and introducing him to contacts. But eventually tensions developed. Kappler's team and Elling would end up as rivals competing for the same sources. In addition, Elling disapproved of Kappler's use of violence at the interrogation center. Elling's main responsibilities were to keep an eye on Vatican diplomats like Sir D'Arcy Osborne and to manage a network of agents who could operate in Rome.

Kappler's expanded network now included a series of wireless operators and agents who were willing to pass on information from a wide range of sources. He had information coming in from many of the different ethnic groups across Rome, including the Albanians and the Yugoslavs.

As the various intelligence operations continued covertly across the city, publicly the Nazi occupation became more conspicuous. As the year ended, the German forces and the Italian police tightened their grip on Rome. A new checkpoint was put in place close to the Vatican, a number of locals assisting the Escape Line were arrested, and spies were placed outside a number of safe houses, among them Henrietta Chevalier's apartment.

As 1943 came to an end, Herbert Kappler had every reason to feel that the New Year would see him shut down Monsignor O'Flaherty's organization and help him finally penetrate the closed world of the Vatican.

Chapter 10

Raids and Arrests

"It has gone on for too long, and it has got to stop."
—Baron Ernst von Weizsäcker,
German ambassador to the Vatican

The New Year was just a few days old when a gold-embossed invitation was delivered to O'Flaherty's desk by a porter. The monsignor was invited to attend a reception at the Hungarian embassy. At first glance the event seemed innocent enough. He was often asked to attend functions in the various national embassies in the city. However, as he knew well, social events at the Hungarian legation were often attended by a good number of German officials who used such occasions for a spot of casual diplomacy.

O'Flaherty knew he was taking a risk in leaving the security of the Vatican and going to the embassy but, characteristically, he wanted to go. As expected, one of his fellow guests was the German ambassador to the Holy See. Personable and articulate, with white hair and blue eyes, Weizsäcker was a familiar sight on Rome's social scene. A powerful and experienced diplomat, Weizsäcker had held the second-highest position in the Reich's Foreign Ministry until his appointment to Rome. That the Führer should appoint such a senior figure to the Vatican illustrated the importance Hitler attached to papal diplomacy. It was Weizsäcker's job to regularly tell him what the Vatican was thinking and to constantly inform the Pope of Hitler's views.

The ambassador would become a figure of controversy during and after the war. He had been involved in the discussions surrounding Hitler's plans to kidnap the Pope, and later in the year he would be named as a member of the plot to topple Hitler himself. Weizsäcker had established a good relationship with Pope Pius XII and was seen by some Germans as too sympathetic to the Vatican. He was not trusted by the Gestapo. However, in January 1944 he was behaving in public as a most loyal Nazi. Shortly after O'Flaherty arrived at the gathering, the German diplomat spotted him and asked if they could go somewhere for a quiet word.

Weizsäcker told the monsignor that the German military authorities knew he was involved in the Escape Line. He continued, "It has gone on for too long, and it has got to stop." Then he offered some advice: "In future you will stay where you belong. If you leave the area of the Vatican you will be arrested on sight. This is a final warning. Think carefully about what I have said."

O'Flaherty smiled and replied, "Your Excellency is too considerate. I will certainly think about what you have said, sometimes." He then left the embassy and returned to his room in the German College where he told Derry about the ambassador's warning. They discussed how seriously he should take the diplomat's words.

It was hardly a surprise that the monsignor was being watched, but what was different this time was the fact that the warning had come in person from one of the most senior German officials in Rome. If O'Flaherty thought he could ignore the threat, he certainly could not disregard the next request he received.

Within hours of his conversation with Weizsäcker, O'Flaherty was summoned to meet Monsignor Giovanni Montini. An influential Vatican figure, Montini worked as a deputy at the Secretariat of State. He was a close friend of Sir D'Arcy Osborne, and while the British representative is unlikely to have told him about the activities of the Escape Line, it is apparent that Montini had a good understanding of what was going on. The Vatican official spoke frankly to O'Flaherty, repeating the German warning and cautioning him about his work with the escapees. The monsignor faced a dilemma. While he could ignore the words of Weizsäcker, it was a different proposition to ignore the advice of the Church and his employers. He had some serious thinking to do.

There was more bad news. Derry's assumed identity as the Irishman Patrick Derry had been discovered by the rector of the German College, and O'Flaherty was informed that the British major had to leave. Moreover, he was told to move him out within a few days. It was felt that Derry's continued presence was threatening the Vatican's neutrality and making a German raid more likely. Derry packed his bags but didn't have far to go. Wearing the clerical garb of a monsignor provided by O'Flaherty, he left the German College and walked to Osborne's quarters in the nearby Santa Marta Hospice. The Escape Line was facing its biggest crisis. Weizsäcker's warning was only part of the Germans' plan to break the organization.

Days earlier a chain of events had begun that would throw the entire escape operation into turmoil. Joe Pollak, who had become a key part of the network, had visited a colleague and been arrested by the Gestapo. The pair were taken in for questioning. It was a major setback and it made O'Flaherty and Derry very nervous. They knew Pollak's arrest could lead to other German raids. Just as worrying was Weizsäcker's warning, which had revealed that the Germans would arrest O'Flaherty should he step outside the Vatican.

The monsignor and the major tried to second-guess what Kappler was planning. Following Pollak's arrest there were many unanswered questions. How much did the Gestapo know? Would the network's safe houses soon be raided? Was the entire operation now threatened? The two men spent much of the next day arranging alternative accommodations for the escapees. The Escape Line was in jeopardy, and the situation was about to get even worse.

In the first week of January, a young Italian communist was being interrogated at Via Tasso. At the interrogation center, housed in a narrow street, Kappler often witnessed the brutal beatings he had ordered. In windowless cells prisoners were subjected to the most inhumane treatment. Some were beaten with spiked mallets, others had their feet burned with gas flames, and it was not uncommon for prisoners to have their teeth pulled out. A specially constructed soundproofed room was used to prevent screams being heard.

The young communist was brutally beaten but had not betrayed his comrades, so Kappler's men tried a different approach. Wearing raincoats and trilby hats, a number of them visited the young man's mother. They pretended they were members of the Resistance who wanted to free her son from the Gestapo prison. Could she put them in touch with other Resistance friends? Convinced her visitors had come to help, she offered up the name of a close friend who, she mentioned, happened to be looking after two British servicemen.

It was another breakthrough for Kappler. The information led two of his agents to an apartment in the city's Parioli district that was part of O'Flaherty's network of safe houses. A leader of the Italian underground called Nebolante lived there, and when he answered the door the Gestapo men again posed as supporters of the Resistance. Nebolante, being satisfied with their replies to his questions, invited them in. Once inside the agents discovered that the Italian's roommates were Lieutenant "Tug" Wilson and Captain "Pip" Gardner—two decorated British officers. Gardner and Wilson were wary of the visitors, and their anxiety increased when the two men stayed for lunch.

After they had dined the guests said their good-byes and left. Gardner and Wilson, convinced their safety had been compromised, were furious with Nebolante for allowing strangers into the apartment. They were right to be suspicious. A short time later the strangers returned, but this time they had armed SS men for company, and Gardner, Wilson, and Nebolante were arrested. Nebolante's cook, who was also in the apartment, was then interrogated by the two Germans. A small, gray-haired elderly man, he was easily frightened and told them about homes in Via Firenze and Via Chelini that were used to house escaped servicemen. The Gestapo men couldn't believe their luck. They bundled the cook into a car and drove him to Via Chelini.

It was after three o'clock, and John Furman was in the apartment that housed him and eleven other escapees. He was expecting Bill Simpson to call. The pair had agreed on a special ring of the doorbell to signify that the caller was a friend, and it was known to all those involved in the Escape Line. Sadly it was also known to Nebolante's cook.

When Nebolante's cook arrived at the apartment with the Gestapo officers, he rang the bell using the special ring. When the door opened, he said he had some bad news. But before he could explain, one of the Gestapo men said that Gardner, Wilson, and Nebolante had been arrested. The visitors were ushered into the dining room without acknowledging their identities, but Furman was uneasy; he didn't like the look of the cook's two companions. There was something about them that didn't seem right, and both men appeared edgy.

Furman questioned one of them and suggested that his trip to the apartment had been unnecessary because the cook could have delivered the news on his own. The German went to leave the room and Furman asked to see his identity card. Then all hell broke loose. The two agents pulled out revolvers, and Furman and the other escapees who were in the apartment put their hands in the air. Within seconds the front door opened and six armed SS men ran in. They arrested John Furman, Sergeant Eaton of the U.S. Air Force, a Yugoslav named Bruno Buchner, and Herta, a young Austrian girl who looked after the escapees. The Germans were delighted. One of the agents declared, "We were too clever for you! We shall have more of your friends to keep you company, besides Wilson and Gardner."

Bill Simpson, who was on his way back to Via Chelini when the SS raided, had a very lucky escape. When he arrived at the apartment, the Germans were already inside. He was about to use the agreed signal when a female porter spotted him and told him to leave because the Germans were in the apartment. That's all the information Simpson needed. He knew that O'Flaherty and Derry had to be informed. He fled the building and walked briskly to the Vatican.

Shortly after four o'clock he arrived at O'Flaherty's room, where the monsignor was sitting with Derry. He told them, "Chelini's had it, and John along with it!" Derry began to pace the room, while O'Flaherty simply looked worried. How could the Germans have discovered the apartments? Derry wondered aloud if there was an informer in their ranks and raised the prospect of a Gestapo raid on the German College. The very thought of Kappler's men entering the building angered the monsignor. "Just let them try it," he said. Once he and Derry had digested the shock of the arrests, they discussed what they should do next. They needed to know how many escapees and their helpers had been arrested and what safe houses were now at risk.

O'Flaherty spent much of the next few hours on the phone asking his network of priests to check if any of the apartments and houses they controlled had been raided. It was a risky strategy. Derry was concerned that if the safe houses were being watched, the arrival of priests might tip off the Germans and lead them back to the monsignor. It was agreed that the priests would not visit any safe house unless they were certain it was not under surveillance.

Across the city Henrietta Chevalier's apartment in Via Imperia was one of the places being watched by the Gestapo. One evening, just before the curfew was about to begin, she answered a knock on her door. A teenager stood before her and told her excitedly that he knew she was hiding British soldiers and that the Germans were going to raid her house when the curfew began. She was suspicious but felt his message couldn't be ignored. She asked the youth to wait as she went back inside to talk to her "lodgers." Was this a trap? Or was it an act of kindness?

The escapees had just minutes to decide. They felt it was better to leave than to risk punishment for Henrietta if they were discovered by the Nazis in a raid. The five soldiers—four Britons and one South African—left the flat with just four minutes to spare.

As the young boy had predicted, the moment the curfew began a team of SS men arrived at the door and demanded entry. Inside they found only the Chevalier family. The German commander apologized for the intrusion and his men left. It was a narrow escape. When Derry heard the news, he insisted no escapee would be allowed to return to the apartment because it was too dangerous. Despite the threat of arrest, O'Flaherty then went to see Henrietta in person to explain their decision.

The raid on the Chevaliers' home wasn't the only problem facing O'Flaherty and Derry. John Furman's capture meant the Escape Line was in desperate need of an organizer, and he was replaced by Renzo Lucidi, an Italian film producer. Lucidi and his wife, Adrienne, were sympathetic to the Allies and had begun providing accommodations for escapees. He was thrilled to take on a bigger role in the Escape Line and became involved in the delivery of food and other supplies to safe houses.

Lucidi also continued to hide servicemen in his apartment in Via Scialoia. In January 1944 he was playing host to Bill Simpson and a new arrival, Major Fane-Hervey of the 4th Royal Tank Regiment. Charming and gregarious, the major was known to his friends as "Fanny." He was an impressive figure: As an experienced tank commander in the North African campaign, he had won the Military Cross for bravery. A veteran escaper, he had first evaded the Germans by walking out of a hospital, only to be recaptured and flown to a prison camp at Fontanellato in northern Italy. From there he led 130 men in an escape in September 1943.

Fane-Hervey and Simpson were relaxing in the comfort of the Lucidis' apartment when a group of armed SS men arrived at the door. Bizarrely the Germans ignored the two British escapees and arrested only Renzo's eighteen-year-old stepson. The next day they returned and arrested Renzo. However, within days both Lucidi and his stepson were released. Even though both men were freed, it was another reminder for O'Flaherty of how close Kappler was getting to the heart of his organization.

The raids and arrests across the city forced O'Flaherty and Derry to rethink the way they were carrying out their operation. They streamlined the Escape Line. A number of the safe houses and apartments that were known to anyone who had been arrested were now abandoned. In a move to prevent more supporters or helpers being arrested, a system of cells was introduced whereby each person knew only the identities of the three or four other people in their cell. A new clearing process was also put in place in a block of apartments near the Vatican where newly arrived escapees were held while their bona fides were checked.

By the end of January 1944, Kappler had enjoyed his best month's work in his personal battle with O'Flaherty, and he felt he was close to shutting down the monsignor's operation. He had severely disrupted the Escape Line, key figures were in custody, and safe houses had been uncovered. But finding Allied escapees and their helpers was now only part of Kappler's mission. Days earlier the Allies had landed at Anzio, on the Mediterranean coast south of Rome, and the struggle to take the capital had begun. Kappler was now a pivotal figure in keeping Rome in Nazi hands. He had not only a city to control but an ideology to uphold.

On the first day of February, Kappler ordered and supervised a mass roundup around Via Nazionale. His presence signified the operation's importance. His men were aided by infantrymen and police officers. Beginning at ten o'clock in the morning, men of all ages were taken off the streets and dragged off trams and buses.

The detainees were to be conscripts and would be used to dig roads, break stones, and build military defenses. Most of those arrested would end up working on fortifications in Anzio. The rest were destined for labor camps across Europe.

By sundown some two thousand men had been picked up. The news of the indiscriminate arrests sent a chill across the city. Shops and offices closed down and many people were too frightened to venture onto the streets. Young men in particular stayed indoors for fear of being arrested.

Kappler's operation to boost numbers in the labor camps coincided with the arrival of a leading Italian Fascist, Pietro Caruso, as Rome's new chief of police. Caruso had started work that morning, and his new office was close to where the arrests were being made. In a bizarre twist of fate, when he stepped outside to watch the raids, he was confronted by a group of SS men. They arrested him, and it took a few hours before his identity was realized. Amid much embarrassment, he was released.

The news of Kappler's roundups heightened fears in the Vatican that the Holy See would be next. As expected, his Gestapo and Pietro Koch's special police unit continued their work. Within days there was a series of raids aimed at discovering refugees and crippling the Resistance movement. Kappler's men raided an apartment in Via Giulia used by the partisans. There the Gestapo struck gold by finding both Resistance fighters and a large hoard of explosives. Among those they arrested were Gianfranco Mattei and Giorgio Labo, key figures in the Resistance movement, who were taken to Via Tasso for questioning. Mattei's grandmother was a personal friend of Monsignor Montini, and when she heard of her grandson's arrest, she went to see the Vatican official to try to secure his release. Montini gave the visitor a sympathetic hearing, and a letter was drafted calling for Gianfranco's freedom.

Father Pancratius Pfeiffer, a Bavarian who worked in the Vatican and liaised between the Pope and the Germans, was given the letter and took it to Kappler. The priest had a good relationship with the German authorities. Even so, the missive he delivered was not well received. Kappler snapped at the Pope's trusted official, tore up the letter without even reading it, and said, "This communist Mattei is extremely dangerous. Now I'm going to turn him over to Lieutenant Priebke, who will get him to talk by physical and chemical methods."

The attempts to have Gianfranco Mattei released were futile. He found the interrogation unbearable and was threatened with having to watch his own wife being raped. After writing a farewell note to his parents, he hanged himself in his cell.

In February Kappler gave his blessing to a search of the Vatican's extra-territorial properties. The plan was hatched by police chief Caruso and his protégé Koch. Together the pair had formed a ruthless band to hunt down partisans and Jews. In their sights was the large Basilica di San Paolo Fuori le Mura, which was revered as the burial site of Apostle Paul; as a Vatican property, it was meant to enjoy protection under the Lateran Treaty. Koch and Caruso were convinced the basilica was being used to shelter fugitives, so around midnight on February 4 they stormed the church. Inside they found young men who were evading military service and a number of Jews, who would ultimately be deported to Auschwitz.

The raid angered Vatican officials, who presented a formal objection to the German and Italian authorities. Significantly, behind the scenes in the Holy See, the arrests on Vatican property reignited the issue of whether the Church's properties should be used to shelter fugitives. Within days orders were issued by the Vatican that all non-clerics should be dismissed from its buildings. The news sparked passionate debate in the Holy See. Those opposed to the move felt the Church was sending many people to certain death if it refused to offer sanctuary. Those in favor felt it was an important signal that the Church was protecting its independence and neutrality, and they argued that the move would lessen chances of further raids. But in the end the advice was no more than that: Some institutions followed it while others ignored it.

These were anxious times for O'Flaherty and Derry. The raids on Church properties and the continuing arrests had placed the greatest strain yet on their organization. On top of that, the two men were unsure how the arrival of the Allies in Italy would affect the operation. Would escapees hiding in safe houses in Rome and beyond be tempted to take risks now that they knew the Allies were close by? If hand-to-hand fighting broke out in Rome between the Germans and the Allies, what would be the role of the Escape Line? As a British organization deep in enemy territory, should they continue to do what they had always done or should they change their role? These were questions that O'Flaherty and Derry were now openly discussing.

Bill Simpson was planning to discuss the Escape Line's position when he visited the monsignor one afternoon. On entering the room he saw the priest with a pitching wedge in his hand. The table had been moved to one side and at the end of the carpet O'Flaherty had placed one of his shoes, which he was using for target practice. The two men chatted about golf and then the monsignor switched on his radio to hear the BBC news. The brief bulletin contained little about the Allies' advance, which simply added to the priest's frustration. He turned to his guest and sighed, "When will the blessed English come?"

From the roof of the British legation, Derry was able to see the smoke of battle in the distance. Help was on the horizon, but when it would arrive was impossible to predict. Rumors abounded that the Germans would abandon Rome once the Allies were close to the city's boundaries. Some weeks earlier O'Flaherty had tried to determine if this talk was true or merely wishful thinking. He managed to get the Kiernans' daughter, Blon, who worked at the Irish legation and was a family friend, invited to tea with Prince Bismarck at the German embassy. Afterwards she returned to the German College and told O'Flaherty that the prince believed the Germans would withdraw rather than fight to hold on to Rome. It was comforting to hear that the Germans would surrender the city so quickly, but the monsignor knew the prince's assertion was no cast-iron guarantee.

By contrast, in mid-February O'Flaherty received some news that was genuinely uplifting. As he ran into Derry's room to tell him, his excitement was obvious. He thrust a small piece of folded paper into the major's hand. Derry opened the note and instantly recognized the writing. It was from John Furman and read: "Back in Rome. Where the hell are you? Only consolation for my sore arse will be when I see your smiling face. John."

Furman had escaped from German custody by jumping from a train and had spent his recent days on a bicycle, which explained his physical ailment. He had managed to make his way back to Rome, and within hours he and O'Flaherty had an emotional reunion. After a series of bear hugs and back slaps, the monsignor greeted Furman as if he were the Prodigal Son: "In the name of

God, it's good to see you back, John. You're paler and thinner, but you're all in one piece. This is surely a happy day for us all."

Furman's return was a rare moment of good news. The next day, far from the city, the Allies embarked on an act of war that would have far-reaching consequences. On February 15, less than one hundred miles from Rome, the sixth-century Benedictine monastery at Monte Cassino was reduced to rubble, an estimated five hundred tons of explosives dropped on it by Allied bombers. The destruction of the abbey, seen by many as one of the most important religious sites in Europe, incensed the Vatican. Dozens of refugees who had been sheltering there also were killed. The Allies insisted that the abbey was being used by the Nazis as an observation post, but the Vatican viewed the bombing as a senseless act of destruction.

Cardinal Luigi Maglione, the Vatican's secretary of state, said the attack was a blunder and a "piece of gross stupidity." It not only shocked the Vatican but changed its outlook on the war. Many in the Holy See had long thought that Rome, as a historic and cultural city, would be immune from destruction, but the attack at Monte Cassino, although some ninety miles away, ended that assumption. Now there were real fears that if Rome stood between the Allies and victory, the Eternal City would become a battlefield. The Vatican had every right to be worried.

Against this uncertain background Kappler stepped up his plans to penetrate the Vatican.

One February day, as Father Michael Tarchnisvili quickly made his way across Rome, an onlooker might have thought that the priest had the look of a contented man. The Georgian scholar had every reason to be happy. He was on his way to meet the first six students who were to be part of his Georgian College in Rome, which he hoped would open shortly. The priest had campaigned for years to open a center for young Georgian émigrés, where they could study in an environment that made them feel at home. Although he hadn't expected the trainee priests to arrive so soon, their arrival in Rome was still a welcome development and showed that after months of delay things were at last happening. The students had come from Germany, and Father Michael had been told by a colleague that they were good Catholics who wanted to study for the priesthood. He made his way to the Hotel Continental and met the young men. The encounter left him shocked. The six charges seemed morose and unwilling to talk. They were the most unlikely group of potential seminarians he had ever met. When they did speak, it seemed they were more interested in talking about women. Father Michael quickly concluded that at least three of them were not suitable for the priesthood.

It was no wonder. The young men had been sent by the German intelligence service to infiltrate the Vatican by using the Georgian College as a cover. The man who had recommended the "students" to Father Michael was Basilius Sadathierascvili, the Georgian Gestapo informer paid by Kappler to help set up the bogus college. Sadathierascvili was to be the college's administrator and the buildings were to house a secret radio transmitter.

Father Michael discovered the plan. The would-be students were sent back to Germany, and when the priest discovered Sadathierascvili's real motives, the two men had angry words. Father Michael was also concerned that some within the Catholic community in Rome regarded Sadathierascvili as a German spy. The undercover college plan was in tatters, and it fell to Karl Haas, one of Kappler's staff, to inform the German intelligence headquarters in Berlin that the operation had failed. Much time and effort had gone into the ploy, but in the end it had relied on too many people to make it work. Kappler now turned to less sophisticated ways to trap his enemies.

On March 15, in his room in the Holy Office, O'Flaherty met one of the Escape Line volunteers, a man by the name of Grossi. He was well known to O'Flaherty, and because the man was providing accommodations for escapees, the monsignor had no reason to distrust him. However, Kappler had discovered Grossi's link to the Irish priest and with the promise of cash and the threat of violence had persuaded him to betray his friendship. Grossi told O'Flaherty that half a dozen or so escapees were hiding in the countryside about thirty miles from Rome. After explaining that one of the men was sick and that members of the Escape Line were unable to bring him or his colleagues into the city, he suggested that perhaps O'Flaherty could do it.

Committed to helping those in need, the monsignor told his visitor that on the following Sunday he could go and say mass at the place in question and bring the sick man into the city. It seemed a straightforward operation. O'Flaherty and his team of priests were constantly getting requests to leave the relative safety of the Vatican and Rome to collect Allied escapees.

Yet O'Flaherty wasn't the only one in Kappler's sights. The day after Grossi's visit, Brother Robert Pace, who worked with the monsignor under the code name "Whitebows," went to a village on the outskirts of Rome to pick up a number of escapees and lead them to a safe house. His purpose was to make contact with members of the U.S. Army and the Royal Fusiliers, who were in hiding. The priest first linked up with two Italians who helped the Escape Line: Andrea Casadei and Vittorio Fantini.

As planned, they all met up in a small hut to discuss the

operation but were overpowered by a number of Gestapo agents. Brother Robert and his two contacts were taken back into Rome for separate interrogations at Via Tasso. Casadei and Fantini were interrogated at length, remaining in custody for eight days. On Kappler's instructions they were later killed. Brother Pace had a narrow escape. After two interrogation sessions he was released and allowed to return to the Vatican that night.

The next day was St Patrick's Day, and in O'Flaherty's room the annual celebration was under way. The monsignor was joined by colleagues including Father Buckley and John May. They were in good voice when, halfway through a noisy rendition of the Irish rebel ballad "Aghadoe," the telephone interrupted. The monsignor took the call, which his guests quickly determined was a cause of alarm to O'Flaherty. For a few moments the monsignor listened and then said, "All right, I understand. God forgive him."

O'Flaherty ended the call and shared the story with his guests. Grossi had betrayed O'Flaherty and had tried to entrap him. The caller was warning him not to leave the city to say mass as planned. Derry had not been with O'Flaherty when he had met with Grossi, so his first thought was to alert the major. They needed to make sure that helpers and safe houses hadn't been compromised by Grossi's betrayal.

Escapees continued to arrive in Rome, and invariably they were brought to O'Flaherty, even though he was now trying to take a backseat in the organization because of his loyalty to the Church. The Swiss Guards, whose job it was to formally protect the Vatican, were understandably nervous of strangers seeking entry to the politically neutral world that O'Flaherty inhabited.

The monsignor would often have to vouch for Escape Line members who were stopped at the entrance of the Vatican. On one occasion Bill Simpson was held by the Swiss Guards, who called the monsignor to come down to testify to the bona fides of the visitor. O'Flaherty spoke to the guards in his fluent Italian and Simpson was waved through. In the privacy of his room, the priest wanted to know the purpose of Simpson's visit. "Bill, what is the trouble?" he asked. Simpson replied that there was no problem, but he had been asked to bring four very important items to Derry. The major needed them urgently, he added. O'Flaherty was intrigued and Simpson rather sheepishly opened the bulging briefcase he was carrying to reveal, to the priest's amusement, four bottles of English gin.

One day in late March as the monsignor, in his usual position, stood on the steps outside St. Peter's, he was approached by three men. One of them he knew, the others were strangers. The familiar face was that of Branko Bokun, who worked for the Red Cross. His colleagues, dressed in ill-fitting suits, which they had bought near an internment camp, were two escaped British officers looking for a safe house. Bokun, experienced in O'Flaherty's line of undercover work, handed the two escapees over to the priest. Before they parted they shared some good-natured banter. The Yugoslav wondered how O'Flaherty, a lifelong critic of British rule in Ireland, could organize such services for escaped British soldiers.

The monsignor laughed. "The English have never understood us," he said. "They are surprised that I am prepared to risk my life to save theirs. They assume to find accommodation, produce false papers, visit them, et cetera, is all just the typical madness of an Irishman. The English never refer to us as 'the mad Irish,' but simply 'the Irish.' To them this automatically means mad. I just want to show them that behind Irish madness there is a certain generosity."

That generosity was being tested as Rome witnessed the darkest days of the war. In the first three weeks of March, the city was targeted by Allied bombers almost every day. The train station at Ostia was hit, as was the capital's gasworks, and a number of churches were destroyed. The windows of the Basilica of San Paolo Fuori le Mura were shattered, and the bombings caused many civilian casualties.

The war that the people of Rome had read about and talked about was now an everyday reality. It was on their doorstep.

CHAPTER 11

Resistance and Revenge

"Make the world tremble."

—HITLER

IT WAS ONE OF THE BRIGHTEST DAYS OF THE YEAR, AND AS THE warm sunshine filled the grandeur of the Hotel Excelsior's dining room, Kappler was enjoying lunch. Each week he met there with the German Armed Forces commander in Rome, General Kurt Mälzer, to bring him up to date on his work in rounding up partisans and Jews and on his attempts to penetrate the Vatican and seize escaped Allied servicemen. Their meetings at the hotel in Via Veneto were routine yet enjoyable, and that day neither man was in a hurry to return to his desk. The date, March 23, 1944, was significant. It was the twenty-fifth anniversary of the founding of Fascism, for on that day in 1919 Benito Mussolini had brought together a large number of like-minded friends in Milan and started a new movement.

In Rome many leading lights in the German-Italian command structure had gathered to celebrate the occasion. Kappler and Mälzer had decided to skip the commemoration and instead opted for their weekly get-together. An alcoholic, Mälzer was as usual drinking heavily, and by the time they were ready for dessert, he was drunk.

As they ate and talked, across the city Rosario Bentivegna, a medical student in his twenties, was pushing a rubbish cart through the streets. It was a hot afternoon, with little cloud cover, and the young man, dressed in overalls, was beginning to sweat. By a quarter to two he had reached Via Rasella. He pushed the cart up the narrow cobbled street, and after he passed a parked truck, he wedged the cart up against the curb to prevent it from rolling away. Now it was simply a waiting game.

Just under two hours later men from the 11th Company of the 3rd Battalion of the SS's Bozen Police Regiment arrived in Via Rasella, and the sound of their voices and boots filled the air. The column of 156 soldiers in battle dress sang a marching song as they slowly climbed the sloping street.

Bentivegna had heard the Germans approach and prepared his reception for them. Using his lit pipe he ignited a fuse, put his cap on the cart, which was a prearranged sign to his watching comrades, and walked away. He had under a minute to find safety. As the soldiers passed the cart, marching three abreast, a powerful explosion ripped through their ranks.

Around two dozen soldiers took the full force of the blast and died instantly. Dozens of their colleagues lay wounded, some critically. The cart, which had been packed with forty pounds of explosives, had disappeared and in its place had opened up a huge crater. Water from burst pipes mixed with blood and flowed down the street. Body parts were scattered across the cobbles. The dead included two civilians. Large chunks of masonry had been blown out of nearby buildings; rubble covered large parts of the road. The blast blew over a nearby bus and pushed it off the thoroughfare. Via

Rasella, one of Rome's quietest streets, was in chaos. The partisans had succeeded in bringing their resistance to the city's streets in their biggest and most public attack.

The deadly assault on the occupying army was not yet finished. The explosions prompted the Resistance team to put the second stage of their operation into action. On hearing the first explosion, three of Bentivegna's comrades, who had been waiting close by, moved into Via Rasella and threw four mortar shells at the soldiers before making their escape. The Germans, assuming they were under fire from nearby buildings, began shooting at the windows of apartments that overlooked the street. Soon the firing ceased, but the partisans had escaped, and amid the dust and rubble both SS men and civilians lay dead and dying.

One of the first to reach the scene was Pietro Caruso. The police chief had been at the twenty-fifth-anniversary Fascist commemorations taking place not far away in the Ministry of Corporations. Looking around, he saw dismembered bodies being gathered up and watched as the survivors stacked their dead colleagues in lines on the pavement. Bewildered and shocked, he simply didn't know what to do. General Mälzer arrived shortly afterwards, following his lunch with Kappler. Like Caruso, he was appalled by what greeted him and immediately demanded the arrest of every resident of the street, including women and children.

Within minutes the most powerful men in Rome's Nazi and Italian Fascist high command, many of whom had been at the nearby commemoration ceremony, descended on Via Rasella. Guido Buffarini-Guidi, the minister of the Interior, arrived, as did Consul-General Eitel Friedrich Möllhausen and Colonel Eugen Dollmann. By now Italian police and German soldiers were going from house to house, breaking down doors, dragging out the

139

occupants, and beating them up. At gunpoint entire families were marched off to the gates of the nearby Palazzo Barberini and were told to stand still with their hands above their heads.

His anger fueled by the lunchtime drinking session with Kappler, Mälzer was now out of control. Sweaty, red-faced, smelling of alcohol, with tears in his eyes, the commander demanded instant retaliation to avenge the deaths of his countrymen. In front of other German officials, he told Möllhausen that he was planning to blow up the entire Via Rasella. The young German diplomat was appalled by what he heard, and he and Mälzer argued in front of the other officers.

Möllhausen knew his opponent was serious, and as he watched explosives being unloaded from a nearby truck, he feared the drunken Mälzer was about to carry out his plan. Angered and feeling uneasy about what was unfolding, Möllhausen decided to leave and return to his office at Villa Wolkonsky. As he was leaving, he met Kappler, who was one of the last to arrive at Via Rasella. Kappler had heard the explosions when he returned to his office from the Excelsior. Although he had received a number of telephone calls explaining what had happened, he had not appreciated the full horror of the attack. As he drew near the scene, he bumped into Möllhausen. The diplomat urged him to rein in the emotional Mälzer, who, he explained, was planning to bomb the entire street.

Kappler also came across Dollmann. The two officers simply had never gotten along. Kappler believed that the colonel was prone to exaggeration. Dollmann viewed Kappler as narrow-minded. In return Kappler was equally dismissive and wondered about Dollmann's precise role in Rome. He considered Dollmann a "drawing room soldier" whose duties were "clear neither to himself nor to anybody else." Yet, as he stood in the street surveying the carnage,

Kappler could hardly take in what he saw. He would later recall: "The scene was beyond description: dead bodies, wounded and ruins. The general confusion was very intense."

The bomb attack was the greatest loss of life the Germans had suffered since they had seized control of the city. Kappler knew he needed to remain calm. He sought out Mälzer and, finding his lunch companion in an excitable state, spoke to him quietly and carefully. Realizing the commander's presence was unhelpful, he managed to persuade him to hand over control and leave. But, as Kappler helped him into his car, the still inebriated Mälzer barked one last order: "They are all to be shot."

Kappler rapidly took command of the situation. One of his first orders was to tell his men to stop firing at "nonexistent" targets. Much ammunition had been wasted by simply firing, at random, into the buildings that lined Via Rasella. He then started to arrange transport for the injured, knowing that the death toll would increase if the wounded weren't quickly taken to a hospital. Kappler began to walk along the street as the full horror of the attack sank in. He collected the remnants of the partisans' grenades and looked at the large pile of dismembered bodies. He would recall: "I thought I would examine the debris myself, but when I saw a little girl's thigh and arm I left the task to others. I felt the same resentment as on other occasions after bombardments."

As the wounded and the dying were taken away, the operation to arrest local people and search houses continued. The residents of Via Rasella felt the full might of the Germans' anger. Many were dragged from their houses and assaulted with fists and rifle butts. By now a couple of hundred people were being held at gunpoint. They were handed over to the Italian police; the majority of them would later be released.

By five o'clock Kappler had pieced together as best as he could what had happened in Via Rasella, and he had no doubt that the Resistance was responsible. He then made his way to Mälzer's headquarters in Corso d'Italia to bring him up to date. He told the general that he believed the explosive device and other bombs had been thrown from the roofs of various houses and that the German death toll had now reached twenty-eight.

By this time news of the attack had reached Hitler, who was enjoying a restful day at the Wolf's Lair. When told of the manner and the number of the German deaths, he was furious. He called for a reprisal that would "make the world tremble." One staff officer witnessed the Führer's rage. "He is roaring. He wants to blow up an entire quarter of the city, including everyone who lives there, and . . . for every German police officer killed, they should shoot thirty to fifty Italians."

Hitler's instruction that the Via Rasella attack must be avenged was quickly relayed to his officers in Rome. As he answered phone calls and talked in his office, Mälzer was now a little more coherent. One of the first to call him was General Eberhard von Mackensen, commander of the Fourteenth Army. They spoke for a while and then Mackensen, knowing that Kappler was in the room with Mälzer listening, asked to speak to him. The general asked Kappler if he had any knowledge or experience with carrying out reprisals. Kappler explained that he had once discussed the matter with General Harster, a senior SS official based in Verona, and they had concluded that if a reprisal should be called for, they would shoot prisoners in their custody who were either already awaiting execution or likely to be sentenced to death.

Mackensen was interested in Kappler's idea and instructed him that for every German killed in Via Rasella, ten Italians should be shot. When the call ended, Mälzer and Kappler discussed what they should do. Neither man had any experience that matched the scale of what they were being asked to do. Mälzer told Kappler that since the German death toll stood at twenty-eight, he should draw up a list of 280 people who would be executed in retaliation.

Kappler knew instantly that finding so many suitable people would be very difficult. He simply didn't have that number of prisoners who met the criteria that he had explained to Mälzer. He also guessed, correctly as it turned out, that the German death toll of twenty-eight would rise, which would mean that his retaliation list would be even larger and his task would become even more difficult.

By now all of Rome was talking about Via Rasella and the roundups that had followed the attack. The explosions had been heard across the city, and word quickly reached the Vatican. Derry was, as usual, in the British legation when he heard the news. O'Flaherty was close by. The first pieces of information the pair received were sketchy, but they soon realized that even if the casualty figures were not correct, the Resistance had still carried out one of its most daring acts to date. The repercussions would be felt far beyond the rubble-strewn Via Rasella.

O'Flaherty and Derry had no doubt that the German authorities would seek revenge. Any escapees hidden in safe houses were now vulnerable to arrest, as were those hiding them. Indeed, any local people found sheltering Allied servicemen would most likely be shot. It was crucial to act quickly. Derry dispatched a series of messengers to the safe houses, and dozens of escapees were moved into temporary accommodations. The major had to be inventive in finding new homes, so some of his charges were put in unusual hiding places, such as public gardens and parks. While Derry knew this would be uncomfortable and possibly unacceptable to many of the escapees, it was preferable to placing host families in danger.

As darkness enveloped the city, Kappler began to compile his list of Todeskandidaten, "candidates for death." He knew he could not reach the latest figure of close to three hundred without help, so he instructed Pietro Caruso to provide fifty names. However, the police chief agreed to submit a list of suitable candidates only after it had been endorsed by his superior, the minister of the Interior.

Sitting at his desk in Via Tasso, Kappler then made a number of telephone calls, including one to General Harster in Verona. Harster was a senior SS officer who had been involved in rounding up Jews in the Netherlands. They talked about the difficulties of reaching the figure Kappler had been asked to provide. Kappler then spoke to a series of legal officials about the legalities of executing prisoners who had been given the death sentence. Permission came from the presiding justice of the German military tribunal. With legal formalities out of the way, the work began.

Kappler called his staff together, including Captain Erich Priebke, who would have a key role in events over the next few hours. Priebke would later recall: "We were told that all records in the office were to be searched and all those persons who had been sentenced to death by German tribunals for offenses against German troops were to be killed."

As he trawled through the files of prisoners, Kappler sat at his desk with his sick dog, which he was nursing. In the quiet of the evening, he began selecting suitable candidates for execution. He would soon have company. Consul-General Möllhausen had discovered that Kappler had been tasked with drawing up a list. He came by and the pair began to discuss the day's events and the imminent retaliation. Horrified at what his host was planning to do, he turned to him and said, "What you are doing, Kappler, goes far beyond patriotism and war. Remember that you will be answerable not only before men but before God."

Kappler replied, "I can only promise you I will do what I am able to do. And this is what it is: For every name that I will write, I will think three times."

Möllhausen's last-minute appeal fell on deaf ears. Kappler remained determined to proceed with Hitler's order for retribution. The instruction was that the retaliation was to be carried out within twenty-four hours, and Kappler planned on adhering strictly to the Führer's timetable. He worked through the night, and by the time daylight streamed through his window, he had assembled 270 names, though he was still 10 short of the original target.

Nevertheless, Kappler felt confident that the remainder would be provided by his allies in the Italian police. He telephoned Caruso's office and reminded his staff that he was expecting a list from them shortly. He also contacted Koch in the hope that he too could provide further names. Caruso still had not managed to list any candidates for Kappler and was beginning to feel the pressure. He felt he needed some authorization before he could hand over details to the SS Obersturmbannführer.

In the bright morning sunshine Caruso was driven along Via Veneto to the Hotel Excelsior, where the minister of the Interior was staying after attending the Fascist anniversary celebrations. He arrived at eight o'clock to discover that Buffarini-Guidi was still in bed. The minister told him to give Kappler exactly what he wanted and warned him that "otherwise who knows what will happen."

Shortly afterwards Kappler spoke to Caruso and was frustrated that the police chief had little to offer except a few common criminals who were being held as prisoners. "Then give us some Jews," he demanded.

At midday Kappler went to see Mälzer in Corso d'Italia to discuss the list and the coming operation. They were joined in the general's office by Major Dobbrick, the commander of the Bozen SS's 3rd Battalion, which had been the target of the Via Rasella attack. Kappler began by explaining what progress he had made assembling the list and how he was still waiting for some fifty names to be supplied by Caruso within the hour. Mälzer then explained why retaliation was necessary, how the order had come from the Führer, and why it was important that Dobbrick should carry it out. The major looked shocked and refused to comply with the general's order. He rattled off a series of excuses, saying that his men were too old, were very religious, and there were not enough of them to carry out a task of such magnitude.

Unsure how to respond, Mälzer telephoned the office of General Mackensen. Mackensen was not available, so his chief of staff, Colonel Wolfgang Hauser, took the call. Hauser listened to Mälzer's account of events and made it clear that extra manpower was not available to carry out the executions. He told the general that since it was the SS that had been attacked in Via Rasella, it would be the SS that carried out the retaliation. Hauser, who was on the verge of being promoted, then ended the call. Mälzer was shocked and relayed the details of the conversation to his two guests. He then turned to the Gestapo chief and declared, "It is up to you, Kappler."

Kappler looked at Mälzer and said nothing. When he broke the silence, he said his men would carry out the executions. Mälzer responded by saying that Kappler's rank demanded that he lead by example and must therefore be involved in the killings. Kappler, he made clear, should not ask his men to do something he wasn't prepared to do himself. In all his years of service, including his experience of arrests and interrogations, Kappler had never actually killed anyone. That would change in a few hours time.

He returned to his office and called together the dozen officers who were under his command. He was direct and brief: "Three hundred and twenty people will have to be killed." All the officers were told they would be involved in the executions. Captain Erich Priebke, who was one of those listening, would later state: "He said that this was a horrible thing to do and that to show the men that they had the backing of the officers, all the officers were to fire a shot at the beginning and a further shot at the end."

Kappler's list of names was a mix of individuals of different backgrounds and ages. There were shop workers, electricians, butchers, soldiers, shoemakers, and secretaries. The collection included Catholics, Jews, and some of no faith. The ages ranged from teenagers to old men. A number of people rounded up in the Via Rasella raids were included, as were two of O'Flaherty's key helpers, Andrea Casadei and Vittorio Fantini, who had been arrested with Brother Robert Pace when he had gone to pick up new additions to the Escape Line. The one category his list had very little of was the easy ones—prisoners facing the death sentence.

Kappler had placed on the list a number of former members of the Italian armed forces, including those who had been actively involved in the overthrow of Mussolini and had become key figures in the Resistance. Thirty-seven officers were marked for execution, among them three generals, a major, and the two captains who had arrested the Italian dictator on the steps of Villa Savoia in July 1943.

One of the most high-profile names that Kappler had written down was a man he regarded as his most dangerous prisoner, the Resistance leader Colonel Giuseppe Cordero Lanza di

Montezemolo. An aristocrat, Montezemolo had gone into hiding in September 1943 and had established a military front to oppose the Nazis and the Italian Fascists. He had also set up Centro X, a clandestine radio network that was used to transmit information about German troop movements and the work of the Resistance.

A distinctive and charismatic figure with gold-rimmed glasses and a moustache, the forty-four-year-old Montezemolo was a deeply religious man. He had been arrested in January 1944 and taken to Via Tasso. For Kappler this was a tremendous coup, and he clearly hoped that Montezemolo would reveal details of Resistance operations, including the names of those who had taken part. The former army colonel had been tortured repeatedly. His jaw was dislocated, his eyes were swollen and bruised, and his lips and face were battered. His beatings were so frequent and his pain so great that he was given a deck chair to sit on in his cell. The Vatican had been informed of his detention and a relative appealed to the Pope.

On March 19 Montezemolo's cousin, Marchesa Fulvia Ripa di Meana, had a private audience with the Pontiff. The marchioness, a mother of six, was a determined soul and had become her cousin's greatest ally since the arrest of Montezemolo, who had smuggled a letter out of Via Tasso telling her to go to the Pope for assistance. Pius XII knew the woman because he had taught her when she was a religious student in the city. Dressed in white and seated behind his desk, he listened as the marchioness detailed how her cousin had been arrested and was now incarcerated in Via Tasso. She pleaded with the Pope to intervene and bring him into the sanctuary of the Vatican. She also explained that, as a military man, Montezemolo could be invaluable in maintaining order on the streets when the Germans left Rome. Pius XII listened carefully and after a while appeared uncomfortable.

"He is in Kappler's hands then?" he asked.

The marchioness replied, "Yes, Your Holiness, and we all know what that means. Montezemolo's tortures have been atrocious." She saw the Pope wince. A few moments later he said, "I promise you we shall do all we can, absolutely all we can." He wrote down the details the marchioness had just given him and she left the Vatican. Later she heard that the Pope had instructed Monsignor Montini to investigate. It would lead to nothing.

The role of the Catholic Church during the Nazi occupation of Rome has been well documented and has provoked much controversy in the decades since the war. The debate has largely focused on whether Pope Pius XII did enough to intervene and speak out against Nazi atrocities.

Journalist and author Robert Katz, whose groundbreaking work has focused extensively on this period, contends that in the aftermath of the Via Rasella attack, the Vatican had been informed that a reprisal was likely. This became the central point in legal proceedings that were brought in 1974 by the Pope's niece Contessa Elena Pacelli Rossignani against the writer. Katz was charged with "defaming the memory" of Pope Pius XII. The case examined a visit made by Colonel Dollmann to a monastery in the hours following the bombing at Via Rasella but well before reprisals were carried out.

Dollmann had left the scene of the attack and, after changing into civilian clothes, went to a Vatican building that housed the Order of the Salvatorians. There he met Father Pancratius Pfeiffer, the Pope's liaison with the Germans. Both were Bavarians and got along well. The Nazi officer told the priest that the Führer was "beside himself with rage" after the bombing and explained that a reprisal was coming. Recalling the encounter some years later, Dollmann said, "It is possible that in order to get the Vatican moving to take some kind of action, naturally as fast as possible, I spoke in terms of a bloodbath."

The colonel proposed a plan whereby the funerals of the Germans would take place and the Pope and Field Marshal Kesselring would speak for peace. He clearly hoped that after a few days the anger of the Nazi high command would subside and a violent reprisal could be avoided. Looking back, he insisted that Father Pfeiffer agreed to take his proposal to the Vatican and ended their meeting by declaring, "Excellent! I am certain the Vatican will be very enthusiastic. And I will go at once to inform them." Dollmann then left and the pair agreed to talk again later.

It is not clear exactly whom Father Pfeiffer informed about Dollmann's visit or when he passed the information on, but it is known that within hours the Vatican was aware of the German plans for a reprisal. A document that lay hidden in the Vatican archives until 1980 confirmed that the day after the Via Rasella attack, the Holy See knew that although "the countermeasures are not yet known: it is however foreseen that for every German killed ten Italians will be executed."

Möllhausen and Dollmann, as evidenced by their visits to Kappler and Father Pfeiffer, respectively, were opposed to a reprisal. Both believed an act of such magnitude would provoke widespread anger. They were also convinced that the Via Rasella bombing was a Resistance tactic aimed at goading the Germans into a violent response. But it seems there was little they could do.

By lunchtime on March 24, Kappler's plans for the mass executions were well advanced. He had spent much of the day solving problems. The first was how to kill and then bury such a large number of people in as short a time as possible. The killings had to be completed by the deadline of 8:30 that evening, so with seventy-four men at his disposal, Kappler concluded that if one prisoner was shot every minute, he would be ahead of schedule. He would later chillingly recall his thinking during his war-crimes trial in 1948: "I calculated the number of minutes necessary for the killing of each of the 320. I had the arms and ammunition computed. I figured the total amount of time I had. I divided my men into small platoons, which would function alternately. I ordered that each man shoot only one shot."

Then there was the problem of where to carry out the shootings. One of Kappler's officers and some engineers were dispatched to investigate a location a few miles outside the city. They discovered the ideal spot, the Ardeatine Caves, an abandoned network of tunnels among Christian catacombs very close to the place where St. Peter is said to have met Jesus. The caves were out of view and were connected by a series of passageways. It was perfect. There was no need to dig a mass grave: The executions would take place in the caves and the engineers would detonate a series of explosions to seal it all up like a massive tomb. Now that he had finalized how the executions would be carried out and where, Kappler began to ferry the prisoners to the site.

The first time the inmates at Via Tasso realized that something unusual was happening was when their cell doors were flung open and they were shouted at in German to hurry up and leave. They were on the move. Rome's blackest day had begun.

CHAPTER 12

Massacre

"The reprisal has been carried out. I know it was very hard for some of you, but in cases like this the law of war applies."
—HERBERT KAPPLER

As HE WAS DRAGGED FROM HIS CELL, KAPPLER'S PRIZED PRISONER could barely move. The Resistance leader, Colonel Montezemolo, had been so tortured by his captors that he was unsteady on his feet. They had, in fact, ripped out his toenails. He was also unused to the bright light, so, flanked by guards, he stumbled and groped his way outside. He was not alone. His fellow inmates were also being pushed and hurried toward the daylight. They were dazed and frightened and had no idea what was happening.

Some thought they were being moved to another jail, possibly the nearby Regina Coeli prison. Their hopes quickly began to fade as their hands were tied with cord; once outside the building they were herded in pairs toward a convoy of unmarked trucks the Germans used to transport meat.

Kappler watched as the prisoners were pushed into the trucks. He spoke to Captain Schutz, the officer in charge of loading the prisoners and overseeing the executions. The Obersturmbannführer had noticed that the prisoners' hands were tied, and he questioned this detail with his captain. Schutz replied that it was a precaution to stop any of them from escaping, and added that the prisoners had not been told what was happening. Satisfied that all was in order, Kappler got into his car and was driven to the Ardeatine Caves.

Before he followed, Schutz called his men together. He told them what was expected of them and that if any man—including officers—refused to take part in the executions, he would be shot for failure to obey a direct order.

Then the convoy set off, slowly heading south. It was dark inside the trucks, but through small rips in the canvas, the prisoners caught occasional glimpses of familiar streets and landmarks such as churches and historic sites. After crawling through the city the trucks were soon in the countryside and climbing high up onto the Appian Way. Onward they made their way until, after a final right turn, they reached the entrance to the caves in Via Ardeatina, where Kappler was standing and waiting. The rear doors were opened and the human cargo was brought out into the daylight.

Blinking and bruised from his beatings, Montezemolo was one of the first to emerge from the darkness. He was still in his forties, but the past few weeks had taken their toll, making him look old and tired, and he had a big mark under his right eye where he had been attacked. Others around him were ashen with fear. Realizing what was about to happen, one of the prisoners cried out, "Father, bless us!"

Back in the city, at the German-controlled wing of Regina Coeli, a group of Kappler's officers had gathered in the section reserved for political prisoners. Eleonora Lavagnino, a lawyer who had been arrested for helping Allied escapees, had been in a bathroom on the first floor. She had been rinsing mess trays under the tap, and as she walked back to her cell, she looked down toward the ground floor.

She would recall: "This was an unusual sight. I then saw four pairs of German officers, in uniform with papers in their hands, going from cell to cell opening the doors and shouting out names."

Umberto Lusena had just shaved and was in his cell when he heard doors being banged and orders shouted. Recently arrived at the prison, he was getting used to his new surroundings, having been transferred from Via Tasso, where he had been tortured. He had worked as a radio operator for Centro X, the underground radio network for the FMCR, the Clandestine Military Front of the Resistance. Lusena, who was known to O'Flaherty, Derry, and many of their friends, had also assisted the Escape Line and often journeyed into the countryside to meet escaped Allied prisoners.

An experienced parachutist, Lusena had been Derry's point of contact with isolated groups of escapees; using his radio skills and aerial knowledge, he had often arranged supply drops by parachute to Allied groups. But the Germans had arrested him and were convinced he was in the Resistance, and so as he languished in Regina Coeli, he was a prime candidate for Kappler's list. He was sharing a cell with Guglielmo Morandi. When the raid began, the two men looked out to see their fellow inmates being dragged from their cells.

Then the Germans arrived at their cell. The door was flung open and the two prisoners stood up. One of the Nazis was holding a list and glanced down to read off the latest name. "Umberto Lusena," he shouted. As Morandi recalled, the name "lay heavily in the air." According to his cell mate, Lusena had the look of a "child who had been caught doing something wrong." As Lusena got ready to go, he picked up a bag and turned to Morandi. He had guessed what was about to happen. They are going to shoot me, he thought to himself. But Morandi, thinking his cell mate was simply being moved to a concentration camp, gave him some bread for the journey.

At the caves Kappler now had some five hours to complete the executions, so he knew they had to start shortly. He was clearly emotional and almost tearful as he called his officers together for a few minutes. He talked about what lay ahead and sympathized with them, but stressed that what they were doing was right.

Close to the trucks stood Captain Erich Priebke. It was his job to check the list of Todeskandidaten. Holding sheets of paper, he asked for their names, scanned his list, and with a pencil crossed off their details. The first five prisoners were taken into the caves. It was dark and torches helped to light the way. The men were ordered to their knees; they bowed their heads as Kappler's officers readied themselves. Schutz then shouted "Fire!" and five shots rang out. The executions, which would stun the world, had begun. It was shortly after 3:30 p.m.

Kappler wanted the process to be swift and straightforward. He had considered bringing a priest or chaplain to the site to offer spiritual comfort to those about to die. In the Great War, at military executions, the condemned soldier was often granted time with a priest, but as Kappler would later recall, he found the idea unattractive. At his trial for war crimes in 1948, he said, "When the chaplain makes contact with these human beings, it is very hard to drive him away after a few seconds. I thought it would be best not to have him."

After the first killings Kappler walked to a nearby truck. He selected a prisoner, as did each of four of his subordinates, and they entered the caves. The prisoners knelt a few yards behind the five fresh corpses. Kappler, along with his colleagues, opened fire, killing the second batch of prisoners. As General Mälzer had insisted, he must lead his men by example. Then it was Priebke's turn. The captain used an Italian machine pistol to shoot his victims. After three rounds of executions, fifteen prisoners had been killed. Kappler's timetable of no more than "a minute per death" appeared to be going according to plan. But this macabre schedule would not last.

The Obersturmbannführer allowed his men to have a rest and some cognac, which had been brought from Via Tasso and was passed around. Far from speeding things up, the alcohol made matters much worse. Soon Kappler's executioners became sloppy. Some of the men ended up firing three or more bullets into their victims. A sizeable number of prisoners were actually decapitated—so many bullets were fired into their heads. Other officers missed entirely, and those who were given uncooperative prisoners found the killings were taking longer than planned. The sheer mass of corpses also began to cause difficulties: The buildup of bodies slowed down the executions, and to save space some victims were ordered to kneel on the corpses of fellow prisoners. As the day progressed, anxiety was setting in among the executioners, and the discipline that had been on display in the early part of the afternoon was being tested.

One of the junior officers, Second Lieutenant Wetjen, refused to take part in the shootings. Kappler took the young man aside and calmly explained what impact his behavior would have on the men under his command. He then asked Wetjen if he would be able to carry out the orders if Kappler stood beside him. When Wetjen said that would make it easier, Kappler again joined one of the execution parties and walked with the officer into the darkness of the caves. To steady his nerves he placed his arm around Wetjen's waist. In the half light they each shot a prisoner.

Like Wetjen, another of Kappler's officers hadn't the stomach to carry out an execution. Lieutenant Günther Amonn arrived on the scene after around two hundred killings had taken place. He was selected to be a member of a firing party and entered one of the caves under Schutz's supervision. When ordered by the captain to fire, the young lieutenant simply could not carry through with the act. He would later recall: "I raised my gun, but I was too afraid to fire. The four other Germans fired one shot each into the backs of the necks of the other prisoners, who fell forward. Upon seeing the state in which I was in another German pushed me out and shot the prisoner I had been detailed to shoot."

At his war-crimes trial Kappler would confirm that Wetjen was the only one of his officers who refused to comply with the order to shoot.

By around four o'clock all the prisoners from Via Tasso and Regina Coeli who had been on Kappler's list had now been removed from their cells and brought to the Ardeatine Caves. The prisoners promised by Caruso had still not materialized. Kappler, now furious, sent two of his officers back down to the city to speed the matter up.

By half past four Caruso's list still hadn't appeared, so one of the officers took things into his own hands: He went to the Trastevere prison and chose the first group of prisoners he came across. The unfortunate souls, who were about to be released, were instead packed into a truck and would become some of Kappler's final victims. Moments later Caruso's list finally arrived. This lottery of life and death was further highlighted by what happened next. Those who had just been randomly taken to the caves were added to Caruso's list while an equal number were removed.

In darkness the massacre at Via Ardeatina was coming to an end as the last prisoners were unloaded from a truck and marched into the caves and shot. By eight o'clock, just within Hitler's twenty-four-hour time limit, the executions were over. In total 335 people had been slaughtered. The final death toll remains controversial to this day. To avenge the thirty-three German deaths at Via Rasella, Kappler had been ordered to execute ten times that number. Yet, despite the detailed paperwork and the use of lists, five extra executions took place.

The full story of the additional five killings remained unsolved for over fifty years. Originally it was attributed to a counting error made by Erich Priebke, who was responsible for checking the list at the Ardeatine Caves. However, in the 1990s Karl Haas, who was Kappler's intelligence chief and who shot two of the prisoners in the caves, gave evidence in a Rome courtroom. He explained that five extra prisoners had not been on the list and had been continually set aside as the executions went ahead. When the killings stopped, the five were left, and it was agreed that since they had witnessed everything they should be killed as well. They were shot simply because they had become witnesses to murder. Kappler would insist later that he did not hear about the five extra deaths until the next day, but this contradicts evidence given by Haas, who insisted Kappler said, "What shall I do with these five men who saw everything?"

Moments after the last five prisoners were killed, Kappler ordered engineers to blow up the entrance to the caves to prevent access to the gory scene inside. A series of explosions brought to an end the events of that grim day.

At ten o'clock that night Kappler addressed his men in the Gestapo mess at Villa Massimo. He told them, "The reprisal has been carried out. I know it was very hard for some of you, but in cases like this the law of war applies. The best thing you can do is get drunk."

Kappler stayed with his men for a while and then made his way to the Hotel Excelsior. At midnight he met members of the Nazi high command, among them General Karl Wolff, head of the SS in Italy, who had flown to Rome that afternoon. Colonel Dollmann was also at the hotel, but had other business to attend to before he met Kappler. He telephoned Father Pancratius, the Pope's liaison officer with whom he had spoken after the Via Rasella attack, and informed him that any diplomatic efforts to avoid bloodshed were too late, as the reprisal had taken place.

Dollmann and Wolff then went to Wolff's suite, where they met Kappler. According to Dollmann, the Gestapo chief, who had just carried out the bloodiest acts of his military career, looked like a "true executioner" with "flaming deep livid eyes." As the most senior officer present, General Wolff requested that Kappler detail the events of the past forty-eight hours. This he did, stating that the order for the reprisals had been carried out. Wolff was not satisfied and said that the number of executions was not enough. He believed the retaliation had been too lenient, for "the people of Rome do not deserve favored treatment."

It was decided that a communiqué must be issued that would place the blame for the retaliation firmly on the shoulders of the Resistance. After much discussion the wording was finally agreed upon and it was then translated into Italian. The late-night conference was still not over; Wolff had other business he wanted to discuss. He argued that the attack on Via Rasella had reinforced his view that the level of anti-German feeling in Rome was becoming too difficult to control. The general insisted that the city should be cleared of Jews and anti-fascists. He then asked his two colleagues for their comments.

Kappler showed little enthusiasm for Wolff's idea of mass evacuation of Jews. He was already tired and knew that the process would be time-consuming and labor-intensive. He argued that many men would be required to search entire districts for Jews and then to escort them out of the city. He had serious doubts about the practicalities of such an operation, just as he had initially raised concerns about the difficulties of policing the deportation of Jews in the autumn of 1943. However, he had eventually carried out such operations.

Dollmann waited his turn to speak. Ever the diplomat, he raised the political implications of such a dramatic move and explained that the Pope was likely to formally object to such large-scale deportations from his own city.

The discussions continued until two in the morning, when Wolff rang Himmler to give him a progress report on the day's events. The two men discussed what should happen next, and after Himmler insisted that the deportations go ahead, Kappler was instructed to draw up a plan. Then the meeting wound up and the men who ran Rome went to bed. Only a handful of people knew the full horror of what had occurred just hours earlier.

The next day, as Romans went about their normal Saturday business, the talk was of what might have happened to the prisoners who had been taken from the jails. Facts were scarce and rumors abounded, so those families with relatives in Regina Coeli and Via Tasso feared the worst. A number of people who lived near the Ardeatine Caves had witnessed some of the previous day's activities, but German guards had kept them well away from the scene of the killings. Nicola D'Annibale saw Germans stopping cars in Via Ardeatina in the afternoon at around the time the shootings began. Others saw similar activity. From a field across from the caves, Celesta Rasa, a pensioner who was gathering food for her rabbits, also saw the Germans. When he spotted her, a German sentry fired a warning shot.

The Vatican was now trying to piece together the events of the previous day. One report came from Monsignor Nasalli Rocca, a papal representative who regularly visited Regina Coeli. Hours after prisoners had been taken away, he had called at the prison to take confession. When he arrived he found the inmates agitated and frightened. He was told by one of the inmates that prisoners had been taken off to be shot by firing squads. The guards also confirmed that some of the prisoners had been taken away but there was no more detail. Monsignor Rocca, who was a prelate attendant to the Pope, took the news straight to the Holy Father. He later recalled: "When I told him what I had learned in prison, the Pope covered his face with his hands." The monsignor added that the Pontiff then replied, "It is not possible, I cannot believe it." Rocca believed that the Pope responded in a way that signified that this was the first time he had been told of this news.

Elsewhere in the Vatican, O'Flaherty and Derry were in a state of anxiety. Around forty escapees and Italian helpers were in the jails that the Germans raided, and the monsignor and the major were desperate to find out if they had been killed. Phone calls were made, but it would be some time before they would eventually discover that five of their Italian helpers had been shot at the caves. Andrea Casadei and Vittorio Fantini, who had just recently been arrested with Father Robert Pace, were among those who had died. So too had Antonio Roazzi and a helper by the name of Bernardini. The death of Umberto Lusena hit Derry hard, since he recalled how helpful the Italian had been to him when he first arrived in Rome.

Like Derry, O'Flaherty was deeply saddened by the news of the massacre. In his grief the monsignor may also have considered that thanks to a mixture of good luck and circumstance, he was not himself a prisoner in Via Tasso or Regina Coeli. Had he been arrested and imprisoned, he would certainly have appeared on Kappler's list and been shot.

As news of the atrocity spread by word of mouth, all of Rome was desperate for confirmation of how many had died and who had been killed. Exaggerated rumors of five or six hundred dead were commonly bandied about as family members traveled across the city to the jails to see if their loved ones were still alive. The desire for news was widespread and palpable.

At noon the German communiqué was finally made public:

On the afternoon of 23 March 1944 criminal elements executed a bomb attack against a column of German police in transit through Via Rasella. As a result of this ambush, thirty men of the German police were killed and several wounded. The vile ambush was carried out by communist badogliani. An investigation is still being made to clarify the extent to which this criminal deed is attributable to Anglo-American involvement. The German Command has decided to terminate the activities of these villainous bandits. No one will be allowed to sabotage with impunity the newly affirmed Italo-German cooperation. The German Command has therefore ordered that for every murdered German ten communist badogliani criminals will be shot. This order has already been executed.

Romans first read the German communiqué at midday on Saturday, March 25, around sixteen hours after the massacre ended. It was published on the front page of the *Messaggero* newspaper. The most chilling words were the concluding ones, which detailed that the order had already been executed. Now the city knew what had happened, but still didn't know who the victims were and where they had been killed, although strong rumors persisted that the shootings had been carried out at the caves in Via Ardeatina.

Hours after the *Messaggero* broke the news, the communiqué appeared in the Vatican newspaper the *Osservatore Romano*. The only legal non-fascist newspaper in Rome, the *Osservatore Romano* had appealed the day before to the city's inhabitants to refrain from acts of violence after the Via Rasella attack, for fear that the Germans would retaliate. In Saturday's edition the newspaper returned to that theme. Part of the editorial read: "In the face of such deeds every honest heart is left profoundly grieved in the name of humanity and Christian sentiment. Thirty-three victims on the one hand; and on the other, 335 persons sacrificed for the guilty parties who escaped arrest."

The wording is worthy of examination. Who were the "guilty parties"? Were they the Nazis who rounded up over three hundred people and then butchered them, or the small gang of Resistance fighters who planted the bomb in Via Rasella? What is clear is that those behind the editorial, viewed by many as the authentic voice of the Vatican, felt they could draw a distinction between the two acts of violence. The statement was also seen by many as another warning that further acts of resistance could lead to more German reprisals.

The questions raised about the behavior of the Resistance prompted a debate across the city. It is an argument that still dramatically divides opinion in Italy. Was the Resistance right to attack the Germans? Was the Resistance responsible for the Ardeatine retaliation? Had the Resistance members who carried out the bombing given themselves up, would the revenge attack have been avoided? Was the taking of thirty-three German lives worth 335 Italian lives?

These questions now consumed the Resistance movement. The Comitato di Liberazione Nazionale (CLN) met in emergency session to discuss the Via Rasella attack and the Ardeatine Massacre. The CLN was an odd mix of six anti-fascist groups united by the common cause of defeating the Nazis. The groups included Socialists, Communists, Christian Democrats, and Liberals, and each was represented on the Military Command. Inevitably the political dynamic meant infighting, which meant that arguments slowed the decision-making process. The Christian Democrats argued that any future military operations must be cleared in advance. The Liberals argued that the CLN should take full responsibility for the Via Rasella attack. The Patriotic Action Group, known as the gappisti, the organization that actually carried out the bombing, took matters into their own hands and issued a statement saying they had been behind the attack and would continue to fight the Nazis until they left Italy.

Ironically, the editorial in the *Osservatore Romano* that prompted much of this debate led to German protests. Field Marshal Kesselring took objection to the newspaper's suggestion that the Italian victims were innocent. Kesselring was desperate to maintain the Nazi lie that those who were killed in the Ardeatine Caves were all prisoners who had been on "death row" awaiting capital punishment. It was a cover-up that would soon be exposed, but in the darkness of uncertainty, Rome's rulers had the upper hand in the propaganda war.

That Saturday, the German dead of Via Rasella were buried. The city's senior Nazis were all in attendance. Kappler, Möllhausen, and Dollmann were among the funeral party and heard a strident speech by Wolff. Kappler would recall how the general promised more retaliation. After their colleagues had been laid to rest, it was down to the business of planning what to do next. The proposal to cleanse Rome of Jews and anti-fascists was uppermost in Wolff's thoughts. Even though he had been warned by Kappler and other officers that the operation would be a drain on manpower, he seemed intent on carrying it through. He would spend a large part of the day in discussions with Kesselring and Mackensen.

As the Germans discussed tactics, the world was beginning to hear the details of one of the worst war crimes committed on Italian soil during the Second World War. By early evening the news of the Nazis' retaliation in the Ardeatine Caves was being widely reported in Europe and the United States. Around the globe readers and listeners received the first accounts of what had happened on that spring day in Rome. It was just a snapshot of what had occurred. The full picture would take months to emerge.

In response to the worldwide coverage, there would be no letup in the Germans' attempts to present their version of events. The next day they issued another communiqué, which focused on the question of whether Rome should be an "open city." For some time there had been much debate on how Rome and its inhabitants could be spared further Allied air attacks and how the city could be protected. In the communiqué the Germans said they would take new steps to deprive the Allies of the need to bomb Rome. There would be "no military traffic of any kind through the city and in the city."

Typically, the directive was not as simple as it seemed. The order stated that if the Resistance used these changes to disrupt matters, the German high command would respond. The statement ended by saying that the fate of Rome and its population was now in the hands of the city's people. Just as the Nazis had blamed the Resistance for the Ardeatine Massacre, so they now said the Resistance would be blamed again if there were further atrocities. It was a classic Nazi statement, designed to put the pressure on their opponents.

By now nature was taking its course in the Ardeatine Caves, and locals began to notice a strange smell emanating from the network of tunnels. The odor of 335 rotting corpses hung over the site, and the pungent stench drew numerous onlookers. One local resident found the smell so overpowering that he contacted the police. The news was passed on to Caruso, who in turn contacted Kappler. Told about the problem, Kappler replied that he would "have the inconvenience eliminated." He needed something to mask the smell of death, so he came up with a novel idea: He ordered that rubbish be dumped at the entrances to the caves to both hide what lay in the tunnels and cover up the foul odor. His plan didn't work.

Relatives of the missing prisoners began to make the journey out of Rome to the caves to see if they could find the bodies of their loved ones. When they discovered the rubbish blocking their access, some simply moved it out of the way. Entry into the caves was still blocked by rubble and stones from the explosions, however, so many visitors simply left flowers at the site and returned home.

Others, however, managed to get inside the caves. Father Don Fernando Giorgi was a supporter of the Resistance and had regularly helped to organize sabotage actions with the Partito d'Azione, a member of the CLN. The Salesian priest was based at the St. Calixtus catacombs, which were contained within the Appian Way, close to the Ardeatine Caves. The priest had been alerted by a colleague who had come across scavengers who had found clothing and spotted a ladder and wire at the caves. Father Giorgi walked over to the site and, with another priest, Father Valentini, lit a torch and climbed down into the caves through a hole in one of the tunnels. In the half light, and almost overpowered by the smell, they

167

discovered a pile of bodies "covered with a thick mould." Six corpses were immediately visible, and they could see that the victims' hands had been tied behind their backs with heavy cord.

The two priests climbed out of the darkness and returned across the fields to the Salesian Institute. They now had confirmation of exactly what all of Rome had suspected. And they knew exactly what they had to do. They contacted the Vatican and journeyed into the city.

While Father Valentini delivered the news to the Pope's staff, Father Giorgi took the opportunity to tell an old friend in person. Father Giorgi and Hugh O'Flaherty had worked together finding safe houses for Allied servicemen. Sitting in the monsignor's room in the German College, Father Giorgi described what he and his colleague had found in the caves. O'Flaherty found it hard to listen to his account. The shocking details would stay with him for years. Even after the war he found visiting the site emotional. One visitor recalled how some years later, when the site became a national memorial of remembrance, they prayed together on the floor of the caves and the monsignor openly wept. The Ardeatine Massacre touched Hugh O'Flaherty like no other event of the war.

Within hours of the two priests' visit to the Vatican, Kappler had discovered that his enclosed tomb on Via Ardeatina had been breached. He knew he had to act fast, otherwise the secrets of the massacre would begin to leak out. He dispatched a truck full of soldiers and engineers to the site, and after a series of explosions the entrance to the caves was again encased in a mix of earth, stones, sand, and rubbish. His aim to create an enclosed burial chamber, away from prying eyes, was complete. The tomb in the Ardeatine Caves would now remain closed for as long as Herbert Kappler ruled Rome.

CHAPTER 13

Clampdown

"That bastard Perfetti has gone over to the Boche."
—SAM DERRY

AS THE SPRING OF 1944 ARRIVED, O'FLAHERTY AND DERRY WERE effectively prisoners of war. The major had been in the British legation since January and was used to being housebound. And the monsignor knew that if he set foot outside Vatican territory he would be arrested. He had been told a few months earlier by the German ambassador that he would be detained by German soldiers if he strayed from the neutral territory of the Holy See. He took the warning seriously.

O'Flaherty had also been informed that Kappler had offered 30,000 lire to anyone who would give information that would lead to his arrest. The move indicated Kappler's growing desperation to close down the escape operation, which so far he had failed even to disrupt. It also underlined his continuing obsession with the monsignor in particular. In cash-strapped Rome, where loyalty had a price, O'Flaherty knew the bounty could prove quite tempting. The reward may well have reinforced his decision to confine himself to the Vatican's rooms, corridors, and gardens.

Nevertheless, in late March O'Flaherty and Derry reached the conclusion that, with planning and a bit of luck, they could still operate without jeopardizing their own safety. In the safety of the priest's room, they would often pore over the escape operation's paperwork and plot how best the organization could look after a membership that now numbered nearly thirty-five hundred and was still growing. This index of escapees, besides helping them keep track of who was under the operation's care, also allowed them to keep officials in London informed about escapees who were now officially "safe."

Meanwhile Derry continued to keep detailed notes of how much money was being spent, still hiding his receipts in buried cookie tins. Osborne, in his role as unofficial banker to the Escape Line, was still very busy contacting London and arranging payments. By now the operation's running costs were around three million lire, or some $40,000, each month.

The escapees being helped by the organization were mainly British, but also included Americans, South Africans, Russians, and some Greeks. Across Rome the operation had around two hundred hiding places at its disposal. A few hundred Russians were being looked after in buildings outside the city. O'Flaherty had secured the services of former Red Cross workers and had also recruited a Russian priest. The monsignor may have been leading a hermit-like existence in the German College, but it didn't stop his appearances on the steps of St. Peter's nor his effectiveness in passing messages on through his network of priests and helpers. He was restricted in what he could do, but he was still the heart and soul of the escape operation.

In late March Rome was tense. After the attacks in Via Rasella and the Ardeatine Massacre, extra German troops swamped the city. For Derry the atmosphere was a very different one from when he arrived in Rome during the winter of 1943. Hiding escapees in the city had become harder than ever, so he was grateful for any extra help he could get.

Enter the man who seemingly could obtain the unobtainable. One day John May bounded into Derry's room and teased the major: "How would you like to get hold of their routine orders when they come out?"

Derry, thinking he had misheard, told May he was talking nonsense. Yet the British ambassador's opportunistic butler had actually established a contact with someone who had access to Fascist police and SS orders, and he told Derry he could get a copy for 1,000 lire.

The major considered May's proposition. Money was tight. There was food to buy for the escapees, and because of rationing, much depended on the black market. The organization was also spending 180,000 lire a month on clothing. Money was still coming in from the British government via Osborne, but Derry knew that whatever he spent it on had to bring worthwhile results. The two men discussed the merits of May's contact, a man called Giuseppe, and Derry, although somewhat skeptical, agreed to the deal. Within days the organization was 1,000 lire lighter, but on Derry's desk sat a detailed transcript of SS and police orders. After days of bad news it was a rare moment of joy. Now, instead of relying on luck or an unofficial tip-off, he and O'Flaherty had a more reliable early-warning system in place should any of their safe houses be about to be raided. The cash payment turned out to be the wisest investment the Escape Line ever made, for Giuseppe's information quickly proved very reliable.

Lists of houses the Germans were about to search usually reached Derry's hand by lunchtime on the day of the planned raid.

This gave Derry and O'Flaherty about five hours to send out warnings and to arrange alternative accommodations. Under Derry's "cell" system only four people knew the addresses of the safe houses: Derry, O'Flaherty (who had originally found many of the Italian helpers), record-keeper Henry Byrnes, and Bill Simpson.

When word came from Giuseppe that a raid was imminent, Derry and O'Flaherty had to drop everything and put their warning system into operation. O'Flaherty had established a messenger service that used priests to pass on notes alerting householders that a search was about to take place. Kappler, however, was well aware of what O'Flaherty was doing, and he was determined to break up his network of clerical activists. Then Kappler got lucky. Kappler's team discovered that one key building lay to the north of the city wall. The church of San Roberto Bellarmino, dedicated to the Jesuit cardinal of that name, was founded by the previous Pope, Pius XI, in 1933. Here priests unofficially offered hospitality and food to escaped prisoners of war. Kappler had all the access points under observation, and his men were ready to stop escapees coming and going.

The crackdown on O'Flaherty's messenger-priests also started to get a little more sophisticated. Kappler knew servicemen on the run usually trusted men of the Church, so he had some of his officers disguise themselves as priests to trap them.

One of Kappler's trump cards was Pasqualino Perfetti. Also known as Don Pasquale Perfetti, the Italian had been one of O'Flaherty's key stalwarts from the early days of the escape operation. He dressed in clerical attire, but he was no priest. O'Flaherty used Perfetti to arrange safe houses. John Furman and Bill Simpson had dealings with him during their early days in Rome. When Derry wrote his speculative letter to the Vatican seeking assistance and clothes for his group of escapees in the countryside, the letter was delivered to O'Flaherty by Perfetti. And when the British major arrived in Rome, it was Perfetti who helped him find accommodation and clothes. Perfetti had been loyal to the Escape Line, so when he was arrested for questioning by Pietro Koch's Italian police unit, little thought was given to it. Within a few days, however, it was clear that his detention had serious implications.

François de Vial, who looked after French escapees, contacted Derry and told him, "That bastard Perfetti has gone over to the Boche." The news was later confirmed in a report from Giuseppe, May's contact, who wrote that Perfetti had been collaborating with both the Fascist and the German police. The news was devastating because Perfetti, having been involved in the Escape Line from an early stage, before security was tightened, knew the names and addresses of the local families who offered shelter for escapees.

De Vial told Derry that Perfetti had initially given nothing away, but after a few days of torture had crumbled. After his release Perfetti had been spotted in various parts of Rome in the company of known Gestapo agents. Derry and O'Flaherty had to act fast. They set about removing escapees from safe houses that Perfetti knew about, though in some cases they were too late. The Italian's information led to the arrest of around a dozen of his compatriots and the recapture of twenty-one escaped servicemen.

The scale of Perfetti's betrayal was enormous, and the escape organization was now under serious pressure as it tried to continue providing safe houses for servicemen. A further problem was that many key activists were now effectively housebound. O'Flaherty and Derry were closeted permanently in the Vatican, and Father Aurelius Borg and Father Kenneth Madden were also confined by their superiors to their religious houses. Father Borg routinely delivered messages to host families and escorted escapees across Rome, while Father Madden was an Irish Augustinian priest who helped escapees move to safe houses and often distributed provisions. Brother Robert Pace, who had recently been released, was also keeping a low profile. While Kappler and Koch hadn't put the escape organization out of business, between them they had certainly diminished its effectiveness.

But in April, much to the relief of Derry and O'Flaherty, new faces came forward to assist the escape operation. The Ardeatine Massacre had prompted many ordinary Romans to offer homes for escapees or to work as helpers and messengers. Deeply angered and hurt by the massacre and by the continuing deportations of Jews, they wanted to do anything to get back at the Nazis.

Rome was still grieving, but now it had another concern to contend with—hunger. Shortly after the Via Rasella attack the German authorities had reduced the city's bread ration, making daily life intolerable for the many thousands of people who were already struggling to survive. Exasperated and hungry, women took to the streets demanding their right to bread. Protest turned to violence, and a number of bakeries were attacked and looted. Inevitably the demonstrations brought clashes with the local police and, ultimately, with the Germans. When the SS became involved, they arrested ten women, who were later shot and dumped in the Tiber River.

Kappler's response to the bread crisis was predictably simple and cruel. Rather than increase the food supply, he preferred to reduce the demand for food through deportations. When, on Easter Monday, three Germans were killed in a Resistance attack, he seized his chance. A week later, before first light, Kappler and a team specially chosen for the task surrounded houses in the Quadraro district, a working-class area that was home to a number of Resistance groups. In the largest roundup since the Germans seized control of the city the previous September, every house in the neighborhood was searched and some 2,000 men and boys were detained. They were marched off to a nearby cinema, where the fittest were detained and the least healthy were released. Around 750 of them were then deported. Their destination was unknown, and the majority of those taken away that day never returned home.

The next day, in a different part of the city, there was another German raid. This one was small-scale compared with the number of men who had been deployed in Quadraro, but it delivered Kappler's hardest blow to date against O'Flaherty's escape organization. When armed SS officers arrived at an apartment shortly after the start of the nighttime curfew, they discovered an Irishman named William O'Flynn, who claimed to work at the Vatican library. O'Flynn was an alias and the man's identity documents were false. Kappler's men had just arrested a member of the escape organization's inner circle.

When he was found at the apartment, Lieutenant Bill Simpson was with an American officer and several Italian black-marketeers. Simpson offered his papers to the SS men and claimed to be Irish. The American, who spoke Italian, claimed he was local. The SS sergeant major was having none of it. He sensed they were not telling the truth, and his men, ignoring the others present, handcuffed the two Allied officers, marched them from the premises, and bundled them into a waiting car. The drive to Regina Coeli prison didn't take long, and once there, Simpson faced a string of questions. He maintained the pretense: "Listen, I am not English. I am Irish, my home is in Dublin and I am an employee of the Vatican. If I don't turn up for work tomorrow morning, there'll be some awkward questions to answer, both for me and you." But his interrogator was well informed and suggested that Simpson was not Irish but Scottish, a fact that his accent could not hide. When this first bout of questioning came to an end, the prisoner was taken to his new home, Cell 321, which he would share with three others.

Bill Simpson's disappearance mystified and then greatly worried O'Flaherty. He and Derry had received no indication that their colleague had been picked up by the Germans, but when he didn't show up for a number of days, they assumed he had been arrested. O'Flaherty telephoned a number of friends and acquaintances. Other messages were sent to contacts close to the prisons and in the Italian police, but they failed to uncover Simpson's precise whereabouts.

In late April it became clear that the Germans knew exactly how the Escape Line was being funded. After a number of uncertain months, Sir D'Arcy Osborne had recently been able to put the organization on a more secure footing. In February, after weeks of phone calls and memos to and from London, he had secured a loan of some five million lire from the government, and money was being channeled through a Jesuit account. The Treasury had also agreed to place a credit of $20,000 in Swiss francs at his disposal in Switzerland. Without Osborne's financial negotiations O'Flaherty knew the group couldn't continue to operate, which made the German discovery even more troubling.

In March the average monthly cost of looking after an escapee in Rome was 122 lire. By April 2.5 million lire had been spent helping nearly four thousand escapees. In addition a growing number of escapees were rearrested, which meant that money destined to help them fell into the Nazis' hands.

The news that Osborne had been identified as the Escape Line's "banker" came from friends in the Swiss embassy. Weizsäcker, the German ambassador with whom O'Flaherty had crossed swords at the Hungarian embassy in January, was clearly well informed. He knew that officials at the Swiss legation assisted Allied escapees and provided cash. He told them that if they continued to do so they would face arrest. The Swiss took the threat seriously and informed Osborne that as of late April they were withdrawing their support for the operation. Weizsäcker's warning was presented in a friendly manner and with a degree of subtlety. The Swiss had no need to fund the Escape Line, he suggested, as that was being done so well by Osborne. He added that the British funding was clearly generous, since Allied escapees were often seen lunching in some of Rome's most expensive restaurants. The diplomat's canny observation hit a raw nerve with O'Flaherty and Derry.

For some time the two men had been concerned about the behavior of a number of the escapees in Rome. Derry had written to some of them after being informed that they had been seen drunk in public. He made it clear that their behavior compromised security and placed at risk the families who were providing safe houses. At the same time the arrests in Rome of Simpson and other escapees and the constant expenditure on food, clothing, and accommodations made Derry rethink the way the organization was being run. The operation had become too dangerous and too costly; something had to change.

Derry wrote to key members of the Escape Line, including O'Flaherty, to explain that the latest information suggested that the Allied forces would not arrive in Rome until the autumn. He also said that the arrests, the rationing of food—bread and meat were scarce and the supply of salt was restricted—and the difficulties in finding safe houses were making the situation in Rome very hard for the escape organization. As a result no more escapees would be billeted in the city. Instead they would be given money and advised to return to the countryside. They would be confined to their billets, and the practice of visiting friends in other safe houses had to stop.

Derry's changes and decision were harsh, but he felt that Kappler and Koch's ever-tightening control of the city demanded a new approach in the interests of security. Specifically, he feared that the next arrest would be the one Kappler desperately wanted above all others—that of Hugh O'Flaherty.

The monsignor's daily routine consisted of working in his room, his activities in the Holy Office, and his forays into other Vatican buildings. He still stood on the steps of St. Peter's every day, but he did not venture beyond Vatican territory. Now Kappler wanted to make his arch-enemy's life even harder. Quite likely at his behest the Germans officially complained to the Vatican authorities about O'Flaherty. Ambassador Weizsäcker continued to make it clear to his contacts in the Holy See that he and his colleagues were well aware of the priest's activities. In an attempt to make O'Flaherty's life more difficult, the Nazis barred all public access to the German College. It was a well-planned move by Kappler and meant that the monsignor's room, which was the nerve center of the escape operation, was now off-limits to non-Vatican staff.

O'Flaherty now had to think up ingenious ways to conduct Escape Line business. He would often meet Derry and the recently released Furman inside St. Peter's, where they could talk discreetly. But it was far from ideal: O'Flaherty was frequently approached there by friends and acquaintances, and sometimes it was hard to carry on conversations away from prying eyes and ears. As so often the case, it was the quick-thinking May who came up with an alternative. He persuaded the ever-present Swiss Guards to allow him to use a guardroom, which was quiet much of the time, for private discussions.

By May a new Allied offensive had begun in southern Italy, and in Rome there was much talk that the liberation of the city was just weeks away. The most asked question was "Quando vengono?" "When will they arrive?" When Furman heard the news of the Allied assault broadcast on BBC Radio, he allowed himself a little celebration. Surrounded by friends, he raised a glass of liqueur and proposed a toast to "the success of the Allies."

If Kappler had serious concerns that his days in Rome were coming to an end because of the Allies' advance, he did not show them publicly. His attempts to break up the escape organization continued relentlessly. His officers stepped up their efforts to catch O'Flaherty's most successful helper, Henrietta Chevalier. They had raided her apartment on a number of occasions but had yet to discover any Allied escapees.

Two armed Germans and an Italian woman took up residence in a café directly across the street from the apartment, from which they had an uninterrupted view of the property. The very next day their patience paid off when two men approached the apartment. The pair, both Allied escapees, had not been notified that the Chevaliers' home was out of bounds. When they knocked on the door, Henrietta told them to leave at once because she had noticed that the apartment was being watched. The two men casually left the building, followed by a Gestapo agent. Aware they were being tailed, they entered a nearby courtyard and then ran from the scene, shaking off their armed escort.

It was a close shave, and when O'Flaherty and Derry learned what had happened, it was clear to them what had to be done. The

Chevaliers' life in Rome had to end, at least for the time being. The family found safety on a farm, where they would remain until the liberation of Rome. The city's war-weary population didn't know it at the time, but the Allies were just over three weeks away from the city.

Under Derry's new regime all Allied escapees were confined to their safe houses and told to stay out of sight. For the time being the only way to get messages to them was to deliver the news in person or by sending a messenger. Normally one of the many priests who worked regularly with O'Flaherty would be called into action, but the monsignor's choices were now limited. On the advice of his colleagues in the organization, Brother Pace was keeping a low profile after being released by the Germans. He had been arrested with the Italians Andrea Casadei and Vittorio Fantini, who were later killed in the Ardeatine Caves. Similarly, Father Borg, whose code name was "Grobb," and Father Madden, or "Edmund," were also staying out of sight after the Germans complained about them. As a result operational duties fell to a number of the remaining priests, among them Father Musters, a Dutch national, who went under the imaginative code name of "Dutchpa."

Walking in the warm air on a day in May, Father Musters had gone out of the Vatican to visit a number of escapees hiding in safe houses across the city. As he left one address and started to make his way to another, he noticed he had company. The priest was being followed by a plainclothes German agent. When Musters paused and looked back, true to form the other man stopped too and glanced into a shop window. Now sure of what was going on, Father Musters made for the church of Santa Maria Maggiore, which, being Vatican extra-territorial property, offered safety.

Before he could get there, however, his escort approached him and demanded to see his identity documents. Father Musters said he would produce them on the steps of the church, which angered the Gestapo agent, who then pulled a pistol from his jacket. The priest pushed the German aside and hurried toward the church, but was brought down by a massive blow to the head. He fell at the door of the church, at which point his attacker turned and left. The priest was helped inside by a guard, who quickly informed the Vatican authorities about the incident. Word came back that Father Musters should remain at the church, where he would be safe, and where he would be picked up the following day and taken back to his religious order. It was bad advice.

Thirty minutes later a squad of SS men arrived at the church to find Father Musters resting. He was ordered to stand up but protested, saying the Germans had no right to be on extra-territorial property. His pleas made little difference, and within seconds he was struck again on the head, this time with a submachine gun. The SS men then dragged him out of the church and ferried him to Via Tasso. Battered and bruised but conscious, he soon realized why his arrest had generated such excitement. The Gestapo believed they had discovered Sam Derry, who often adopted the disguise of a priest. They were convinced they had captured the man who, as a British Army major and the most senior officer involved in the Escape Line, had military responsibility for the whole operation. A brutal interrogation followed in which Father Musters was repeatedly asked to admit that he was an English spy. Then he was shown an up-to-date operational chart of the escape organization and ordered to point out what role he had in the operation.

"Tell us all or you die tonight," barked the interrogator, but the priest had nothing to say. Producing the diagram showed how current Kappler's information was and highlighted his determination to break the escape organization, even as Nazi rule in Rome was nearing an end. Father Musters's incarceration would last thirty-five days. He would later be put on a train to Germany, and like so many of the Allied soldiers he had helped, he would follow their lead and dramatically escape, in his case at Florence. When he returned to Rome the city would be in different hands.

By now many within the German-Italian Fascist leadership realized that the Allies would start arriving in the city within days. Monte Cassino had fallen into Allied hands and U.S. troops were within sight of Rome. For the city's rulers time was running out. In his final days of power, Pietro Koch had been giving serious thought to what would happen to his family when the Allies arrived. However, he had a survival plan, so he sent a messenger to the one man who he thought could help—his longtime enemy Hugh O'Flaherty.

The monsignor was startled by the message from Koch, and at first he thought he was being led into a trap. In his office in the German College, he listened as his visitor explained that he had been sent by the police chief. "He wants to make a bargain with you," said his guest. "He says if the monsignor will arrange to place his wife and mother in a religious house when he goes, he in exchange will ensure that the monsignor's friends are left in Regina Coeli instead of being transported to Germany."

O'Flaherty thought for a moment. This proposal was full of risk, and he needed some indication that Koch would stand by his word. Was it worth chancing it? He decided to test the police chief's intentions. Some days earlier the monsignor had received written confirmation that Bill Simpson was alive and was being held in Regina Coeli, which made it only natural that Simpson would be one of those included in any deal. The priest responded to the offer, saying, "Tell Koch I agree to his suggestion on one condition. As evidence of his good faith, he must first deliver safely to me the two British officers who are in Regina Coeli—Lieutenant Simpson and Captain Armstrong. If he does that I shall make the arrangements he desires for his wife and mother."

O'Flaherty's visitor left the Vatican and took the offer back to Koch, who agreed to it instantly. However, the deal struck a snag. In custody, Simpson was still pretending he was an Irish citizen named William O'Flynn, so when the prison authorities looked for him they could find no record of a Lieutenant Simpson. O'Flaherty then told Koch's contact to search the prison records for an inmate using the name Simpson had assumed. For days nothing was heard, and the monsignor and Derry were convinced that the deal had broken down.

Then one day as John Furman and Renzo Lucidi sat in their apartment working on safe-house accounts, the doorbell rang. They both jumped up in fear, because the caller was using the secret signal. They were not expecting anybody, so they naturally wondered if it was a trap. Whoever was outside had some kind of inside knowledge. But who was it? When they tentatively opened the front door, they both cried out with happiness on seeing a familiar face. Bill Simpson was a free man.

On June 3 it became clear that the German occupation of Rome was about to end. Weizsäcker made a last visit to the Vatican to meet Monsignor Montini and his colleague Monsignor Tardini. He confirmed that the Germans were leaving and said he wanted the Vatican to act as an honest broker with the Allies to effectively secure a safe passage for them as they withdrew. The German ambassador proposed that parts of Rome should be designated an "open city," free of military action by either side, in order to safeguard the many historic buildings. The Vatican was suspicious of Weizsäcker's plans but, tired of the war and accustomed to German doublespeak, reluctantly agreed to pass the offer on.

The retreat was now in full swing. Offices were cleared, bags were stuffed with cash and valuables, and those who had ruled Rome for the past nine months said their good-byes and left. Colonel Eugen Dollmann took one last long walk around the city he had enjoyed for seventeen years. He then headed for Florence. Kappler's deputy, Captain Erich Priebke, had just returned to Rome from Germany and went to visit a lady friend who wanted to escape with him, but he left Rome without her and headed to Verona. Members of the "Koch gang" made for Milan; Pietro Caruso drove out of Rome early one morning with jewelry and watches hidden inside his car.

Allied planes flew over the city, but this time their payload was innocent. Thousands of leaflets rained down bearing a message from General Harold Alexander, the deputy Allied commander. He declared that the liberation of Rome was at hand and urged local people to safeguard public services such as the telephone service and the railway network. He asked that street barriers be removed so that the Allies could arrive unhindered. "Rome is yours! Your job is to save the city, ours is to destroy the enemy," said the leaflet.

Herbert Kappler spent his final days in power destroying incriminating documents at Via Tasso. Dozens of prisoners would be left locked up as the Germans retreated, unaware that they would soon be free. One inmate who was released, by Kappler himself, had long feared he wouldn't live to see the Allied liberation. In one of his last acts in the city, Kappler freed Giuliano Vassalli, a partisan commander, telling him he could thank the Pope for his liberty. The

Germans had promised the Vatican that before they withdrew they would free many prisoners. As Vassalli was being led away, Kappler remarked, "Don't ever let me see you again."

The Allies were now just twenty miles from Rome. German tanks and trucks packed with troops thundered through the streets, heading north. British forces had reached the Pope's summer villa at Castel Gandolfo, and Allied commanders were anxious to discover what would greet them once they arrived on the streets of Rome. When they made contact with the Vatican radio station, Derry came on the line. Surprised to find a British officer in the Vatican, they were grateful for his briefing on what he knew of the situation. Derry then asked the question that much of Rome had been asking for months: "When will you arrive?"

"Maybe tomorrow or the next day," came the much anticipated reply.

Hundreds of German soldiers were now on the move. Looking tired, forlorn, and bedraggled, they slipped away from the city, in marked contrast with their triumphant arrival less than a year before. Some Romans offered them sympathy, prepared to momentarily suspend their anger and forgive the injustices of the occupation. Other citizens saw the German retreat as a chance for revenge, and gun battles periodically raged. The occupiers were leaving, but their rule had not completely ended.

One German truck pulled out of Rome with a cargo of prisoners on board. Its number included Captain John Armstrong, the man O'Flaherty had hoped would be freed as part of the arrangement with Koch. It was a deal that would never be realized. Outside the city the truck stopped and the prisoners, with their hands tied, were forced to their knees. In an act that mirrored the horror of the Ardeatine Massacre, each was shot once in the head.

185

Armstrong's grave would lie unidentified for fifty years. Documents in the National Archives in London suggest that Armstrong was not his real name and that he was working undercover, taking many secrets to his grave.

In the panic and fear of June 1944, such details mattered little to the retreating Germans. The morning after the killings, Herbert Kappler walked out of Via Tasso for the last time. His war in Rome was over.

CHAPTER 14

Liberation

"Welcome to Rome. Is there anything I can do for you?"
—HUGH O'FLAHERTY

MANY ROMANS GOT THEIR FIRST SIGHT OF FREEDOM AS THEY perched on rooftops and balconies. Squinting into the distance, they were able to make out the arrival of the Allies as a cavalcade of tanks and troops moved toward them. On the top floor of the British legation, Derry and Osborne stood and watched history unfold. Too anxious and excited about what was about to happen, they had not slept the night before.

In the chapel of the Santa Marta Hospice, Monsignor O'Flaherty was on his knees praying. There was much to be thankful for. He had survived Kappler's rule, but over the past nine months he had lost many dear friends. His beloved Rome had suffered much during the bombings, though he was relieved that in recent days the city had been spared major damage. His life, like those of the colleagues around him who for months had worked in secret, was about to change. From now on, the monsignor's days would be very different.

In the amber glow of a June evening, American tanks rolled into the city. Once the target of German artillery, now all the Allied forces faced were cheers, kisses, and flowers. For many children it was the first time they had found the sight of tanks reassuring. They climbed aboard the Armored Division's vehicles and asked for sweets and chewing gum from their liberators. Soldiers found themselves the center of female attention, and there were hugs and handshakes at every corner. Rome was relieved, delighted, and quickly grew drunk on emotion. That night a power outage struck the city. It would take a few more hours before the full story of freedom would emerge.

From dawn the next day the U.S. Fifth Army, led by General Mark Clark, moved deeper and farther into the city. The American commander was driven through the streets in his Jeep, and in what was probably the most satisfying journey of his military career, he indulged in a bit of early-morning sightseeing. For Clark this was a personal and professional triumph. For months he had plotted and planned this moment, and he intended to enjoy it.

Clark and his entourage arrived at St. Peter's, where the general stopped for some photographs. O'Flaherty, as on every previous morning, was in the square, reading scriptures, thinking, and talking. He saw Clark in his Jeep and approached him. More photographs were taken, then the monsignor greeted the American: "Welcome to Rome. Is there anything I can do for you?" Clark replied that he wanted to go to the Campidoglio on Capitoline Hill. The square was now busy with crowds, so O'Flaherty arranged for a boy on a bicycle to guide the general. This unique convoy set off with the boy pedaling hard and telling the crowds to part because General Clark was on his way to Capitoline Hill.

When he arrived at his destination to the sound of ringing bells, Clark called a press conference and declared to the assembled war correspondents and photographers, "This is a great day for the

Fifth Army and the French, British, and American troops of the Fifth, who have made this victory possible."

Delia Kiernan, the wife of the Irish minister to the Holy See, discovered Rome's new occupiers by chance. After breakfast she went for a walk with her daughter Blon, and outside the railway station they came across a group of soldiers. Assuming they were Germans, she walked on until one of them spotted her and called out, "Say, sister. Come and park your arse beside me." She knew then that the Nazi occupation was over.

Harold Tittmann also met the new arrivals that morning. As the chargé d'affaires stood with his family and watched the morning unfold, a series of American Jeeps drove by. One stopped and the family shouted words of support in English. Delighted to have come across some fellow countrymen, a soldier handed them chocolate, cigarettes, and a magazine before resuming his journey. Before the day was out the Americans would get used to dispensing gifts to a population long deprived of treats.

The Stars and Stripes and the Union Jack now flew across the city unchallenged. British soldiers were also in Rome now, and like General Clark and his troops, they began to explore their new domain.

After weeks of fighting it was a chance for some rest and recuperation, and David Cole was in need of a haircut and a drink. The signals officer with the 1st Royal Inniskilling Fusiliers wandered into the Hotel Excelsior, formerly the Nazis' social center in Rome. It was the hotel where Kappler and Mälzer had dined and plotted. It was also where General Wolff held a late-night conference hours after the Ardeatine Massacre. As Cole made himself at home in surroundings untouched by war, one Roman asked the day's most repeated question: "Why were you so long in coming?"

For O'Flaherty this was the moment he had talked about and prayed for. He would now be able to do what he had been prevented from doing under Kappler's rule. In simple terms he was no longer a prisoner in the Holy See. He could now walk out of the Vatican without worrying.

Sitting in his study the Pope had listened as the liberation began, and amid the rumble of army trucks and the dull thuds of war, he heard the unmistakable sound of bagpipes. A Scottish piper made his way into St. Peter's Square and let rip with one of his most requested tunes. He played "Lillibulero," a refrain that soldiers routinely marched to. The words of the song refer to the Williamite war, during which the Catholic King James was defeated at the Battle of the Boyne in 1690. For this reason the tune was popular with Protestants who were members of the Orange Order, and if the Pope was listening carefully, he may have enjoyed the piper's mischievousness.

As the Vicar of Rome, Pope Pius XII knew he had to speak about the changed circumstances, and that night thousands crammed into St. Peter's to hear his address. Flags and messages were held aloft as ordinary Romans, members of the different Resistance groups, and Allied soldiers in battle dress squeezed into the square.

On the roof of the British legation, Osborne, Derry, May, and two of O'Flaherty's priests looked on. As the early-evening sunlight streamed across the crowd, the Pontiff appeared on the balcony to rapturous applause. His address was short and to the point. He appealed to the crowd to dwell on the future, not the past, and said God had saved Rome. He urged the crowd to forget any thoughts of retaliation but to reach out to those who had been their enemies. He blessed all those present before leaving the balcony and then, to the sound of cheering, disappeared from view.

It marked the end of a remarkable day. As the applause subsided, May felt a celebration was in order. He turned to his friends and, with a smile, duly informed them, "We do have some extremely good champagne downstairs, gentlemen." May's colleagues needed little persuasion and followed him to Osborne's quarters, where the liberation of Rome was toasted. Over the coming hours there were many such parties to celebrate the end of Nazi rule. The Lucidis, one of O'Flaherty's most reliable host families, put on a large celebration. In a farmhouse outside the city, Henrietta Chevalier and her family also marked the arrival of the Allies. In the Grand Hotel, another haunt of Rome's prominent Nazis and local Fascists, Derry and the leaders of the escape organization got together in their biggest-ever social gathering. They drank and ate and thought of absent friends.

One of those who may have been in their thoughts was on his way back to Rome. Father Musters was on the move, hitchhiking slowly back to Rome after dramatically escaping the clutches of the Germans. "Dutchpa" would find much had changed during his enforced absence.

Hours after the Allies seized Rome, the war would take a dramatic turn off the coast of northern France as Operation Overlord was put into action. Thousands of Allied troops landed in Normandy on June 6, D-Day. This opened up a new front against the Third Reich and marked a defining moment in the conflict, which still had nearly a year to run.

The arrival in Rome of the Americans and the British changed the battleground in Italy. Chased out of the city, the German forces moved northward and regrouped. They had lost the Italian capital, but they were far from defeated. Field Marshal Kesselring intended to fight along the "Gothic Line," which stretched across northern Italy from coast to coast, touching the Apennine Mountains in the east.

As Romans relished their newfound freedom, Kappler took a vacation and tried to relax and forget about the stress of leaving the city in such a hurry. Although the manner of his departure hurt, he knew he had to leave behind the memories of a place that had been his home for five years. He had some time before his next posting, which would be in Maderno, in northern Italy, where he would work as the Verbindungsführer, liaising between General Wolff and the local Italian police chief.

The full story of Kappler's reign in Rome would take many months to emerge. In the early days of the Allied liberation, a series of reports was compiled for the British and American intelligence agencies. In July 1944 one official assessment viewed him as a "typical Nazi, self-assured and confident that if he orders a thing to be done it will be done." The authors were skeptical of Kappler's abilities, declaring that "he has obviously impressed his superiors by a modicum of hard work and some very effective window dressing and although his own work was originally straightforward police liaison work he now regards himself as an expert on spy matters."

The report also suggested that "the failure of his most ambitious schemes for Rome will make him all the more eager to run better ones in Northern Italy." Kappler's obsession with Hugh O'Flaherty was also noted. The report stated that "during the last few months he was firmly convinced that the Vatican was his chief enemy and that the British Intelligence Service was centered there in the person of Monsignor O'Flaherty, the Red Cross delegate in charge of prisoners of war. He suspected the genial and garrulous O'Flaherty of having a V-man inside the SD (German Police)."

The target of Kappler's obsession found himself with a new role once the Germans had left Rome. O'Flaherty now turned his attention to looking after local families who had helped the escape organization as well as Italian prisoners of war. The monsignor also put pressure on the American commander, General Clark, to make sure that the many hundreds of German troops who were captured in the battle for Rome were now being treated properly. In this O'Flaherty showed the same evenhandedness he had applied back in 1942 when he visited British POWs across Italy.

Even though the Germans had gone, there was still much work to occupy Derry's days. At the time of the liberation, nearly four thousand Allied escapees were being housed in Rome and outside the city. Now there was the huge task of their repatriation to be managed.

O'Flaherty had also helped Jews hide in Rome during the Nazi occupation. Unlike the operation he maintained for servicemen "on the run," a precise figure for Jewish civilians has not been documented. What is clear is that the monsignor used the same tactics to assist Jewish refugees as he did for Allied escapees. It seems likely that hundreds of the former were offered shelter by O'Flaherty, since we know that he used a series of safe houses and church buildings to house Jews fearful of being rounded up by the Gestapo. One building he routinely used belonged to the Franciscan order, and he often sent fifteen or so Jewish refugees there at a time. He also used a building run by Canadian nuns, where Jewish women were given false identity documents.

In the aftermath of the Americans' arrival in Rome, Derry got a new job as the military attaché to Sir D'Arcy Osborne. The escape organization was moved out of the Vatican and was now based in an apartment at Via Scialoia. Numerous Italians who had hosted

Allied escapees came forward clutching handwritten IOUs they had been given by their visitors during the Nazi occupation. The administrative system that Derry had pioneered during the early days of the organization helped tremendously, and eight months' worth of receipts and invoices were delicately retrieved from the cookie tins he had buried in the Vatican's gardens.

O'Flaherty, Derry, and Osborne had discussed how those who had assisted the Allied Escape Line should be rewarded. They concluded that each helper should be recognized for his or her efforts. Ultimately a commission would be established that would report after the war ended. Gemma Chevalier, the daughter of Henrietta Chevalier, who bravely hid many Allied escapees, would be one of those asked to help the new commission.

With Rome free from German interference for the first time in nine months, the business of justice began on several fronts. For the families of those killed in the Ardeatine Caves, the prospect of retrieving the bodies of their loved ones moved closer. Every day pilgrimages were made from the city along the Appian Way and then Via Ardeatina to the caves. A seemingly endless procession of mourners armed with candles and flowers choked the route. In the summer sunshine they stood and prayed, overcome with grief amid an overpowering smell of death. Three months after the tragedy, they were still waiting to bury their dead. The move to exhume the bodies started with Colonel Charles Poletti of the U.S. Fifth Army, who set up a commission to conduct an inquest, which would ultimately lead to the recovery of the bodies. The grisly, painstaking task of identifying rotten corpses covered in larvae would last six months.

The first to be held to account for his role in the Ardeatine Massacre was brought to trial in September 1944. Like many of the Nazi and Italian Fascist leaders, Pietro Caruso had escaped from Rome before the Allies arrived. Later the former police chief crashed his Alfa Romeo into a tree and sustained serious injuries. He was taken to a hospital in Viterbo and was later captured by the partisans and returned to Rome. In a twist of fate, on his return to the city he was held in Regina Coeli, the jail from which he had ordered prisoners to be taken for execution in the Ardeatine Caves.

As the city's head of police, Caruso was charged with supplying to the Germans a list of inmates who were subsequently killed. He publicly repented and was pictured in his cell reading the Bible. He was later found guilty, convicted, and sentenced to death. In a police wagon he was taken to Fort Bravetta, where the Germans had carried out executions during their occupation of Rome. The *New York Times* correspondent Herbert Matthews witnessed the scene and reported that, before he was shot by a firing squad, Caruso's last words were "Aim well!"

There was a constant demand to bring to justice those who had supported and carried out Fascist rule in Rome. Regina Coeli now housed those who once denounced their neighbors and friends. Aldo Zambardi as well as Pasqualino Perfetti, who had betrayed members of the Escape Line, were now prisoners in the jail. The two men initially had been recruited by O'Flaherty and had helped a number of Allied escapees settle into life in Rome, including Derry. Another inmate was Dr. Cipolla, who had worked as a double agent. They would all be spared execution. Despite their betrayal O'Flaherty was not prepared to condemn them, and he told Derry, "They did wrong but there is good in every man."

Life for the monsignor was as busy as ever. As well as his day-to-day work in the Holy Office, the impact of the war still took up much of his time. O'Flaherty's reputation for looking after prisoners of war meant he was continually in demand. With thousands of Italian servicemen still being held in camps in South Africa, he was contacted by many relatives who wanted to get messages to their loved ones. It took him back to his days before the Nazi occupation when, as a Vatican official, he went to visit Allied POWs in Italian camps. He decided to set up links between the Vatican and the camps in South Africa in the same way, but he was frustrated because it was proving very difficult to travel there and see the conditions for himself. Derry solved his problem. The major spoke to Field Marshal Alexander and a military flight was arranged for O'Flaherty. Another flight was also arranged to take the monsignor to Jerusalem, where he spent some time finalizing the resettlement of Jews who had escaped from the Germans.

O'Flaherty's former opponent, Herbert Kappler, was adjusting to life in Maderno. While his new surroundings did not have the grandeur or atmosphere of Rome, Kappler still had power and influence. The Verbindungsführer was heavily involved in the arrest and interrogation of Resistance members, political dissidents, and other anti-fascists.

Kappler's onetime ally Pietro Koch, alongside whom he had worked in Rome, was now in charge of a special unit of Italian police in Milan. Koch had continued his reign of terror in the northern city, and his abuse of power quickly caught the attention of others. Milan's chief of police was a man named Bettini. A Mussolini loyalist, he was appalled by the behavior of Koch's staff, who, Bettini discovered, kept prisoners in tiny, unclean cells, routinely tortured them, and robbed them of their possessions. The police chief also received evidence that Koch's men took drugs and drank while on duty, and that those who made the arrests were given bonuses. Bettini prepared a seventeen-page report that he sent to Mussolini and then he arrested Koch. The move angered the Germans. Bettini argued that if Koch's men were allowed to continue in their actions, their presence would turn local Italian opinion against the regime. His move was supported by Mussolini, who had also been told of Koch's misdeeds by Pier Pisenti, the minister of Justice. Pisenti gave strict instructions that Koch should remain in prison while the public prosecutor investigated the charges against him.

Kappler was sent to negotiate the release of his old friend Koch. He traveled to Salò on Lake Garda, where Mussolini had established his headquarters. Inside the building Kappler met Pisenti and began by telling him of the "good work" Koch had done in Milan and, before that, in Rome. He talked of how anti-fascists had published a leaflet that had defamed Koch's character.

The meeting was not going well and became quite heated. Kappler asked his host, "Surely the Italian government does not intend to leave me with the impression that because of a scandal campaign organized by the enemy at home and abroad it is going to stop its police doing a job of the highest importance?"

Kappler's appeal did little to influence Mussolini's minister of Justice, who was convinced there was strong evidence that Koch and his team had committed serious crimes. Pisenti turned to his visitor and said, "I am not going to be intimidated or prejudiced by public clamor; I am going to see that justice is done, and that evidence from medical and legal sources is above suspicion."

"If you put Koch on trial it will be a scandal," Kappler replied.

Pisenti was unmoved by the argument, and just before the German left he informed him that steps were being taken against Koch. Kappler's appeal had failed and his former colleague would remain in prison. It was a sign that the Obersturmbannführer's power was not what it had been. It also illustrated the tensions that now existed between the German leadership and Mussolini. The Italian dictator had been angered by news of frequent German attacks on Italian prisoners and was becoming convinced that his compatriots were being viewed by Italians as enemies rather than allies.

General Wolff, Kappler's superior, did not intervene and demand Koch's release. He had other matters on his mind. The Allied advance through Italy was slow but seemingly unstoppable, and Wolff had concluded that the war was lost. In August the Germans had surrendered control of Florence, and the general knew that it was only a matter of time before other cities in northern Italy fell to the Allies.

In the New Year, Wolff and Dollmann began secret negotiations with the Allies, using Cardinal Ildelfonso Schuster, the archbishop of Milan, as a mediator. The cardinal had suggested to the two men that the growing strength of the partisans and the steady advance of the Allies meant the Germans could not win the war in Italy. The discussions, conducted behind Mussolini's back, would ultimately lead to negotiations in Switzerland involving Wolff and senior Allied officers that would drag on for weeks.

In the meantime the Allies continued to advance through Italy, and by late April the Germans had lost control of Bologna. At two o'clock in the afternoon on April 29, a document of complete German surrender was signed. A ceasefire was due to take effect starting May 2. Wolff had negotiated the truce without the approval of Hitler or Kesselring. The Führer had previously ordered Kesselring to fight to the death. That simply wouldn't happen.

Events were now moving at an alarming speed. The North Italian section of the Comitato di Liberazione Nazionale pronounced a death sentence on Mussolini. The partisans then seized the dictator and shot him before publicly hanging him in Milan.

General Wolff moved on to the next stage of the agreed plan and unilaterally sent out surrender notices without informing Field Marshal Kesselring.

By now Hitler had taken matters into his own hands. On the morning of April 29, as Mussolini's body was being taken into Milan, he married his longtime companion Eva Braun, who had been at his side for the past twelve years. The next day the couple ended their lives. In keeping with Hitler's wishes, their bodies were burned and no trace was ever found. The Second World War in Europe was entering its final days. As the light ebbed away at sunset on the second day of May, Italy's ordeal was over.

That night many Allied soldiers enjoyed their best sleep in months, knowing that for them the war had ended. Daylight ushered in a new era of peacetime, which brought a series of huge tasks. There was the job of reconstruction and recovery, in which many troops would be asked to participate. Italy's battered towns and cities were in dire need of new public services. The partisans and the Resistance had to be disarmed and demobilized, and there was the colossal problem of dealing with around 150,000 prisoners of war. On May 9 Herbert Kappler became one of them.

The Gestapo chief's war ended when he surrendered to the Allied forces and was taken into custody in Florence. It was the beginning of a life behind bars that would last for over thirty years. To the Allies he was a prized prisoner, and there was much his interrogators wanted to know. Over the next few weeks he was questioned on a wide range of subjects, including missing Allied servicemen, allegations of torture in Via Tasso, and the details of his use of intelligence sources. What became clear from the early interviews was that he was prepared to speak freely and at length about his activities as head of Rome's Gestapo.

Inevitably questions about his role in the Ardeatine Massacre began to emerge. Kappler admitted that he had played a leading role in the killings. Indeed he was clear and almost clinical in his responses. Questioned about whether some of the dead could have been British or American subjects, Kappler was adamant that no Allied personnel had been killed in the Ardeatine Caves. He confirmed that he vetted all but sixty of those who were shot.

As Kappler's role in the massacre began to emerge, so did the role of Pietro Koch. Ironically, on the first anniversary of the liberation of Rome, Koch was back in the very city he had ruled with Kappler. The former police chief was found guilty of torture and of handing over to the SS numerous people who were subsequently killed in the Ardeatine Massacre. He was sentenced to death.

While he was being held in Regina Coeli, Koch was visited by Monsignor Nasalli Rocca, who had been a regular visitor to the prison during the German occupation. Rocca brought him a rosary from Pope Pius XII after Koch had sent the Vatican a letter of apology for his part in a raid on St. Peter's Basilica. Koch told the monsignor that his hands were drenched in blood and were not worthy of touching the Holy Father's rosary. Later that afternoon he was given the last rites and then executed by a firing squad at Fort Bravetta.

As the authorities in Allied-controlled Rome continued to punish those responsible for war crimes, O'Flaherty continued to do the things that mattered most to him. He spent much time inside the Vatican on religious and pastoral matters and frequently visited Italian and German prisoners. However, his work during the Nazi occupation had not gone unnoticed. Official confirmation of this fact had appeared in the *London Gazette* back in April 1945, when he was made a commander of the British Empire. The award of a CBE made little difference to the monsignor. In fact it probably caused him more amusement than pride. He shunned such honors and neither sought nor wanted reward for his work. But, as a proud and patriotic Irishman who had once opposed all things British, he likely enjoyed the irony of the *London Gazette*'s announcement. His family played down the award, and the story gained little publicity in Ireland. O'Flaherty was also honored by the United States. The citation accompanying the U.S. Medal of Freedom, a rare award for a non-American, praised him for "his untiring energy and efforts, often at the risk of his own life."

The Italian president also awarded O'Flaherty a medal for military valor and described him as a man who had given a shining example of "valor and service." The monsignor was also awarded a pension by the Italian authorities, which he never collected. O'Flaherty was a modest man, and the medals were put away in a bottom drawer in a chest in his room in Rome. He rarely looked at them, and they were eventually sent home to his sister in County Kerry.

O'Flaherty was not alone in the honors list. There were awards, too, for Brother Robert Pace and Fathers Borg and Madden. Sam Derry, who already had the Military Cross, was awarded the Distinguished Service Order, and Bill Simpson and John Furman were given the Military Cross. Others who had assisted O'Flaherty during the Nazi regime were also honored. Henrietta Chevalier, who hid dozens of escapees for the monsignor, was given the British Empire Medal. There were further celebrations for the Chevalier family when Gemma married Corporal Kenneth Sands of the Hampshire Regiment. Appropriately, the wedding service was conducted by Monsignor O'Flaherty.

For O'Flaherty the return of peace also meant that, after being confined to his room for some twelve months, he could now become reacquainted with his golf clubs. The scratch player took to the fairways as if he had never taken a break, and his powerful driving and precise putting were once again a regular sight at Rome's golf clubs.

One day as the monsignor and the British ambassador were enjoying eighteen holes, Osborne sliced his shot and the two men went in search of the ball. Walking off the course, the priest came across a number of derelict cottages and a damaged church. Nearby were hungry and poorly clothed villagers whom it seemed the Allied liberation had passed by. The discovery alarmed O'Flaherty, who promised them he would return shortly with food. He abandoned his game and drove back to Rome to collect clothes, food, and drink, then returned with them that day. The derelict church and the villagers became the priest's latest passion. He made sure they regularly received food, and over time he organized the church's restoration. It was rebuilt and painted, a new bell was placed in its tower, and eventually services resumed there. The restoration project gave the monsignor a renewed sense of purpose. He had never worked as a parish priest, and this was as close as he would ever come to having his own church.

By this time O'Flaherty had been promoted from Scrittore, preparing reports and translating documents for others, to Substitute Notary at the Holy Office. This new job gave him more responsibility within the Holy Office and meant his ideas and his thoughts on Church teachings carried greater weight with his superiors. The end of the Nazi occupation also meant that the monsignor could receive visitors from home, and his sister Bride Sheehan traveled from County Kerry to stay with him. The monsignor was a fine host, and in addition to showing his sister the sights of Rome, he proudly took her to the restored church beside the golf course.

The liberation of Rome also allowed the monsignor to travel to Ireland more regularly, and in the late summer of 1946, he returned home. In August he met up with his friends Thomas and Delia Kiernan, who were also vacationing in Ireland. They had lunch with a priest friend in County Kildare, who had also invited along a talented young singer named Veronica Dunne. The priest, Father Campion, wanted Delia Kiernan to hear the teenager sing.

Veronica, who came from a musical family, told the monsignor that it was her ambition to go to Rome to train as a singer. O'Flaherty agreed to visit her parents to discuss the idea, and within days he was at their Dublin home. A feast was prepared for the monsignor but he ate little, as years of rationing had diminished his appetite. They discussed Veronica's ambition, and the monsignor offered to help her find both training and accommodations in Rome.

The young singer arrived in the city in September 1946 after a twelve-hour journey that took her from Ireland to England, then across to France, and finally into Italy. Exhausted but excited, she was greeted at the airport by the monsignor. The priest had a warning for her. Conscious that he was now responsible for her welfare and also aware that the pretty eighteen-year-old could be the subject of unwelcome male attention, he offered a fatherly warning: "Now do you see that plane over there? If I see you with any Italian men you will be back on it."

Life for Veronica Dunne would never be the same again. For the next few years she received top-class musical training and, thanks to O'Flaherty's influence, was invited to the cream of Rome's social events. The monsignor became her guardian and would regularly call her to check that she was pursuing her studies. Every Friday she would have lunch with him in his room in the Vatican, where they would catch up on the week's events and he would quiz her on what she had been studying.

One Friday morning in 1947 Veronica traveled to the Vatican to meet O'Flaherty for their weekly lunch. However, on this occasion he wanted to do something different and told his guest, "There is something I want to show you."

The monsignor wanted to go to the Ardeatine Caves, a place that he had never visited. Three years after the massacre he was at last ready to see what his former arch-enemy Herbert Kappler had done.

Veronica and the priest traveled out to the caves, and she later recalled: "I remember going in and he said nothing." Inside the dimly lit caves, as they stood together, they were struck by the odor: "the overpowering smell of flowers. He said we will say the rosary, which we did. Then I looked at him and there were tears on his face."

O'Flaherty's grief was perhaps all the greater because he knew that, had circumstances been different, he also could have been a victim of Kappler's butchery. He spent some time at the graves of the dead, including those who had assisted the Escape Line. He and Veronica then walked out into the daylight. It was Hugh O'Flaherty's first visit to the site, and it would be his last. Soon the secrets of the caves would be revealed to the world.

Chapter 15

Conviction and Conversion

"I'd like to tear out those eyes that saw what was done to my father and my brother."
—A relative of victims of the Ardeatine Massacre

DRESSED IN A DARK SUIT, HERBERT KAPPLER SAT MOTIONLESS and quiet as he gazed at the crucifix on the courtroom wall. A few feet away in the public gallery sat relatives of the victims of the massacre in the Ardeatine Caves. They had crowded into the military hearing in Rome to hear firsthand how their loved ones had died. They wanted to look into the eyes of the former SS lieutenant colonel and listen to his account of that March day when 335 people were pushed into trucks at gunpoint, driven out of the city, and systematically murdered. But they had come for one thing above all else: justice.

By the summer of 1948 Kappler had privately given Allied interrogators a detailed account of his role in the killings. He was also no stranger to giving evidence in public. In November 1946 Kappler had been in Allied custody for more than a year and was a witness for the prosecution in the trial of General Eberhard von Mackensen and General Kurt Mälzer. These two senior men had been interrogated in England, where they had been held as prisoners of war, and then had been brought to Rome to face a British military tribunal. They faced charges relating to their role in the shootings at the Ardeatine Caves. The atmosphere in the courtroom was tense and very emotional, and the proceedings were occasionally punctuated with shouts from the relatives watching from the public gallery. One woman screamed toward the dock, "The blood of my husband claims justice!" Another family member simply shouted, "Butchers, murderers!"

Mälzer and Mackensen tried to pin the blame for the massacre on Kappler, asserting that he had compiled the list of victims, who, he had told them, were prisoners under sentence of death. This was the centerpiece of the two men's defense, and they maintained that Obersturmbannführer Kappler had misinformed them.

Kappler listened intently to much of the evidence offered by his former colleagues. He sat quietly, often rubbing the scar that creased the left side of his face. He told the court that he had written his death list after talking to both Mälzer and Mackensen. Questioned as to why 335 people were shot as opposed to the 320 that had been demanded, Kappler explained, "Somebody must have sent them as extras."

The arguments put forward by the defendants' attorneys made little impact, and the two generals were found guilty and sentenced to death. The verdict pleased the watching relatives and reduced many to silence. One word could be heard: "Grazie." Although there was a sense of relief among the crowd and across Rome, many who had hoped that their loved ones' lives would be avenged by the deaths of their killers would ultimately be disappointed. The death penalty was not carried out: Mälzer and Mackensen were given life imprisonment instead.

Three months later Field Marshal Kesselring, who had been the German supreme commander of the Southern Front, was the next to face a military court. His trial was held in Venice. He was charged with responsibility for the Ardeatine Massacre and also faced an unrelated charge of inciting men under his command to kill around one thousand civilians. Kesselring used similar arguments to those that Mälzer and Mackensen had relied on during their hearing. He claimed it was Kappler who had told him that the victims of the Ardeatine shootings were already under sentence of death and that therefore he, Kesselring, had been convinced that "innocent" people were not going to be shot.

The court was not swayed by Kesselring's defense, and he was found guilty on both counts and sentenced to death. However, as with Mälzer and Mackensen, the sentence was commuted to life imprisonment.

Five months after Kesselring's case wrapped up, the Allies handed Kappler over to the Italian authorities in Rome. He had been held in the infamous Dachau prison camp and also in Naples and Ancona, but was now back in the city he had once controlled. Like Rome's former head of police, Pietro Caruso, Kappler was sent to the prison where many of the Ardeatine victims had been housed before they were murdered. Held in custody in Regina Coeli for ten months, he had plenty of time to think about both his time in the city and the future he faced. He became a prolific letter writer, but his correspondence wasn't confined to his lawyers, family members, or friends. He decided to write also to the man who for years had been his archrival on the streets of Rome.

Hugh O'Flaherty received Kappler's note, and the two men began to correspond. Just what was Kappler's motivation in contacting his old enemy? What is now clear is that he was questioning some of his past actions and seriously thinking about becoming a Catholic. He clearly saw O'Flaherty as the person who could help him make this transition. Kappler needed a sounding board and a confessor, and the monsignor fitted the bill. Kappler also happened to be in need of some allies.

After he received one of Kappler's letters, O'Flaherty took a step that would have far-reaching consequences. He agreed to meet the man who years earlier had planned his assassination. For the Irish priest, extending the hand of friendship to Herbert Kappler seemed the most natural thing in the world. Forgiveness lay at the core of his personal and professional life. Just as he had been prepared to forgive the actions of those who had betrayed him during the war, he was now willing to do the same in peacetime.

The Vatican official was no stranger to visiting jails; after all, much of his time had been spent in the company of prisoners of war. His meeting with Kappler was low-key but nonetheless symbolic for both men. It marked the first time they had laid eyes on each other since the war had ended. O'Flaherty treated Kappler the way he would have responded to anyone. Kappler had watched O'Flaherty from afar during his time as head of the Gestapo in Rome. At that time he had wanted him kidnapped, interrogated, and even killed. But now, as he looked across at the priest, Kappler wanted his help.

O'Flaherty never wrote or spoke about this first private encounter with Kappler, but it seems likely that he would have played it down and regarded it as routine. The two men talked about many things, including religion and literature, and after their first meeting agreed to see each other again. According to O'Flaherty's friends, on future visits the monsignor brought Kappler books. By all accounts their meetings were good-natured and enjoyable for both parties. Their rivalry and shared experiences created a bond, and wartime rivals slowly became peacetime friends.

Veronica Dunne, who met the monsignor every week during her time in Rome, remembers him talking about his visits with the former SS officer. "He took a great liking to him. He used to joke that, 'here I am, this man who had 30,000 lire over my head for information, and now we are sort of pals.' They became good friends apparently. They would laugh together and speak in English."

O'Flaherty and Kappler spent part of their time talking about their days in Rome during the German occupation. But Kappler had more on his mind than just reminiscing with his newfound friend. Kappler made two demands of him, as the priest's nephew, also named Hugh O'Flaherty, recalls: "At some stage Kappler sent for him and said he had two requests. One was that he wanted to be converted to be a Catholic. My uncle advised him against this step, saying that it would be construed as if he was trying to curry favor. His other request was that he wanted him to be present at his execution. My uncle wouldn't have been capable of being present at the execution of a mouse."

A fervent opponent of the death penalty, the monsignor hated violence of any kind and was notoriously squeamish. He remained convinced that Kappler was not going to face a firing squad or the hangman's noose. On one visit he shared his thoughts with the prisoner, reassuring him, "You are not going to be executed."

In prison Kappler had much time to consider his wartime activities, but now his thoughts were moving to a more spiritual level. Raised as a Protestant, he was serious in his desire to convert to Roman Catholicism. But he decided to take O'Flaherty's advice and wait because, in the spring of 1948, other matters were foremost in his mind.

More than four years after the Ardeatine Massacre, it was Kappler's turn to publicly account for his actions. He and five codefendants appeared before the military tribunal of Rome, each charged with the deaths of 335 people in the incident.

Absent from the courtroom, however, was Kappler's colleague Captain Erich Priebke, who had also taken part in the killings. He should have been on trial with Kappler, but he had escaped from a prisoner of war camp in Rimini. With the help of sympathetic Catholic clergy who ran an escape network nicknamed the "Rat Line," he would eventually find his way to Argentina and would live there happily for nearly fifty years until he was discovered by an American television journalist. Eventually Priebke would be extradited to Italy and face a court in Rome in 1996—over five decades after the massacre.

Herbert Kappler's trial began in May 1948. He faced two charges: One was related to the killings in the Ardeatine Caves; the other charge was related to his demand for gold from Rome's Jews in September 1943. On the opening day of the trial, about one hundred relatives of the dead stood in the courtroom, with a line of carabinieri standing between them and the six defendants. Kappler and his codefendants sat at the front of the court, their faces lit by the spotlights of the watching press photographers. When the charges were read out, a woman in the public gallery screamed at Kappler, "I'd like to tear out those eyes that saw what was done to my father and my brother."

Four years of hurt and anger were etched on the faces of those looking down at the defendants. Kappler, who rarely displayed his feelings, was clearly struck by the woman's outburst and the hostile atmosphere that was building up in the courtroom. He reached for his handkerchief and put it to his mouth, then dabbed a few beads of sweat from his brow.

On the last day of May, his defense began its case. Kappler addressed the court in his native German. He related the events of March 24, 1944, in a matter-of-fact way. It was like a technician describing an operation or a student detailing an experiment. His account was precise, detailed, and emotion free. His detached, almost uncaring manner angered the relatives of those murdered in the massacre. He described how he ordered his men to shoot the victims in the Ardeatine Caves, and then he explained how he refused them religious assistance because he felt the intervention of a priest would have slowed down the executions. This was too much for some in the public gallery, and the courtroom echoed to shouts of "Schweinehund." Some of those present surged toward Kappler, but the protective cordon of carabinieri kept him safe.

The proceedings were now in serious danger of getting out of control as Kappler became the crowd's focus of attention. The growing hostility of the relatives and their constant interruptions began to alarm court officials. Grief was now mixed with rage, and Kappler's evidence was punctuated by bouts of weeping in the public gallery. Family members were warned that if the noise continued the courtroom would be cleared. Some relatives replied that they could not contain their feelings.

Kappler's defense team put forward the argument that the original Via Rasella attack carried out by the partisans was illegal and that the reprisal was a legitimate response, supported by the 1907 Hague Convention.

Kappler spoke for eight days. He stated that he was carrying out an order and that his actions should be viewed in military terms. He told the court: "As a German soldier I entrust my honor to Italian soldiers and Italian judges." He added, "The judges wear on their chests the badges of honor. Thus they know that in war orders cannot be discussed but only carried out. I am, therefore, certain that whatever the verdict may be, it will be the judgment of soldiers on a soldier."

However, the five judges of the Italian military tribunal concluded that the killings in the Ardeatine Caves were not legitimate and did constitute a war crime. On July 20 they made public their findings. After six hours of deliberations the head of the tribunal declared Herbert Kappler guilty of both charges and sentenced him to life imprisonment. It was the toughest sentence that could be imposed under the workings of the new postwar Italian constitution. Moreover, the sentence allowed little chance of parole. Kappler was also given an additional fifteen-year sentence for extorting gold from Rome's Jewish community. It seemed that Italy's most hated man was going to lose his liberty for the rest of his life.

Kappler's five co-defendants were much luckier. All were acquitted.

Although Kappler's life sentence pleased many of those who felt justice had prevailed, parts of the court's ruling caused concern. The judgment examined the attack on Via Rasella and concluded that, while it was courageous, the bombing by the partisans was illegal because the group was an unlawful organization. This meant that their action was an "illegitimate act of war." By definition that meant a reprisal could be justified. However, the court concluded that the German reprisal in the Ardeatine Caves did not qualify as legitimate under international law because of the way in which the victims were killed. Ten of the 335 victims who were killed were outside the authority of the order given by the German state and five others were killed by mistake.

To some the judgment seemed muddled and contradictory, and it was a ruling that would have lasting effects and would lead to a series of legal challenges. It also provided Kappler with an opportunity to begin his attempt to overturn his sentence. With time on his hands he put his energies into drafting correspondence to his lawyers seeking information in preparation for an appeal. He also began to write to a local woman who visited him and became a friend. His letters to her, which were uncovered in the 1990s and handed to a reporter, provide an insight into his early years in custody.

After his trial Kappler was moved to the military jail at Fort Boccea in Rome. He welcomed the move inasmuch as his new surroundings gave him more space and he had a place to read and write. But the transfer caused him some sorrow, as he wrote to this female friend: "I was very happy to move to a place where air, sun, running water reign and where one can work, move around, write, and study. But I must confess that at the same time I thought sadly that this transfer meant moving away from the nearby Gianicolo and from your little house."

The two of them became more affectionate as the weeks went by, and their notes to each other, which were once quite formal, soon developed into full-blown love letters. Like most prisoners, Kappler missed his creature comforts, so his new girlfriend would routinely send him little gifts to cheer him up. Just over three weeks after his trial ended, he received a parcel that especially pleased him. He wrote, "Tell me, how did you know I needed slippers? And with the two pairs of shorts I could even go to the Lido! I'm slowly becoming the most elegant prisoner in the Forte."

Being stylish was not the only thing on Kappler's mind. Before his trial he had begun to question his religious convictions. By the autumn of 1948 his thoughts turned again to faith. In September he wrote to his girlfriend, "Our Christian doctrine does not forbid us from taking pleasure in those modest joys that this earthly life might offer us. So forget about worrying that this joy will bring us sorrows. We must, however, endure the pain that comes from my current material status with dignity and I am grateful to you my dear for wanting to help me."

Kappler also wrote about his beliefs. "I assure you that in my entire life I have never knelt disheartened before that which God wishes to knock me with. And I will always seek to endure with humility to God, but with pride to men, everything he sends to me. Just as I hope to be able to take pleasure from human joys without harming a soul."

So where had this newfound faith come from? Had Kappler turned to God simply because he was facing a life sentence and it was convenient to pretend he was remorseful and to seek public sympathy? Or was there an influence in his life that made him genuinely think in a way that he had never done before? What is clear is that Hugh O'Flaherty now had an important role in Kappler's life. He was his only regular visitor and had become a confidant and friend. Was Kappler's former rival now the guiding force in his desire to become a Catholic?

O'Flaherty was not a proselytizing cleric and would not have pushed Kappler toward Catholicism, even though they discussed his desire to convert. What is known is that the monsignor always had a relaxed view toward those who didn't share his faith. Allied servicemen who worked with him in the Escape Line who were non-Catholic or of no religion often remarked that he never attempted to preach to them. Sam Derry recalled: "I lived under his care and he never once tried to sell religion to me." Even when O'Flaherty was approached by people who wanted to be admitted to the Church, his watchword was caution. His nephew Hugh O'Flaherty recalls that when he was told of a family friend who was planning to give up a well-paid job and go and train for the priesthood, the monsignor replied, "Why? Aren't you doing fine? Why change?"

Right From an early age Hugh O'Flaherty made no secret of his desire to become a priest.

Below As a young student Hugh O'Flaherty blossomed in the structured environment of Mungret College in Limerick. He is pictured here (front row, third from left) as a Senior Apostolic.

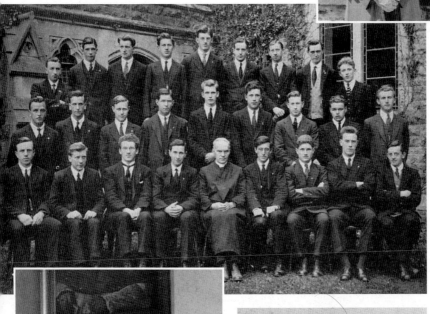

The young O'Flaherty arrived in Rome in 1922 and began working at the Vatican.

Golf was one of Monsignor O'Flaherty's passions. During his time running the Escape Line, his code name was appropriately "Golf."

Herbert Kappler was viewed as clever and ambitious by his superiors, who sent him to Rome to work with local fascists and organize intelligence operations.

ver six feet tall with a ready smile and a twinkle in his eye, Hugh O'Flaherty made an
stant impression on anyone he met.

Right Away from work Herbert Kappler enjoyed the finer things in life, such as good food and expensive wines. Here he is socializing with fellow Nazi Karl Haas.

Pope Pius XII would spend much of the war worrying about the Allies bombing Rome or the Germans taking over the Vatican.

At Gestapo headquarters on Via Tasso, Herbert Kappler's men interrogated and abused those opposed to Nazi rule. The building was associated with torture and brutality.

Above Key members of the Escape Line: (l-r) John Furman, Sam Derry, Henry Byrnes, and Bill Simpson. Henrietta "Mrs. M" Chevalier (top inset) and John May (bottom inset). All would provide invaluable help and assistance to O'Flaherty during the Nazi occupation of Rome.

Left In the hours following the Resistance attack on Via Rasella in 1944, which killed thirty-three German soldiers, dozens of civilians were rounded up and arrested.

ght In revenge for the ack at Via Rasella, 335 ilians were massacred at Ardeatine Caves by a it led by Herbert Kappler. is memorial service took ce to mark the 29th niversary in March 1973.

Below The Allied bombings of Rome destroyed many buildings, and Pope Pius XII feared that parts of the Holy See would be damaged.

Above U.S. General Mark Clark (front left) drives through the streets of Rome hours after the Americans liberated the Eternal City.

Above After months of Nazi rule the sight of Allied tanks in June 1944 brought thousands of Romans out onto the streets.

Right Well done. Honors often came to Hugh O'Flaherty, although he never sought them. Here he is being commended for his wartime work by U.S. Army General John C. H. Lee.

eedom and relief. The Allied liberation of Rome in 1944 brought great joy to the streets.

r his role in the Ardeatine killings, Herbert Kappler was sentenced to life imprisonment.
ere he is pictured at his trial in 1948 (front left). Kappler was given an additional fifteen-year
ntence for extorting gold from Rome's Jewish community.

Left Herbert Kappler and his wife, Anneliese. They married in prison i[n] Italy in 1972. In 1977 she smuggle[d] him back to West Germany where [he] died in 1978.

Below Monsignor Hugh O'Flahert[y,] Major Sam Derry, and Eamonn Andrews at the 1963 recording of t[he] BBC TV program *This Is Your Life.* [It] was the last time Hugh O'Flaherty and Sam Derry would be together.

Right Resting place. Hugh O'Flaherty is buried in the graveyard of the Daniel O'Connell Church in Cahersiveen in County Kerry.

In Loving Memory of
RT. REV. MGR. HUGH O'FLAHERTY
BORN 28 - FEBRUARY 1898
ORDAINED 20 - DECEMBER 1925
DIED 30 - OCTOBER 1963
R . I . P

By September 1948 Kappler and his girlfriend were involved in a discussion over when he would finally convert to Catholicism. In one letter he tells her, "You can serenely ask me: When will it be? I am happy to answer you. My wish to be admitted into the Church will be articulated when the whole legal matter has ended, however that may be—sentenced once and for all or acquitted."

Kappler clearly wanted to delay his conversion until the legal issues surrounding his case were resolved. He was now involved in an appeal against his sentence. It was a process that he probably didn't realize at the time would take many years to complete.

For the rest of that year, Kappler continued to write his weekly letters to O'Flaherty, and the two men met to swap books and chat. In December, facing another Christmas as a prisoner, hundreds of miles from his home, Kappler was in a nostalgic mood. He pined for the days of old when he and his sister and his parents stood "holding hands around the green tree with tiny lights sparkling on its dense branches as we sing our solemn song together with the little ones: 'Silent Night, Holy Night.'"

On Christmas Eve, most probably feeling a little lonely and in need of some affection, he wrote a love letter to his girlfriend. "It has been a dark year for me: a year of affronts, of incomprehension, and of humiliation, but these darknesses along the path were pushed to the edges of my memory by the light of your heart."

The New Year brought further reflections. Again writing to his girlfriend, Kappler turned to the events of March 1944 and in particular the Ardeatine Massacre. "You know well that it pains me greatly to have been part of an act of war that caused so much pain but I would feel the same regret for my own life if—as a pilot—I had to rain death on the towns of any country. It is not, then, the pride of a criminal or the rebel spirit against human law that speaks

215

with my tongue, but these are just my thoughts—a natural expression of human dignity."

This is the only time in his letters to his girlfriend that Kappler talks directly about the murders. He still sees the role he played in March 1944 as that of a soldier involved in normal military action. He seeks to justify his behavior by equating it to the way bomber pilots behaved during the Second World War. What is also interesting about the letter is that Kappler's tone is different from the cold and somewhat clinical manner in which he testified at his trial. He is still trying to explain his behavior but for the first time there are glimpses of sorrow, and this letter is the first documented indication that he understands the pain and suffering caused by his actions.

Kappler's world revolved around the weekly visits of his woman friend and O'Flaherty, letter writing, exercising, and reading. He drew much comfort from the frequent messages of support sent by his former SS colleagues. His friend Erich Priebke, who had helped to carry out the Ardeatine Massacre and was now hiding in Argentina, brazenly wrote to him expressing such support.

With a great deal of time on his hands, Kappler inevitably reflected on what had happened in wartime Rome, and it is clear from his letters that he still had scores to settle. In late 1949 he wrote of his feelings toward those Catholic clergy who had assisted the Allies during the German occupation of the city: "Now I will say a few words about the monsignors. What a part many individuals from that community played—anything but spiritual. Everyone knows it by now. Some were even decorated for gallantry by the Allies. And I could list many, many cases in which the extra-territoriality was taken advantage of and I never spoke of it." Kappler does not name him, but it is obvious that he is referring to Hugh O'Flaherty. Yet, despite the criticism, he clearly wanted to continue his friendship with the monsignor. He felt comfortable with him and looked forward to his visits.

Throughout 1949 Kappler and O'Flaherty remained in contact, and Kappler asked his girlfriend to pass on his letters to the monsignor. Contact with the priest was now an important part of Kappler's life. In February 1949 he asked his girlfriend, "Sorry, did you manage to send my note to Monsignor O'Flaherty?" The two men had grown very close and Kappler would later write of the Irishman: "to me he became a fatherly friend." He also had dealings with other priests, and in one letter to his girlfriend, he wrote, "Today then, after Mass in the truly wonderful new church, I was able to speak to Father Vincenzo and in the evening I was also visited by Father Giuseppe."

Kappler's wish to become a Catholic remained undiminished, and he began to rethink his decision that he should convert only once his appeal had been concluded. It was now increasingly clear that he would have to wait many months for his case to be heard. Feeling frustrated, he decided to act. He wrote to O'Flaherty, who visited him as Kappler had requested in his letter. However, this was no ordinary meeting for the two friends. Behind closed doors they prayed together. Then O'Flaherty received Kappler into the Catholic Church. It was a quiet, simple affair, and afterwards the monsignor slipped back to the Vatican.

Herbert Kappler had achieved what he had wished for. He could have asked another priest to carry out the ceremony, but he had wanted Monsignor O'Flaherty. In a matter of minutes Italy's most notorious Nazi had been welcomed into the Church by the very man he had tried to kill. At first glance it reads like a scene from a Hollywood blockbuster, and some years later it would become a headline writer's dream. But for the time being, only a handful of people knew. Even though Monsignor O'Flaherty's precise role in Kappler's conversion would remain secret for years, the growing friendship between the two men was about to become public.

O'Flaherty's visits to Kappler had not gone unnoticed by the press, and the Italian newspaper *Avanti* highlighted their close bond, suggesting that the priest was campaigning for the release of the country's most notorious inmate. The reporter also wondered whether O'Flaherty was motivated by his own Christian desires to see Kappler embrace Catholicism or had been instructed to convert him by the Vatican. The newspaper concluded that the monsignor had become Kappler's number-one protector and was "moving heaven and earth to free the executioner of Rome from his imprisonment."

There is no evidence to suggest that O'Flaherty was actively lobbying for Kappler's release. It is clear, however, that he knew that his association with an imprisoned former Gestapo chief would make him unpopular with the press or with some within the Vatican. Nevertheless, he continued his visits to Kappler while pursuing his Church work. He was particularly busy in 1950, which was a Holy Year, and he put his knowledge of both the Vatican and Rome to good use by co-authoring with Bishop John Smit, the canon of St. Peter's, a walker's pocket guide to the city. The book was a great success and brought praise from the *New York Times*, whose reviewer declared it comprehensive, easily read, and better than many other guides to Rome.

In 1953 Hugh O'Flaherty was appointed a Domestic Prelate by Pope Pius XII, an honor given to priests whose work has impressed the Vatican establishment. Even though this appointment pleased O'Flaherty, he knew that within the Vatican he had a number of enemies who had objected to his wartime role and more recently to his links with Kappler. Others within the Holy See were jealous of the Irish priest's high profile and felt that he got more credit than he deserved. O'Flaherty was aware of the discussions going on behind his back and confided to Veronica Dunne, "You think politics is bad. Religious politics is worse."

As O'Flaherty began to enjoy his new role in the Vatican, Kappler's lawyers were finalizing their work on his appeal. In December 1953 his case was heard in the Supreme Court in Rome. Kappler's legal team argued that the sentence imposed some five years earlier was flawed. Yet after all the work and waiting, the highest court in Italy backed the original verdict and sentence. Kappler seemed destined to remain behind bars for the rest of his life.

Yet he refused to give up his dream of freedom, and in 1957 he was still trying to overturn his original sentence. The argument for his release was the same, though his surroundings were now different. By this time, and possibly as early as 1948, he had been moved to Gaeta, a coastal town midway between Rome and Naples. Home for the former Nazi was a cell in the town's impressive stone fortress.

Having exhausted the legal process, in 1957 Kappler appealed to the Italian state for a pardon. He argued that the order for the reprisal that took place in the Ardeatine Caves had been given by Hitler, and that the memory of the executions had remained with him and his men for a long time. He claimed that he was simply following orders that, as a soldier, he could not evade. He said it was Hitler who had stated that ten Italians should die for every German killed in the attack on Via Rasella. After his plea for a pardon failed, Kappler's options were slowly running out. Italy was simply not prepared to let its most notorious mass murderer walk free.

Even thirteen years later the country's memories of what happened that spring day in the Ardeatine Caves were still raw.

In 1958 Monsignor O'Flaherty was preparing to go through his own memories of that same day by doing something he had so far studiously avoided. Having been approached by a journalist, he was getting ready to talk about his wartime experiences. A reluctant interviewee, the monsignor had eventually agreed, after six days of negotiations, to speak to the Irish journalist J. P. Gallagher. The result would lead to the publication, nine years later, of Gallagher's book, *Scarlet Pimpernel of the Vatican.*

Soon after his interview O'Flaherty again found himself in the media spotlight, when the story of Kappler's conversion to Catholicism appeared in the papers. Characteristically the monsignor played it down and teased some of the reporters that their scoop was over a decade old. He said to one correspondent, "Why, that is not news," adding, "that's something which occurred a very long time ago." The story may have been old, but its news value was obvious, and headline writers made hay with reports about the priest and the prisoner.

Kappler was rarely out of the public eye in 1959, particularly in Italy, as it marked the fifteenth anniversary of the Ardeatine Massacre. He asked for permission to make a pilgrimage to the site to pay homage to the victims. Not surprisingly, his request was refused. The news coverage of the massacre and Kappler's conversion to Catholicism coincided with O'Flaherty's latest promotion. The monsignor was made Head Notary of the Holy Office, which meant that all publications endorsed by this body carried his name. He didn't know it at the time, but it would be his last job in Rome. In 1960, after he had been in the post for about a year, the prospect arose of O'Flaherty's becoming Papal Nuncio to Tanzania. He discussed the move with his superiors but, sadly, it would never happen.

In June that year he had just completed mass in the Holy Office when the ushers noticed he was somewhat unsteady on his feet. They persuaded him to go to a nearby hospital run by the religious order, the Little Company of Mary. The nuns were affectionately known as the Blue Sisters because of the color of their tunics, and many of them knew O'Flaherty. The monsignor was no stranger to the building, as he had used it to hide Allied escapees during the Nazi occupation. Situated in the center of Rome and able to care for one hundred or so patients, it had provided adequate hiding space. It was regarded as one of the best hospitals in Rome and was favored by American, British, and Irish priests because the staff spoke English. After the war O'Flaherty often visited the nuns for a chat and a cup of tea.

In the autumn of 1957 O'Flaherty had been admitted to the same hospital with the flu. He had been well treated and given his own room—complete with a telephone. The monsignor was a reluctant patient, however. He had an aversion to taking medicine and studiously avoided injections. When he was taken into the hospital in June 1960, his health was already deteriorating. He was now in his sixties, and it was clear that his lifestyle had to change. Sister Elizabeth Matson, who worked in the hospital, remembers the monsignor. "He came in with heart problems and although it was serious he was a happy patient and he was always talking. He liked talking to you and in particular he loved chatting about golf, but he also talked about the war and how he had helped people escape."

When doctors examined O'Flaherty they found he had suffered his first stroke and concluded that his long-term prospects were not good, as Sister Elizabeth Matson recalled: "He was going downhill. He was elderly and he was falling apart."

In September Monsignor Hugh O'Flaherty retired from the Church, at the same time ending a relationship with the city that had begun nearly four decades earlier. After spending a number of weeks in the hospital, he had decided that there was only one place to go. Home.

CHAPTER 16

Kerry Calling

"I believe all our wanderings abroad teach us to live a better life at home."

—HUGH O'FLAHERTY

HUGH O'FLAHERTY STEPPED OUT OF THE CAR AND PAUSED OUT-side Sheehan's brightly colored hardware store in Cahersiveen. As he stood in the cold Atlantic air, he was back on familiar territory and among family and friends. In the shadow of the Beentee Mountain and in view of Valentia Harbor, he had returned to the southwest corner of Ireland. The monsignor had swapped the hustle and bustle of city life in Rome for the rural landscape of County Kerry, one of the most scenic parts of Ireland. Life was now going to be much slower and quieter.

Cahersiveen, a village of just twelve hundred souls, was dominated by one building. The Daniel O'Connell Memorial Church, the only Catholic Church in Ireland to be named after a layperson, took its title from the town's most famous son. The political leader was known as the "Liberator" because he had fought against British rule in Ireland and campaigned for Catholic emancipation in the first half of the nineteenth century. The handsome granite construction was the focal point for many of the townsfolk. It would also become Hugh O'Flaherty's place of daily worship.

Home for the retired monsignor was now a series of rooms above his widowed sister's shop on Cahersiveen's main street. The old-fashioned store sold all manner of goods, including kitchen items, tools, and household appliances. Bride Sheehan ran the business and after the death of her husband was clearly pleased to have the company of her brother.

O'Flaherty soon established a daily routine. As had been his habit throughout his life, he rose early and by 8:30 a.m. was saying mass in the church, which was a short walk away. Afterwards he would return home for breakfast and then he would read the morning papers and often pop downstairs to chat with customers in the store.

After lunch he would sometimes go out and meet with friends, or if the weather was agreeable, the local golf course would often prove irresistible. His handicap was not what it once had been, but his love of the game remained undiminished. And even though the stroke had made his left arm stiff, he was still able to play. Effectively he became "a one-handed golfer." He told a visiting *Sunday Express* journalist that his disability would not deter him. "The doctors say it may be OK. Anyway I intend to keep on playing. I used to have a handicap of six. I am not that good now, but I enjoy the game and that is the main thing." Just as it had sustained him in his childhood and during his time in the priesthood, golf was now providing a refuge for O'Flaherty in his retirement.

At home in County Kerry his world now revolved around "the three Fs": faith, family, and the fairway. Even though he was retired he continued to assist the Church both at Cahersiveen and abroad. He was asked to travel to the Diocese of Los Angeles, and although the journey would be arduous and he was not in good health, he agreed to make the trip.

In California he found himself taking confession when the regular priest was away, and he clearly made an impact on the youngsters of the parish. When one teenager remarked, "Who is that new priest who is taking Father Collins's place today?" his friend replied, "I don't know who he is but he sure is terrific!"

The American work was enjoyable but it was physically too much, and when O'Flaherty returned to County Kerry, it would be for good. He seemed publicly content to be back in Ireland and told one reporter, "I believe all our wanderings abroad teach us to live a better life at home." Privately, though, he probably missed the buzz of his old life in Italy. His niece Pearl Dineen seems certain that he found life in Kerry too quiet. "I think, to be honest, he missed Rome terribly. If the television came on and there was any mention of Rome, he would get all emotional."

Danny O'Connor got to know the monsignor well during his days in Cahersiveen. An altar boy at the Daniel O'Connell Church, the young man saw the retired cleric every day and helped him to prepare mass. Away from church duties, the pair would often go for drives in the countryside. Danny recalled that the monsignor was an anxious passenger. "He was always very nervous. Going round any bend he would have you hooting the car all the time." O'Flaherty's concerns about the quiet roads of Kerry seem strange since the monsignor had decades of experience of rather more chaotic driving on the streets of Rome.

On their journeys to local scenic spots, the two men would talk about sports, most often about golf and the fortunes of the Kerry Gaelic football team, for which O'Flaherty had a lifelong passion. One thing they didn't talk about was the war. However, the retired priest found it difficult to avoid being reminded of his past life. Following the publication of war memoirs by John Furman in 1959 and Sam Derry in 1960, which chronicled the Rome Escape Line and the monsignor's role in the operation, Hugh O'Flaherty was much sought after by reporters and writers, and his bulging mailbox reflected a growing interest in his wartime activities. What concerned him most was that if too many of his old pals from Italy sent him mail, he would not be able to reply to each. "I try hard to answer everybody, but it's a tough job. I don't know how I got to know so many people. You know, I have even had to discourage some of the Rome escape boys from writing. It is not that I don't want to hear from them, but I would not like to let their letters go unanswered." In truth he was also a little embarrassed by all the attention.

By 1962 O'Flaherty's health was declining rapidly, and his friends and family feared what the next few months had in store. The singer Veronica Dunne, whom he had helped in Rome, had now returned to Ireland. She was working on her career and traveled down to Kerry to visit him. "He was a shattered man. It was like the body was there but he could not believe that life could kick him like that. He was shattered."

News of the central role O'Flaherty had played in the Escape Line had by now reached the offices of one of his native country's most famous journalists. Irish broadcaster Eamonn Andrews was making a name for himself in Britain as host of the popular BBC TV program *This Is Your Life*. Andrews had read about O'Flaherty's exploits and wanted him to be the subject of one of his shows, so he called his colleague and friend Fred O'Donovan, who ran Andrews's recording studio in Dublin. The two men had a successful partnership recording radio programs, and Andrews wanted O'Donovan to gather research material on O'Flaherty. A perfect choice to help with the program, Dublin-born O'Donovan was a producer who had been trained by the BBC and had gone into show business after serving in the RAF during the Second World War.

The surprise nature of *This Is Your Life*—the person didn't know that he or she was the subject of the show until they were in front of the TV cameras—meant that the information had to be gathered in a secretive way. Andrews was convinced that if a British researcher went to meet O'Flaherty directly, the retired cleric would quickly uncover their intentions, so the plan to get background details on the monsignor had to be handled cleverly.

Fred O'Donovan decided that he would tell O'Flaherty that he was making a film about Rome and he wanted to meet him to discuss it. Andrews hoped that O'Donovan's RAF background might make O'Flaherty less suspicious. So the operation to make Hugh O'Flaherty the subject of one of Ireland's favorite TV programs secretly swung into action.

O'Donovan left Dublin and traveled to the Great Southern Hotel in Killarney where he stayed for a few days before making contact with the monsignor. By the time he met O'Flaherty in person, he had already learned much about the "Vatican Pimpernel." The former RAF man had spent some time talking to the hotel doorman, who was a source of much information, and he spoke to others in Killarney as well.

When they met in the hotel, O'Flaherty and O'Donovan got on famously, as the TV producer recalled: "We chatted and he told me quite a bit. He obviously loved his period in Rome. I did a whole bluff about the film and then I drove to Cahersiveen and he invited me to play golf. I went out to the golf course, but I am the worst golfer in Ireland."

O'Donovan got all the information he needed, and his background in the armed forces clearly put O'Flaherty at ease. "He was chatty. We were on the same wavelength and there was something about him that I felt it was like talking to one of my fellas in the RAF."

Andrews's decision to call an old friend had paid off, for O'Donovan proved to be exactly the right person for the job. Within days a file containing the details of O'Flaherty's dramatic wartime career was on the desk of the *This Is Your Life* producers in London.

Both Andrews and O'Donovan were delighted because they sensed that they had found a charismatic individual whose life story would make a great piece of engaging television. But a week passed and O'Donovan heard nothing from London about the plans for the program. Then one morning Andrews called, and it was clear that there was disappointment in his voice. O'Donovan recalled the conversation: "Eamonn rang me and said there had been a change of plans. He said, 'I don't think we are going to do the program on the monsignor, we think he will cop on. We are going to do it on Sam Derry.'" Eamonn, in other words, believed that O'Flaherty would catch on to O'Donovan's motive and realize that something was up besides research on the war.

O'Donovan sensed that his friend wasn't telling him the full story. "Eamonn was upset because he thought highly of Monsignor O'Flaherty. I knew how much he wanted to make the program about him. Eamonn wouldn't have confided in you completely. I had a feeling Eamonn had a row with the producers." Yet, if Andrews had clashed with the producers over who should be the subject of the program, he kept it private.

Senior BBC staff decided that the program would feature the life and work of the British Army officer Sam Derry, and Hugh

O'Flaherty would make a contribution rather than being the subject. It is possible that O'Flaherty's poor health may have had a bearing on this decision. Concerned that the retired priest might not be able to travel to London, the BBC dispatched a film crew to County Kerry to record his interview. This took place in a room above Sheehan's shop, and Danny O'Connor was there. "I remember the BBC coming to film. They filmed an interview with him and we were excited about the whole thing. I was excited about it because *This Is Your Life* was a big program."

The whole town was talking about the BBC show, but O'Flaherty was clearly unaffected by the attention and downplayed the interest in him. As Danny recalled: "He would shy away from it. He wasn't a thrill seeker or anything like that or looking for attention or notice. He was very quiet."

The film crew returned to London struck by O'Flaherty's contribution, and when the producers watched a recording of his interview, they knew his words would add greatly to the strength of the program. So it was then decided that O'Flaherty should be featured more in the broadcast after all—if he was well enough to travel to London for the final surprise recording featuring Derry and others connected with the Escape Line. A BBC researcher went to County Kerry to see if he could make the journey and be the surprise guest who would be revealed toward the end of the program. Hugh O'Flaherty, the monsignor's nephew, remembers the persistence of the BBC representatives. "The BBC kept coming back and wondering if there was any chance he would come to London. I am glad they did because in the end he agreed."

Knowing that his health was failing and the trip to London may be his last opportunity to be reacquainted with his wartime friends, Hugh O'Flaherty gave in to the BBC's request.

In February 1963 Danny O'Connor drove O'Flaherty to Cork Airport, and the retired cleric boarded a flight to England. In London he was taken to the BBC studios. Derry, who had been taken by surprise by Eamonn Andrews some hours earlier, was now sitting in front of an audience being interviewed. Andrews then explained that the Rome Escape Line had been founded by a priest called Hugh O'Flaherty, who was now retired and living in his native Ireland, but who was unable to travel. The presenter then introduced the monsignor as "one of the most extraordinary characters to come out of the war."

Derry remembers looking up at the screen and seeing a white-haired man speaking in a halting, quavering voice. O'Flaherty addressed him and spoke about the danger of life in wartime Italy some two decades earlier. "Hello, Sam, it seems a long time since we were together in Rome." He continued, "These were dark days and I shall always remember the difficulties we had in trying to keep one step ahead of the Gestapo. Sam, when you came to Rome you arrived at the right moment. Events were getting difficult for me. I needed a British officer with some authority, and when I mentioned your name and when he saw you, the British minister said to me you were the right man."

O'Flaherty ended his contribution by praising Derry's absolute unselfishness and wishing him and his wife every blessing.

When the film stopped rolling, Eamonn Andrews turned to Derry and said, "He was quite a character too, I gather." Derry, struck by seeing his old friend for the first time in twenty years, simply said, "He was marvelous."

The very nature of the show ensured that, in many cases, the subject was reunited with people he or she had not seen or spoken to for a considerable time. The producers had done some detective work and tracked down Norman Anderson, a Cameron Highlander who had become seriously ill with appendicitis in Rome during the Nazi occupation. Anderson was given emergency treatment and placed in a safe house thanks to the efforts of O'Flaherty and Derry. After Andrews announced that Derry had not seen Anderson for years, the former soldier was brought on stage, and he used the occasion to thank Derry for his work. Derry was probably wondering what would happen next as the host told him, "You are getting a few surprises tonight." Derry laughed, perhaps nervously, and replied, "It is terrible." Unknown to the former major, the producers had planned one further surprise.

Backstage Hugh O'Flaherty had watched the proceedings well away from the audience and the invited guests. As the recording moved to its conclusion, Andrews, clutching his famous "Red Book," turned to Derry and said, "We have time enough for one more guest. This is the man whose guidance you so often relied on during those strenuous months in Rome. You paid him a great compliment a few moments ago, not on film this time but here in the flesh. Monsignor Hugh O'Flaherty CBE."

To a background of music and applause, Hugh O'Flaherty stepped forward. Derry looked up in amazement as his friend emerged from behind the screen. "Suddenly the monsignor appeared and slowly walked on stage. Blinking in the limelight he grinned and threw his arms around me. We both wept for joy."

It was a poignant moment, giving a very public glimpse of what two very different men had been through. Here were two remarkable individuals bonded by friendship and touched by personal memories of war and peace.

Fred O'Donovan watched it all being filmed from backstage but deliberately stayed away from the monsignor. "He didn't come near me, so I kept in the background," he later recalled. He didn't want to be recognized as the man who had done the secret research.

When the show was aired, it was watched by around eight million viewers. O'Donovan remembered that it was regarded as one of the highlights of the series: "Everybody thought it was magnificent. It was one of the best. This man was a real hero and so was Major Derry."

The trip to London gave Hugh O'Flaherty a final chance to see his Escape Line friends. After the recording there was an opportunity to relax and reminisce. He was able to catch up with old friends and relate hair-raising tales of how they had outfoxed Obersturmbannführer Kappler during the Nazi occupation.

The monsignor's nephew Hugh O'Flaherty remembered going to Dublin Airport to collect his uncle when he flew home from London, and inevitably the program and the after-show celebrations dominated their conversation. Hugh O'Flaherty said his uncle was in great form: "He was chuffed [pleased]. He enjoyed his time. I asked was there a party. He replied with a smile, 'Oh there were several parties.'"

It was O'Flaherty's last major trip away from County Kerry, and he knew he would never see his wartime friends again. It was his swan song. His poor health had motivated him to make the journey to London because he knew time was short. The BBC program had a profound impact on him, though he had never sought publicity or recognition for his work. Veronica Dunne said that the experience was very timely. "He was embarrassed yet he was very moved by it. I think it was the best thing that ever happened. It showed him at the end of the day all these people were alive and they came to him and said we were grateful."

Hugh O'Flaherty spent the last year of his life in Cahersiveen, modestly and quietly. Danny O'Connor managed to take him out for the occasional drive along the coast, and they would often go to a nearby beach and chat, either sitting in the car or outside if the weather was good. For the retired priest it was a quiet, simple existence, surrounded by the people who had known him all his life.

In May 1963 he suffered another stroke, and although he never spoke about his health, by the summer his family and friends knew his life was near the end. He had high blood pressure, hardening of the arteries, and was now in the final stages of prostate cancer. In October he would take another turn for the worse. It was understandably upsetting for his family but hardly surprising. He was confined to bed in his room above his sister's shop. Danny O'Connor was with Hugh O'Flaherty during his final hours. "He was just quiet and peaceful. I think he died in late afternoon and I can remember when he died that I stayed with him. I dressed him in his robes and I stayed the night for the wake. There was a steady stream of people coming in and I sat in the room with him all night."

The news of the death of Cahersiveen's most famous resident traveled across Ireland and Britain and quickly reached Rome. In the Vatican there was understandable sadness at the death of one of their own. Cardinal Alfredo Ottaviani, who was now working in O'Flaherty's old department of the Holy Office, described him as a "personal friend." The official said that the greatest tribute he could pay was to say that "the monsignor always strove to do some good."

In the hours that followed, hundreds of friends and well-wishers journeyed to O'Flaherty's hometown to take part in the wake as lines formed outside Sheehan's shop. *The Times* in London reported his death, as did the *New York Times,* and both newspapers inevitably highlighted the priest's wartime activities in Rome.

O'Flaherty's popularity and diplomatic connections prompted the biggest funeral Cahersiveen had ever seen. In the Daniel O'Connell Church, where O'Flaherty had been a daily communicant, Monsignor Lane celebrated mass in front of ranks of mourners. The church was packed. Along with O'Flaherty's family and friends were members of the Catholic Church, dignitaries from the Irish and British governments, and local politicians. The service was a celebration of Hugh O'Flaherty's life, and the congregation of mixed nationalities and faiths reflected a career in the service of the Church that had spanned four decades and taken him to several continents.

After mass had been said, Monsignor Hugh O'Flaherty was buried in the graveyard adjoining the church, and as the mourners filed away, wreaths were placed on his grave. In addition to flowers laid by his family and friends, there were floral tributes from a number of British Army regiments whose men he had helped. One wreath bore a familiar name. It was signed by the man who had stood alongside the monsignor during the darkest days in Rome and who months earlier had embraced him on national television. It was a simple tribute from a retired major—a man better known as Sam Derry.

CHAPTER 17

Dear Herbert

"He answered all my questions but I didn't go as far as to ask why he was still a POW."

—ANNELIESE WENGER

AMID THE FAINT RUMBLE OF TRAFFIC, THE PROCESSION MADE ITS way up to the Ardeatine Caves. Relatives, friends, politicians, and trade unionists walked together, and on a spring afternoon, high above Rome, they stood and prayed. In silence they remembered the 335 men, women, and children who had been murdered in the caves. People just like them—students and professors, shopkeepers and office staff, farmers and lawyers, Catholics and Jews—a cross section of Italian life.

It was March 1964 and the occasion had been planned to mark the twentieth anniversary of the massacre, a ceremony that had been announced for weeks on posters and leaflets across the city. As the people of Rome paused for reflection, along the coast in the picturesque town of Gaeta about sixty miles away, Herbert Kappler sat in his cell. The date of the anniversary had not passed him by. He had been in captivity for nearly twenty years.

Kappler still had a legal team busy seeking his release and return to West Germany, but they were making little progress.

Talks between the Italian and German governments routinely took place, and although the Kappler case was mentioned, there was little appetite among Rome's politicians for releasing the man who had ordered the Ardeatine Massacre. Kappler's mother and his legal team had made a series of written appeals to the Italian authorities, and almost yearly throughout the 1950s and early 1960s, his release had been raised during diplomatic discussions. Across the world other Nazi war criminals were being released, notably by the French and Belgian governments, but in Rome opposition to the release of the former head of the city's Gestapo was too great.

Without success Kappler made a series of personal appeals for release. He even asked the prison authorities to allow him to travel to Rome to visit the Ardeatine Caves to pray for the victims, but this request was also turned down. Time had done little to diminish the official view that Herbert Kappler should remain in prison for the rest of his life.

Since the death of Hugh O'Flaherty, few people visited Kappler in the walled prison at Gaeta. His father had died and his elderly mother and sister lived in West Germany, so his only means of keeping in touch with the outside world was through letters and parcels.

Back in 1961 Kappler had received an unexpected gift through the mail. The sender, who wanted to remain anonymous, had written him a letter and included a small box of chocolates and some cookies in the package. Weeks later his mystery admirer wrote again but this time gave her name and address. Kappler replied, thanking the sender for such kindness, and over the next few months they became regular correspondents. It was the start of a relationship that would change both their lives.

The secret pen pal was a blonde German in her mid-thirties named Anneliese Wenger. From a middle-class family, she had been a Red Cross nurse during the war. Now she worked as a natural-health practitioner and had learned about Kappler's existence when one of her patients mentioned that she was sending him a parcel.

On a rainy day in the town of Soltau, in Lower Saxony, West Germany, Anneliese Wenger had been sitting at her desk in her consulting room seeing patients and completing paperwork. One of her new patients knocked on her door and explained she could not wait any longer for her appointment because she had to get to the post office by six o'clock. The patient explained that she needed to send a parcel to a German POW. Anneliese was shocked that such a person still existed. "There have not been any prisoners of war for years; the last ones in Russia were released years ago."

Anneliese's visitor quickly informed her that there was a German officer by the name of Herbert Kappler who was being held in Italy, in the fortress at Gaeta. As she prepared supper that night, Anneliese told her family about Kappler, and over the next few days she began to make inquiries about him. She was fascinated by the man's existence and surprised that, long after the war had ended, he was still in custody. She telephoned the patient who had first told her about Kappler, seeking confirmation that her story was true.

The news of Kappler's predicament reminded Anneliese of the Second World War. She told her patient, "I could send parcels too. During the war, we often sent parcels to the front." She wrote down Kappler's address and ended the call. Within hours she was at the post office with a small box of treats destined for the most famous prisoner in Italy. She had decided she would send the package anonymously.

Later, after she had given Kappler her address and he had written back to her, Anneliese began the process of finding out a little more about her new correspondent. She would later recall: "He answered all my questions but I didn't go as far as to ask why he was still a POW. Soon letters were flying back and forth, becoming imperceptibly longer and more personal, and friendlier too. I asked him what basic things he missed and he just asked for a tin of milk and some butter. So I told him I would bake him an apple pie using my grandmother's recipe."

Kappler's room was basic, with an iron bed, a large folding table with a Formica top, a chair, a stool, and an iron locker. On another, smaller table sat his typewriter, and here he would compose letters to the authorities and to his family and friends.

Anneliese quickly learned that Kappler's mail was censored, but there was little in their correspondence to concern officials. The prisoner wrote about his interests and passions. He discussed history and religion with Anneliese, particularly the history of the Etruscans, which he had researched during his time in Rome. He also wrote about astronomy and told Anneliese how he was designing aids for children who had problems with mobility.

Kappler was keen on ornamental fish, and the prison authorities allowed him to keep some in a pond that he had built himself. It is clear the fish were therapeutic. He told Anneliese, "When I watch them, it is as good as taking a walk through the woods."

Also in Kappler's mailbox were frequent requests for interviews from journalists and writers. In April 1967 Guido Guidi became the first Italian reporter to sit down with him in the prison at Gaeta and ask him about his wartime career in the Gestapo. Inevitably the discussion centered on his role in the Ardeatine Massacre, and Kappler insisted he was not the only one responsible for the "tragedy," as he described it. He told his visitor, "I followed an order, and I assure you it was extremely difficult. I wouldn't wish it on my worst enemy to find himself in those circumstances, in my situation."

The journalist asked, "But why didn't you refuse to carry out the massacre?"

Kappler, clearly uncomfortable and uneasy with the question, answered, "Do I really have to talk about this? Please don't keep on with these questions. There is a separation deep inside me by now."

Undeterred, the reporter persevered: "And if you went back, Kappler, would you act in the same way?"

The response, when it came, was delivered very quietly: "I would never again accept any occupation that didn't allow me to be myself."

It was a theme that Kappler would return to in interviews with other journalists. He often claimed that during the German occupation of Rome he was a man caught up in a situation not of his making, and that he was, using that time-worn phrase, "simply following orders." Sometimes during interviews he portrayed himself as the victim. On one occasion he urged a reporter to be careful with the story he was writing: "Now do not write that Kappler has a call to martyrdom. I would not feel right under a martyr's halo."

By the time they had exchanged a few dozen letters, Kappler's relationship with Anneliese had developed into more than just friendship. She was now a regular visitor to the Kappler family home in Stuttgart, where Herbert's elderly mother and sister Gretl lived. As they sat in the living room, the three women would talk about Herbert, swap family photographs, and read aloud his prison letters. It was there that Anneliese would learn more about his past and, remarkably, what she was told did little to diminish her feelings.

After over six years of writing to each other, it was clear that the two long-distance correspondents felt they had a future together. They were both single and were clearly in need of company. While he was in custody Kappler had divorced his wife, to whom he had been unhappily married since before he went to prison. Anneliese was separated from her husband and had reverted to using her maiden name.

In 1968 Anneliese took her relationship with Kappler a stage further when she wrote to Italy's minister of Defense seeking permission to see the prisoner in Gaeta. The authorities granted her request, and on a wet Tuesday in March, she flew from Hamburg to Rome, then took a train to Formia, and from there traveled by car to Gaeta.

Jutting out into the Mediterranean, Gaeta lies at the end of a small peninsula. The tenth-century castle, once home to popes and kings and queens, dominates the town. By the late 1960s it was no longer a luxurious residence but the military prison holding Kappler. When she arrived in the town, Anneliese was taken to the Mirasole, a hotel with which she would become very familiar in the years ahead.

Gaeta felt warm in the spring sunshine. In the picturesque harbor fishing boats were tied up, while in the town it was market day, so tourists and day-trippers had come to browse the clothing and jewelry stalls. Before she settled in for the night, Anneliese went for a walk to find her bearings and work out where she had to go the next day. With a number of Renaissance churches and medieval streets, there was much to take in, but Anneliese had only one building on her mind: the castle. Some weeks earlier Kappler had sent her a visitors' guide, and following his advice she climbed Monte Orlando, which gave a wonderful, uninterrupted view of the harbor and the prison.

The next morning Anneliese ate her breakfast, then made the short journey to the castle. Wearing a dark-blue corduroy skirt and a white silk blouse, and clutching her prison pass, she was ushered into the visiting room at the stroke of ten o'clock. The prison commander explained that he was waiting for a senior officer to arrive to supervise the pair, and the visit would not go ahead until he was present. The waiting area was large and damp smelling, and the plaster on the green walls was crumbling. What paint remained was flaking off, and high above Anneliese two naked lightbulbs hung from the ceiling. Surrounded by tables and chairs, she waited patiently close to the door. After a few minutes she heard footsteps, and then the man she knew so much about and had dreamed about meeting was suddenly in front of her.

Anneliese would recall the moment vividly. "The first thing I noticed were his sparkling eyes and his finely chiseled features. We held hands and it felt natural." As it turned out, the two of them were allowed to stay together until the senior officer arrived on condition that they did not speak. The official arrived and their vow of silence ended. For the next two hours they chatted and drank coffee that Kappler had made and brought in a flask. As they sat on wooden chairs in a room with bare walls, Anneliese must have found the surroundings very basic. Slowly she and Kappler started the process of getting to know each other.

It was an unusual occasion for them both. Kappler rarely received visitors and Anneliese was unused to seeing the inside of a prison. Even at this early stage in their relationship, it is clear from Anneliese's recollection of the meeting that she was smitten by the former Gestapo officer. Even though every word of their conversation was being listened to carefully, Anneliese tried to subtly drop in endearments aimed at Herbert, in the hope that their chaperone might miss them.

Then, in a loud voice, the supervising officer declared that the visit was over, and Herbert and Anneliese were escorted out of the room. They were taken back to the entrance through a series of rooms and a courtyard and then the prisoner was taken away by the guards. Anneliese got one last look as the door closed behind him and she was ushered toward the exit. She was given back her prison pass and then, in a routine that would never change, she squeezed through a small door within the iron entrance gate and stepped outside the prison into the midday sunshine. Her first visit with Herbert Kappler was over.

Known to millions as the butcher of the Ardeatine Caves and a convicted war criminal, Kappler was loathed throughout Italy. Yet, after writing to him and now seeing him in person, Anneliese viewed him differently. She had just spent two hours with the man she was in love with, the man who would become her husband.

Anneliese went back to her hotel, but she had no plans to return home. She spent the next two days in Gaeta and then on Saturday was back at the prison gate with her visitor's pass in her hand. This time, as she was ushered into the visiting room area, Kappler was waiting for her. He looked much smarter this time, wearing a stylish new dark suit. Anneliese, who had dressed up for the first visit, was more casually attired and felt scruffy in comparison. Kappler found the situation amusing and, ever the charmer, told her, "I did not want you to fall in love with the way I look; that is why I wore the oldest clothes I could find last Wednesday."

In the damp visiting room Anneliese and Kappler picked up where they had left off three days earlier. Under the watchful eyes of a senior officer, they chatted and sipped coffee. When the visit ended, they said their goodbyes and Anneliese returned to her hotel to collect her belongings and begin the journey home.

Back in West Germany she traveled to see Kappler's mother and sister in Stuttgart to tell them how her first visit had gone. The

Kapplers were interested to hear that Herbert was in good spirits. However, Gretl had some bad news. That morning the family had been visited by Dr. Rudolf Aschenauer, a Munich lawyer who had been fighting to win Kappler's freedom. It now seemed likely that a plea for clemency would not be granted.

Over some five years Dr. Aschenauer had put together a legal case arguing that at the Ardeatine Caves Kappler had been faced with orders that he could not have avoided. The lawyer also insisted that Kappler had endeavored to propose a reprisal quota that could be met using prisoners or those under sentence of death. He also argued that Kappler had opposed the roundups of Jews in Rome. However, by 1968 it seemed that Aschenauer's arguments had little chance of success.

Kappler was not the only Nazi war criminal being held in the fortress at Gaeta. Walter Reder, formerly an SS Sturmbannführer, or major, was another inmate. He had been convicted of ordering the deaths of hundreds of people in Marzabotto, a mountain village near Bologna in northern Italy, in September 1944. An Italian military court said he had given the order for at least six hundred of the eighteen hundred killings that took place in the villages of that region. The victims included women and children, some of them only a few months old. The court sentenced Reder to life imprisonment in 1951.

The massacre at Marzabotto was one of the most brutal events of the Second World War in Italy, and the Italian government regarded it in much the same way as it viewed the killings in the Ardeatine Caves. The prison authorities essentially saw Walter Reder and Herbert Kappler as men from the same mold. The two had similar backgrounds and both were serving life sentences. They would end up spending time together, sharing meals, and exercising outside.

Reder and Kappler became Gaeta's most famous residents, and no guided tour of the town was complete without a reference to their incarceration in the imposing fortress prison. The building could be seen for miles around. One good vantage point was the Villa Irlanda, sited on the Formia coast, which was a summer retreat used by students and priests attached to the Irish College in Rome. The impressive villa, situated close to the water's edge, afforded a panoramic view of Gaeta and its fortress. New arrivals at the retreat would be told about Monsignor O'Flaherty's relationship with Herbert Kappler and would be taken to one of the balconies and shown where the former head of Rome's Gestapo was being held. Every summer fit young seminarians staying at the villa would compete to see who could swim around the coast to Gaeta.

During the late 1960s and early 1970s, Anneliese became a regular visitor to the town. She traveled there from Germany every two months, staying at the same hotel and going through the same ritual with the prison guards. She also devised a system where she could see Herbert without going to the prison. Using binoculars she was able to look down on the prison from a vantage point on Mount Orlando, the place she had visited before she first met him. At a prearranged time they would signal to each other as Kappler walked in the exercise area.

Anneliese's letters to Herbert became longer and more intimate, and on occasions she sent him three or four parcels a day. They decided to marry in Italy, and in April 1972 Anneliese traveled there to oversee the preparations. Kappler's impending wedding was front-page news, and magazine and newspaper editors dispatched numerous correspondents to cover the event in Gaeta. On the morning of April 19, the day of the ceremony, Anneliese's hotel was besieged by reporters, some of whom had managed to get inside the building. When she entered the lobby she was surrounded by journalists and photographers and struggled to reach a car waiting for her outside the hotel.

Anneliese was at the prison shortly after nine o'clock, and an hour later the registrar arrived to conduct the wedding ceremony in the visiting room where the bride and groom had first met. Journalists were prevented from witnessing the proceedings, but one enterprising newspaper reporter had a plan. Keen to secure an exclusive story, Franco Bucarelli left his apartment in Rome after breakfast and drove the seventy-five miles to Gaeta, arriving at the prison in plenty of time for the wedding. Smartly dressed like a guest, he told the guards he had been invited to the ceremony and was ushered inside.

He recalled going into the wedding: "I went into the room and saw Herbert Kappler and Anneliese, and there was a photographer there taking pictures. So I took out a little camera that I had and I started taking pictures, but I didn't use a flash. Just then Anneliese heard the click of my camera and turned around and said to me in perfect Italian, 'What are you doing?' I was then politely taken out." The film was removed from Bucarelli's camera and he was escorted off the premises, lucky not to be arrested.

Apart from the odd uninvited guest, the wedding went according to plan. It was a brief and simple ceremony, after which the couple and the witnesses said the Lord's Prayer. A decade after she had first discovered that Herbert Kappler was a prisoner of war, Anneliese Wenger was now his wife. Five months short of his sixty-fifth birthday, Herbert Kappler became a newlywed for the second time in his life. His bride was eighteen years his junior. After the registrar left, the new Mr. and Mrs. Kappler had coffee and chatted, and Herbert gave Anneliese a brooch with tiny splinters of diamond set in it. In return Anneliese gave her new husband three red roses, which she said were to represent faith, hope, and love.

Their time together as a couple was limited, and after they had chatted Herbert was taken back to his cell and Anneliese left the prison to return to her hotel. Outside the jail she again had to dodge reporters' questions, and similarly back at the hotel the lobby was full of journalists desperate for a quote. She was asked what it was like to marry a murderer, a question she avoided. However, she did confirm that she was delighted to be the new Mrs. Kappler. She added that if her husband were freed he would join her in Soltau and live quietly on "his military pension."

As Anneliese quickly discovered, to be married to a man who was a prisoner in another country was an unconventional arrangement. After the wedding there was no grand reception, no honeymoon, and little chance that she would ever share much time with the husband she so wanted to be with. The new Mrs. Kappler would spend the early months of her married life doing what she had done for the past five years. She continued to write to her new husband, sometimes daily, and traveled many times between Soltau and Gaeta.

Public interest in Kappler's story remained undiminished. Journalists continued to write articles about him, and in 1973 Robert Katz's compelling book, *Massacre in Rome*, which examined the attack at Via Rasella and the killings in the Ardeatine Caves, was made into a film of the same title. The director was Carlo Ponti, who cast Richard Burton as Herbert Kappler.

Politically the Kappler case continued to cause diplomatic waves between Italy and West Germany. The West German authorities argued that Kappler should be repatriated, and Chancellor Willy Brandt was quoted as saying that the Italian government was hypocritical for refusing to release the former Nazi. He recalled how the Italians had been Germany's allies in the Second World War although "they withdrew a little earlier." His remarks caused amazement in Rome. The Italian Foreign Ministry insisted that Kappler should serve his full sentence in Italy.

The German war criminal's story showed no sign of losing its appeal, and in February 1974 Kappler gave a number of interviews to broadcast and print journalists. He told one correspondent that he could not have refused Hitler's plans for a reprisal massacre in the Ardeatine Caves and that "I knew that if I had refused to obey they would have executed it just the same under someone else." In a broadcast interview he said, "If I might have been able for certain to avoid the massacre of so many innocents, I would not have hesitated to have given a refusal, aware of the terrible consequences I would have met." In a plea for forgiveness he also said he was asking for a "pardon of the dead."

After spending nearly three decades in captivity, Herbert Kappler was now feeling that he would end his days within the fortress at Gaeta. However, a discovery in 1975 would change his life and alter his living conditions. A health check revealed that the sixty-eight-year-old was suffering from stomach cancer. He was eventually taken by ambulance from Gaeta to Rome, to Celio Military Hospital. Anneliese continued to write and send parcels and fly back and forth between Germany and Italy, but now her destination was Rome.

Her husband's new location suited Anneliese. Situated close to the Coliseum and the busy Lateran Square, the hospital was only a short drive from the city center and so was easier to reach than Gaeta. The huge hospital, which had more than one thousand beds, backed onto the Irish College, a handsome sand-colored building surrounded by orange trees that was home to priests and students. Hugh O'Flaherty had often frequented the college during his time in Rome, and he had been a guest there on St. Patrick's Day and at Christmas and Easter. During the Nazi occupation part of the college had been used as a hospital. The college's proximity to Celio Military Hospital meant security staff often used the college grounds as a shortcut into and out of the hospital.

When Kappler was a patient in the hospital, Monsignor John Hanley was vice rector of the Irish College. He remembers security staff routinely bypassing the official hospital entrance and that "if discipline required that they stay in at a certain time and they didn't want to exit on their own property, they would come across the wall into the Irish College and they would walk out the front gate." Monsignor Hanley's observations are worth noting since security at the hospital and the guards' behavior would later become a political issue.

The more Anneliese Kappler made the journey from West Germany to Italy to see her husband, the clearer it became that his long-term prognosis was not good. On the positive side, because of his deteriorating health she was allowed extended visits to his bedside. In this way she became a familiar face at the hospital and was soon on first-name terms with most of the staff. She established a routine whereby she would arrive at the security gates and often be acknowledged by the guards, and then she would make her way into the main building. She would walk into the reception area and either take the elevator or walk up the stairs to Herbert's room, where she would sit for hours. Often she would stay in the building until the small hours of the morning, and she would occasionally leave a bottle of wine or some other small gift for the staff. Even though it was a military hospital and Kappler was technically a prisoner, the security regime was relaxed and so Anneliese felt like she was visiting a normal hospital.

Anneliese feared that Herbert's condition would cause his death before any legal campaign to have him freed could succeed. Determined to secure his freedom, she continued to lobby for his release. Letters were dispatched to political leaders in West Germany and Italy, and an appeal was even made to the Pope. Anneliese wrote, "Holy Father, I beseech you to lend your urgent support to the numerous requests made by the German Federal Government for the release of my seriously ill husband Herbert Kappler, back to Germany, before he dies in Italy."

In March 1976 Anneliese received the news that she had been praying for. It was made public that Italy's Prime Minister Aldo Moro had received a telegram from Chancellor Helmut Schmidt of West Germany urging his Italian counterpart to release Kappler. The pressure on the authorities in Rome increased further three months later when over two hundred German politicians across all parliamentary groupings appealed to the Italian government, saying that the time was right to release the prisoner. It looked like the lobbying and the letter-writing campaign were beginning to pay off.

In November there was more good news for Anneliese. A military tribunal sitting in Rome ruled that since Herbert Kappler had spent twenty-eight years in custody, which was the minimum tariff for those jailed for life, he should be released. The hearing said it had taken into consideration his illness and his good conduct in custody. It was the moment Anneliese had waited over a decade to experience.

While the decision naturally delighted the Kappler family, it sparked a series of protests across Rome. Several hundred demonstrators went to the Ardeatine Caves and then gathered at the gates of Celio Hospital. The protest was largely peaceful, but at one stage some fifty demonstrators got into the hospital grounds, only to be turned back by armed guards. Eventually two protesters managed to get inside the hospital complex, where they caught a glimpse of Kappler. Rosetta Stamme, who had had a parent killed in the Ardeatine Massacre, saw Herbert lying in bed with Anneliese at his side. The protester told reporters, "He had the look of a shattered man." Her description was accurate. Kappler had lost much weight. He was very frail and spent much of his time in bed. Anneliese had become his unofficial private nurse and would help him to eat his meals and dress him. She was sure time was running out.

Anneliese's son, Eckerhard, a child from her first marriage, also saw that Kappler's time on earth was drawing near. The teenager, like many boys of his age, was intrigued by stories of the Second World War. His father had been in the German Army, as had his grandfather, and he was fascinated by the role Herbert Kappler had played during the conflict. But Eckerhard had more than a passing interest in the plight of his stepfather. He was well aware of the twists and turns of the campaign to free Kappler, and very soon he would become actively involved in an operation to bring him home.

The decision of the military tribunal was the best news Anneliese and the Kappler family had received for many months. They felt that they could now begin preparations to bring the ailing Herbert back to West Germany.

With Kappler about to be freed, the former SS officer Walter Reder, who was still imprisoned in Gaeta, would be the only Nazi war criminal in an Italian jail. The news of Kappler's imminent release prompted Reder's legal team to step up their efforts to win freedom for their client.

However, as Anneliese began to finalize her husband's travel arrangements, she received devastating news. A month after the tribunal had granted her husband provisional liberty, Italy's highest military court overturned the decision and ruled that he must remain in prison. There was also disappointment for Kappler's colleague Reder: The court turned down his application for early release.

In December 1976, as Kappler and his wife prepared to spend Christmas together in the hospital, rather than in West Germany as they had hoped, their disappointment about the latest court ruling was obvious. Herbert would declare, "Why can't I die in my own country, revisiting the places that were dear to me and which have been constantly in my thoughts during all those years in prison?" His frustration was shared by Anneliese, who said she was worried that Herbert would take his own life, although she would later claim that she had considered getting hold of poison so he could kill himself.

By mid-1977 Kappler's condition had worsened, and Anneliese decided that she had to act. One summer's evening she was in his room in the hospital. After chatting for a bit, Anneliese followed Herbert into the shower room, knowing that no one outside the room would be able to hear their conversation. Anneliese asked Herbert if he trusted her. He replied that he trusted her with his life. She then explained that she had a plan that she hoped would bring him back home to West Germany.

CHAPTER 18

The Great Escape

"Tomorrow night you will be sleeping in your own bed!"
—ANNELIESE KAPPLER

ON A COOL AUGUST EVENING IN 1977, ANNELIESE KAPPLER DROVE into the grounds of Celio Military Hospital in a rented red Fiat 132. She stopped and spoke to the security guards and then parked her car as close as she could get to the building that housed her husband. She walked into the complex, made her way as usual to the third floor, and entered room number two. It was exactly what she had done dozens of times over the past year and a half. Away from the gaze of the guards, she embraced her spouse. This was the moment she had planned, the opportunity she and Herbert had talked about for days. He was weak, tired, and worried. He asked if they were going ahead with the plan and Anneliese confirmed that they were, telling him, "Yes, tonight, if it is all quiet."

The pair began to gather up clothes, and Herbert slowly dressed himself in a suit that, because he had lost weight, was too big. Thirty minutes later they were nearly ready, and Herbert was becoming nervous about what lay ahead. He asked his wife, "Do you really believe we can do this?" Anneliese replied confidently, "Tomorrow night you will be sleeping in your own bed!"

What happened next has been the subject of endless speculation, and over the past thirty years at least three different versions of events have been reported. What is known is that Anneliese left the room first. She made her way down to the ground floor and went outside, then was seen putting a large suitcase into the car. Reportedly she met a guard who asked her where she was going, and she told him she was going to get some medicine.

At around one o'clock in the morning, Anneliese is thought to have re-parked the car so that it was now just five steps from the building. She had hired the Fiat at the airport two days earlier, when she had flown in from West Germany, choosing it because it was spacious. With the car in place Anneliese returned to the upper floor, having left some good German wine on a table for the guard. In Herbert's room the couple completed their final preparations. Together they made the bed and placed a pillow under the covers so that, at a cursory glance, it would look like it was occupied.

By now Herbert had written on a piece of paper, in Italian, "Please do not disturb me before 10 a.m." He handed the note to his wife and she attached it to the door of the room so that anyone going into the room or just passing by would spot it.

It seems most likely that it was at this point that Anneliese and Herbert left the room together. It was very dark outside, and holding each other tightly they began to walk down the stairs. Anneliese had wrapped a blanket around her husband. They walked slowly, mindful that the slightest noise could alert a member of the staff and end their escape. There was no guard on the ground floor, so they slipped quickly into the darkness outside. It was a still night; all that could be heard was the faint hum of traffic in the distance.

The cold air caught Herbert in the face, and as Anneliese held him they walked the few steps to the car. Herbert eased himself onto the backseat and lay down, and Anneliese then stretched the blanket over him. She was now ready for the most dangerous part of the entire operation: driving past the security gate without Herbert being discovered.

Anneliese lit a cigarette, turned the stereo on, and drove toward the exit. She arrived at the barrier to the strains of Domenico Scarlatti. The main gate was locked, as it always was, and the guard on duty recognized her and came over for a chat. It was an opportunity to break up the monotony of the late shift but also a chance to practice his German. The guard was quickly joined beside the car by a colleague. This was the moment of truth.

Anneliese was determined not to panic. There was no reason why the guards would suddenly want to inspect the back of her car. But what if they did? What would she do?

She remained in the driving seat, with the engine running, looking relaxed with a cigarette in her hand. She knew that if she came across as nervous this would alert the guards, who had stopped her and chatted with her on countless occasions. This had to be like any other departure. However, it was obvious that the longer she stayed at the barrier the greater her chances of getting caught. Anneliese told the guards she was in a hurry because she had to get some medicine for her husband. She then asked them to pass on a letter to a priest she was due to meet the next day. Finally the two men waved her on.

The gates opened and Anneliese drove out of the hospital complex. She had done it. As the guards closed the barriers and watched the car's taillights disappear into the night, Herbert Kappler was experiencing his first moments of freedom in three decades. The man who had once terrorized the city and who had been jailed for overseeing an act of systematic murder was now at liberty.

Not surprisingly, Herbert Kappler didn't feel particularly free. He was uncomfortable, weary, and in need of some air. However, his predicament did not last for long. Anneliese knew exactly where she was going and she planned to get there quickly.

Rome was quiet at this time of night. It was a holiday weekend, the traditional August break of Ferragosto, which commemorates the Assumption of the Virgin Mary, and many people had decided to go away for a few days.

A regular visitor to Rome, Anneliese knew the nearby streets very well and drove past Via della Novicella and then along Via Druso, passing the Roman baths. The city seemed empty and there was almost no traffic. At one point she stopped the car and asked Herbert if he was all right, and he said he was. The journey then continued until they reached the Grand Hotel, where they had arranged to meet Anneliese's son, Eckerhard. There Eckerhard came over to the car and asked if everything had gone according to plan. Anneliese told him to look in the back, and there he saw Herbert. She was uneasy about staying any longer at the hotel, so she drove to a nearby car park as her son followed in her Opel, which he had driven from West Germany. Out of sight of late-night revelers who were sitting at nearby picnic tables, they swapped cars. Herbert Kappler was gently helped from the Fiat and into the front passenger seat of the Opel. Even though the hired car was faster, Anneliese preferred her own. She said good-bye to her son, then drove out of the car park and headed north.

Anneliese's decision to swap cars later proved fortunate. The Fiat developed engine problems, and Eckerhard decided to abandon it in Bolzano in northern Italy and complete his journey back to West Germany by train.

As Herbert Kappler enjoyed his first few hours of freedom, Anneliese, at ease driving her own car, quickly navigated her way through the center of Rome and took the road for Florence. She had carefully planned the journey back to Germany and had even taken steps to evade the eyes of passing policemen and border guards. She had shaved her head and was now wearing a snow-white wig, one of a number she would use during the journey. She had also taken the precaution of registering the Opel in her son's name and changing the number plates.

Anneliese drove at great speed, often reaching 125 miles per hour as she headed north toward Florence and then to Bologna over the next few hours. Still, she had to be careful because, even in Italy, her speed could alert the highway patrol. Her first scare came when she spotted blue lights on the horizon. She slowed down to within the speed limit. Was this the moment their escape bid would end? Had the police spotted them because she had been driving too fast? Herbert had noticed the police as well and became anxious. But it was a false alarm, and it became clear that the officers weren't interested in them when the patrol car pulled off at the next exit.

The Opel was thirsty and Anneliese's high speeds burned up the fuel quickly. She stopped at several gas stations to top off the tank. Each time she kept conversation with the attendants to a minimum and kept Herbert well hidden in the car. As daylight arrived they approached the Austrian border. Ahead of them a line of cars had slowed and the drivers were talking to the border guards. Anneliese told to Herbert to pretend to be asleep and he duly obliged. Determined to drive as normally as possible, she slowed down and was waved on by the first official. She then encountered another checkpoint and was waved through. At the third checkpoint Anneliese held up their passports and again they were told to drive on. They were now leaving Italy.

Anneliese shouted with joy, "Austria," and her husband joined in, "Yes, Austria, my God, yes." He had now left the country that had held him prisoner for nearly half his lifetime. A country that he was told he would never be allowed to leave, except in a coffin. The Kapplers were excited and happy. Italy was now behind them, and the next frontier they would encounter would be the one with West Germany. They were now more than halfway home.

Anneliese pressed on, desperate to reach the border as quickly as possible. She knew they had at most three hours' grace before her husband's escape would be noticed in Rome, and then security at national borders would most certainly become more intense. As they drove toward Innsbruck in the August sunshine, the Austrian countryside looked pretty. "Just look at the meadows, everything is so green and lush. And there are cows, real cows, it all looks so beautiful," said Herbert. After half a lifetime of imprisonment his new surroundings were slowly dawning on him.

By seven-thirty, as the morning traffic began to increase, they reached the West German border, and Anneliese again told Herbert to pretend to be asleep. As she had done at the Austrian frontier, she held up their passports and they were told to drive on. It was a simple instruction but one of huge importance. They had made it. Anneliese and Herbert Kappler were in Germany. She had succeeded in bringing her husband home.

After a short distance Anneliese stopped the car so that she could embrace her husband. For the first time in thirty-two years, Herbert Kappler was on German soil, and he began to cry with joy. Anneliese told him to stay in the car as she went in search of refreshments. In a public restroom she changed her dress and put on a new wig, then returned with cups of lemonade.

An hour later they reached Munich Airport and Anneliese parked the car. Herbert was finding his new surroundings difficult to take in. He asked his wife, "Am I really free now?" and later said, "Munich, my God, I can hardly believe it."

Before long, Kappler's disbelief would be shared by politicians, journalists, and relatives of the victims of the Ardeatine Massacre when the news broke of his escape.

Arm in arm, Anneliese in a new dress and Herbert in his crumpled, baggy suit, the pair made their way to one of the airport's restaurants. They were tired and very hungry, having been on the road for nearly eight hours. Herbert ordered a breakfast of ham and an egg washed down with a glass of Munich beer. It undoubtedly tasted good.

Friends had booked two tickets on a flight to Hanover for the couple, who checked in and boarded the plane. At Hanover they were picked up by a taxi and taken to Soltau. Exhausted, they walked from the taxi and slowly climbed the stairs to Anneliese's apartment, where her friends were waiting. Herbert slumped into a chair. The journey was over. He was home.

As the pair began to get used to their new circumstances, the world Herbert Kappler had left behind in Rome was about to be thrown into chaos. Shortly after ten o'clock on the morning of Monday, August 15, a member of the nursing staff was doing rounds at Celio Military Hospital. Sister Barbara paused outside Herbert Kappler's room and read the note that kindly asked nurses not to enter before ten.

Keen to see how Kappler was, Sister Barbara knocked and then pushed open the door. She was startled by what she discovered. The patient was nowhere to be seen; instead a pillow had been arranged to give the impression that someone was in bed. Herbert Kappler was most definitely not in his room. So where was he? Inquiries were made to see if the cancer patient had been taken out for a walk or had gone out on his own. But he was not found on the grounds or elsewhere in the complex. The country's most notorious Nazi war criminal was now officially missing.

At around eleven o'clock the headquarters of the carabinieri was informed and at the same time members of the Italian government were told. Many of those charged with running the country were away from their desks for the day enjoying the mid-August public holiday. The minister of Defense, Vito Lattanzio, was relaxing with his family in Fregene on the Tyrrhenian coast when he was told the news. He hurried to Rome to hold talks with the Ministry of the Interior.

By now police stations across Italy had been informed of Kappler's escape, and border controls were being put in place. Some officials wondered whether the escapee had got very far because he was so frail, but they quickly discovered where the former Gestapo chief now was. Whatever plan the Italian authorities were going to put in place was simply too late. From the safety of West Germany, Anneliese Kappler had telephoned officials in the German government and had also contacted a group that looked after repatriated war prisoners. She told them her husband was now back on German soil. She didn't reveal where he was but simply said she was taking him home. The news quickly filtered back to the Italian government.

It was a major embarrassment for the Italian authorities, and the politician who was first on the firing line was the minister of Defense. At a tense press conference in Rome, Lattanzio was quizzed on how the escape could have happened, particularly because hand-picked members of the carabinieri were supposed to have been guarding Kappler. Lattanzio had little to say except that Anneliese Kappler was seen loading a heavy suitcase into her car at around one o'clock in the morning. This would prompt suggestions that Herbert Kappler had been placed in the suitcase and then driven out in the boot of his wife's car.

The Italian media naturally covered the unfolding developments in full. As a story it had everything. The affair was laced with drama and intrigue and posed a series of difficult questions about the Italian police, the government in Rome, and their counterparts in Bonn. In simple terms Italians were asking the same things. How could the country's most high-profile Nazi war criminal simply disappear? Where were the watching guards? Who helped him escape?

The news went around the world, and the reports that Kappler had escaped in a suitcase gave the affair the feel of a spy story. But it was in Italy that the reporting was at its most critical. *La Stampa* described the escape as a "humiliating scandal," while *Corriere della Sera* called it a "humiliating defeat." Kappler's escape had slashed a hole in the fabric of Italian political life.

In the hours after the escape, the streets surrounding the hospital were filled with carabinieri. There was much interest in the goings on among staff and students at the adjacent Irish College. Journalists and photographers descended on the narrow lanes that ran alongside the college, and the hospital complex was cordoned off as a crime scene. Unable to gain access to the hospital or its grounds, enterprising cameramen, desperate for a picture of Kappler's escape route, went knocking on the door of the Irish College. Monsignor Eamonn Marron, who was the rector of the college at the time, recalled the arrival of the media: "I was inundated by people coming into the Irish College and asking, would I mind if they went up to the roof to get a photograph as the hospital was off limits? From our roof they could get a lovely photograph of the building."

Those who had lost relatives in the mass killing in the Ardeatine Caves three decades earlier took the news of the escape the hardest. The day after the story broke, around 250 family members made the journey to the caves. They were there to express their anger at what had happened and to demand answers.

Mario Passarella, whose grandfather had died in the massacre, found the reports that Kappler had escaped in a suitcase simply too far-fetched. He told one reporter: "This is a strange kind of flight. Somewhere along the line there had to be help." Other relatives shared his skepticism. Passarella's cousin Mario Fanatana was also at the protest rally at the caves. He rejected any suggestion that Anneliese Kappler had acted alone: "She must have been accompanied by someone, at least a nurse. The story is just too incredible."

The theory that Kappler had escaped in a suitcase simply added to the embarrassment that senior political figures in Rome were experiencing. When it became clear that Kappler was now in West Germany, the calls to have him extradited to Italy to resume his sentence began. Rome's mayor, Giulio Carlo Argan, said the affair was a test for the authorities in Bonn and that "The Italians will judge German democracy on its behavior in this case."

The two governments had been due to hold a summit meeting in Verona between Chancellor Helmut Schmidt and Italy's Prime Minister Giulio Andreotti, but Kappler's escape and the resultant tension between Bonn and Rome forced the postponement of talks until the autumn. Andreotti made his feelings clear when he described Kappler as "a symbol of the cruel Nazi occupation of Rome." He instructed the Italian ambassador in Bonn to begin extradition proceedings. It was an academic exercise. The West German constitution forbade the extradition of German nationals who faced legal action abroad. Herbert Kappler was staying put.

In Rome the carabinieri were feeling the heat after Kappler's escape. The three officers who had been guarding him that night were questioned by a magistrate and charges over "violating orders" were being considered. The high-profile Nazi's escape was a major blemish on the reputation of the revered carabinieri. The force, some eighty thousand strong, was involved in some of the most important security operations across Italy, including the fight against the Sicilian Mafia.

The officers investigating Kappler's escape were gathering a growing amount of information as the hours passed. An abandoned car found at Trento, 370 miles from Rome, turned out to be the rented Fiat that Anneliese Kappler had driven out of the hospital. It was now known that two men who were believed to be her accomplices—another man had accompanied Eckerhard—had tried to have the car repaired and then continued on with their journey.

Just as the story was big news in Italy, in West Germany it dominated the front pages and the television and radio broadcasts. There was some support for Anneliese's actions. The right-wing newspaper *Deutsche National-Zeitung* ran the headline "Bravo, Mrs. Kappler" and in an editorial praised her for helping her husband and showing "exemplary service to humanity in general."

In Soltau, northeast of Hanover, Herbert Kappler's new residence was the focus of attention. Outside the apartment reporters lined the pavement while inside the telephone was constantly ringing. There were constant requests for interviews, phone calls from friends and relatives, and inquiries from officials. The Kapplers' attempts to get some rest were proving impossible.

Herbert Kappler's whereabouts were now so widely known that the local police had to deal with a series of bomb scares. They were initially treated as hoax calls, but when they continued, authorities made the decision to move the couple to another location. They were taken to a hospital and it would be ten days before they would be back home.

On a summer's evening in late August, as the light was disappearing, Herbert and Anneliese Kappler once again walked up the steps to their apartment. Herbert turned to his wife and described their return as "a new homecoming." Even though they had been married for more than five years, this was the first time in their relationship that they had actually lived together.

The Kapplers' arrival in Soltau provoked a variety of emotions. The small town was home to around fifteen thousand people, and the news traveled fast that Italy's most wanted man was now living freely among them. Herbert Kappler's new home was an apartment above a pharmacy, where he was guarded by police officers twenty-four hours a day. Supporters and friends left flowers outside the building to welcome him home, but the street also became the target of protests from anti-fascist groups.

Just as she had nursed her husband in prison, Anneliese was determined to keep him as healthy as possible for as long as possible now that he was at home. She routinely prepared his medications and put him on a strict diet of natural foods with no preservatives or artificial coloring. She made sure he ate organic vegetables and cut down his red meat intake. He gave up smoking and she tried to get him out into the open air as often as possible. Even though he was frail, walks in the nearby woods would prove an enjoyable way to help his health.

As the Kapplers began to adjust to their new life together, back in Italy the political fallout continued. Days of debate in the Italian parliament and weeks of unfavorable headlines put Andreotti under intense pressure. The prime minister's Christian Democrats had formed a coalition with the Communist Party in July, and Kappler's escape was now testing that agreement. The police officers who had been tasked with watching Kappler in the hospital in Rome were transferred, and then, on September 18, 1977, a month after the escape, the Italian premier demoted his minister of Defense and close friend Vito Lattanzio to minister of Transport in a move aimed at placating the Communists, who claimed that Lattanzio should take responsibility for Kappler's escape. Although the move took the pressure off Andreotti, some Communists still felt uneasy with Lattanzio still in the cabinet. The demotion may have quelled political dissent to some extent, but it did little to push Kappler off the front pages.

The West German government formally rejected Italy's request to have Herbert Kappler extradited on the grounds that German law prevented it. However, in what was seen as a face-saving exercise, the authorities in Bonn publicly agreed to begin legal proceedings against Kappler with a view to holding a trial in West Germany. This would involve Italian officials providing their German counterparts with legal assistance and documentation. Behind the scenes officials in Bonn hoped this move might reduce some of the tension between the two countries. Privately, however, there was a belief that a trial in West Germany was unlikely because of Kappler's deteriorating health.

Aside from the diplomatic communiqués some key questions still remained about Kappler's escape. In November 1977 Anneliese

Kappler tried to provide some answers in her first interview after bringing her husband back from Rome. She claimed initial press reports that suggested her thin and ailing spouse had been hidden in a suitcase and had then been carried out of the hospital were wrong. She offered a different explanation: that he had lowered himself out of the third-story window by using a climbing rope.

While this account still poses a whole series of questions, it does appear to be marginally more credible than the original suitcase theory. The escape by rope was the version of events that Anneliese Kappler would stick with for the next two decades. However, in an interview in 2007 with the journalist Franco Bucarelli, she changed her story, saying she and her husband had simply walked out of the hospital room and she had driven him out of the grounds. She explained, "I wrapped the colonel up in a blanket and we slowly moved toward the stairs, going down one step at a time without making the slightest noise. If we had taken the lift the carabinieri would have got suspicious and they would have noticed. When we reached the car I lay my husband on the backseat and covered him with a blanket. It was pitch black in the entrance to the building. I started the car and the guard ran to open the main entrance as he did every night. I told the soldier I was going to get urgent medicine so it did not arouse suspicion that I was going fast."

This last version of events seems to be the most likely, but why did Anneliese Kappler give different accounts over the years? The suspicion remains that she was helped by individuals whose names she did not want to reveal. By inventing a cover story, was she trying to throw investigators off the scent? It has been speculated that former Nazis helped free her husband from the hospital, but it is a suggestion she firmly denies. She insists she got no assistance from others and that "the escape was entirely planned by me and carried out by me with the slight help from my son."

By the winter of 1977 the story had largely disappeared from the headlines, but Anneliese Kappler occasionally made the news. Newspaper photographs of Herbert Kappler in the woods near Soltau went around the world; their publication both angered and intrigued. Images of a war criminal enjoying his freedom understandably upset many.

Other newspaper readers were fascinated by what appeared to be a remarkable improvement in the former Nazi's medical condition. Anneliese Kappler, a longtime advocate of homeopathic treatments, claimed she had helped her husband improve his health by making sure he always took the medicines she prepared. The regime of home-produced remedies, a diet of organic vegetables, no smoking, and regular walks in the countryside may well have prolonged Herbert Kappler's life for a few months.

Anneliese also tried to protect her husband in other ways. She would not let him watch television or read newspapers, claiming that if he came across any coverage of his own case it would upset him. She accepted that his time was limited and admitted that he could die "right under my hands any day, any hour."

But Anneliese was not just fighting to keep her husband alive, she was also battling to keep him at her apartment. She was worried that fresh legal proceedings would result in his being taken into custody. A move by the West German authorities was unlikely, but the thought of it still made her anxious. She was adamant that her husband would not be removed, that "this will only happen over my dead body."

In fact the death of Kappler himself was not far off, for he was losing his battle with cancer. Over the Christmas holiday his condition worsened, and by the New Year he was failing fast. Anneliese would spend most of each day sitting with her husband, who was now bedridden and frail. Ironically Kappler had become a prisoner again. Outside in the street two policemen in plainclothes stood guard night and day to protect him from attacks. He was now, according to Anneliese, "very, very wretched."

On the first Saturday in February, she sent word to a doctor in Stuttgart. That night Kappler's general practitioner arrived by train and spent the next few hours sitting at his patient's bedside. The doctor's assessment was bleak, and there was little he could do apart from try to make his patient as comfortable as possible.

Kappler knew he was dying. According to Anneliese it was around this time that he spoke about his life in wartime Rome and asked for forgiveness. She says he told her, "Soon I will appear before God and I will beg for his mercy."

For the next few days Anneliese sat with her husband around the clock. Kappler was lucid and they chatted occasionally. On February 9, with his wife and stepson at his side, he died. Anneliese then contacted the doctor, and over the next few hours a series of visitors arrived at the apartment.

The news of Herbert Kappler's death filtered out to the world, and once again camera crews, photographers, and journalists camped outside Soltau's most famous address. In between making arrangements for her husband's funeral, Anneliese embarked on a round of interviews with reporters. Just as his escape had made headlines in Italy and West Germany, so too did his death.

CHAPTER 19

Good-bye

"You did what every German officer would have done."
—MOURNER AT HERBERT KAPPLER'S FUNERAL
IN FEBRUARY 1978

IT WAS A COLD WINTER'S DAY, WITH SNOW ON THE GROUND, AS around one hundred people gathered inside the small church beside the old cemetery in Soltau. Outside, friends and relatives mingled with journalists, photographers, and television cameramen. The last journey of Herbert Kappler would soon be reported in great detail, and the images of his funeral would be shown around the world. In death, just as in life, he had planned meticulously and now his final wishes were about to be carried out.

Kappler had been a practicing Catholic ever since he had left the Protestant faith and been converted by Hugh O'Flaherty in prison in Italy. During his final days he had told Anneliese of his plans for the funeral, and he had asked for both Catholic and Protestant ministers to conduct the service. With the church packed with mourners, proceedings were relayed through loudspeakers to the crowd outside. The two ministers told the congregation that the former Gestapo officer had wanted reconciliation. It was a message Anneliese desperately wanted the world to hear.

Looking out across the packed pews, Dr. Ernest Wilm, the Protestant clergyman, spoke about Herbert Kappler. He explained how he had met him during his years in prison and he recalled their times together. The minister said that people should "be a just judge" and then asked that God would "grant our brother a new life." He spoke of Herbert Kappler's faith and told the congregation, "the common word of God united us." Standing within yards of the coffin, Dr. Wilm was joined by a Catholic army chaplain, and the two men jointly led the congregation in prayer. After the words of the clergymen, a quintet and a singer provided the music, and the church echoed to "Ave Maria" and Beethoven's *Fidelio* Overture. Then, following the benediction, the coffin was slowly taken outside to the adjoining graveyard.

In the compact cemetery mourners and journalists competed for space. Some photographers had climbed trees to get a better view; others stood close to the graveside and trained their lenses on Anneliese, who was dressed all in black with a shawl covering her head. As the grieving widow she was the focus of attention, and it was assumed it would be her image that would later dominate the television bulletins and the front pages.

In the chilly February air the ornate wooden coffin covered in flowers was maneuvered toward the grave by a group of men wearing black capes and black top hats. The whirr of cameras and the sound of flashbulbs were drowned out as a trumpeter started up behind one of the trees. He played "The Good Comrade," the traditional tune favored on Remembrance Day in West Germany. As the funeral moved toward its conclusion, everything was going according to plan—Herbert Kappler's plan.

Unexpectedly, when the music stopped, a figure wearing sunglasses emerged from the crowd, threw some earth into the grave, and then gave the Nazi salute. The cameras that had been trained on Anneliese quickly switched to the man on her right and captured the moment. Standing by the coffin, the mourner, wrapped in a scarf and a sheepskin coat, called out to Kappler and praised him in the name of the "countless comrades of the Greater German Wehrmacht armed forces." His public tribute continued and he shouted, "You Herbert Kappler acted on orders. You did what every German officer would have done."

The mourner was not alone, and another man also offered up a Nazi salute. Nearby a small group of anti-fascists whistled in protest and pointed to their heads in the sign for insanity.

Anneliese's son, Eckerhard, then confronted one of the Nazi mourners, saying, "Have you no shame? You do not know the first thing about Herbert Kappler. Go away, you have no business here!"

Surrounded by cameramen and photographers, Anneliese Kappler had hoped that the words of reconciliation from the church service would be reported by the press. She wanted the message of forgiveness to be the headline from her husband's funeral. As she stood by his graveside, she knew another story was about to be written. The Nazi salutes were understandably newsworthy, and dramatic images of the impromptu graveside tributes would soon land on the picture desks of the world's leading newspapers and subsequently be published widely. Herbert Kappler may have planned his own funeral in detail, but the world was not going to allow him to bury his past.

Inside the cemetery and outside the church, wreaths were laid bearing messages from former soldiers. One tribute read, "My only comrade," while another simply declared, "Your sacrifice, our obligation." As the graveyard emptied, the police quickly tried to find those who had given the Nazi salute, an illegal act in West

Germany. The watching policemen had been taken by surprise at the display, as one officer confided: "These people weren't known to us. We never expected it to come to this." Two men were arrested, a former soldier and a journalist, and they would be charged with having used symbols of an "anti-constitutional organization."

Herbert Kappler's death abruptly ended the diplomatic debate that the Italian and the West German governments had engaged in since his dramatic escape from Rome the previous year. However, his demise did not bring to an end the story of the man who had brought fear to the streets of Rome.

Over the years since the war, the relationship between Obersturmbannführer Herbert Kappler and Monsignor Hugh O'Flaherty had fascinated more than just reporters. By the 1980s the story was generating interest among film producers, who felt the wartime episode should be brought to a wider audience. The exploits of the monsignor and the Gestapo chief and their personal battle during the Nazi occupation of Rome was made into a film. *The Scarlet and the Black,* released in 1983, cast Hollywood legend Gregory Peck as O'Flaherty and dramatized his duel with Kappler from the early days of the occupation right up until Rome's liberation by the Allies in June 1944. The film, which would become a firm favorite of television program directors in both the monsignor's native country and the United Kingdom, was based on J. P. Gallagher's book, *Scarlet Pimpernel of the Vatican,* which had been published in 1967.

For many journalists and political commentators in Italy who had followed the Kappler story in the 1980s, his dramatic escape from Rome left a lot of unanswered questions. Rumors persisted that the Italian state had had a hand in assisting the former Nazi's flight to West Germany.

Ambrogio Viviani, the former head of Italy's military secret service, believes that Kappler received some assistance. In an interview conducted for this book, he insisted: "It was definitely a dirty operation; that means the kind of operations led by the secret services but in a hidden way." Viviani maintains that a political agreement was reached between West Germany and Italy. However, precise details to back up this claim have never been forthcoming.

Kappler's escape from Rome and his death in 1978 meant that now just one Nazi war criminal was being held in Italy. Former Gestapo major Walter Reder, who had spent much time with Kappler, remained behind bars in the fortress in Gaeta. Reder's legal team had followed the path taken by Kappler's and begun a series of appeals to have him released. The two men's cases shared striking similarities. Both had been senior Nazis and had been jailed for war crimes perpetrated in Italy. Like Kappler, Reder's health had deteriorated in custody—he had lost part of his stomach because of an ulcer and was suffering from arteriosclerosis. Like his former colleague, he also wanted to end his days in the country of his birth rather than remain in Italy.

As 1984 drew to a close, Reder appealed to the relatives of the six hundred Italians who had been murdered by the Nazis at Marzabotto in 1944. He wrote a letter to the town's mayor and explained that he had wept for the victims and was now contrite. "I only have the desire to be able, when I return to my country, to die in silence," he stated. He spoke of the dead and wrote that "nothing is further from my soul than to forget the sacrifice of those martyrs." The remarks echoed Kappler's appeal back in 1976 when he asked to be allowed to return to West Germany after being diagnosed with cancer.

Now, just short of his seventieth birthday, Reder wanted to return to his native Austria. After the Marzabotto relatives received his letter, they met to discuss his appeal. There was little doubt about what they wanted, and after an emotional meeting they voted 237 to 1 against freeing him. However, their decision did little to influence senior politicians in Rome, and a month later, in January 1985, Reder was released amid great secrecy and flown to Graz. Predictably, comparisons with the Kappler case appeared in the press. Among the relatives of the victims, there was anger and disbelief that Reder had been freed. Their pain was compounded when Reder was officially greeted on his arrival in Austria by a senior member of the cabinet, who was quoted as saying that the majority of Austrians would be pleased to see him return.

In Rome the Italian government simply said the move was authorized under international agreements that allowed for prisoners of war to be repatriated, particularly for health reasons. The story marked a watershed in Italy's postwar history. More than four decades after the Third Reich had first arrived and violently controlled large parts of the country, the last convicted Nazi had finally left Italy.

Back in Soltau, Anneliese Kappler had resumed her career and, most of the time, was left alone by journalists and photographers. It seemed that she was now seeking a quiet life away from the attention that had accompanied her during the media's coverage of her husband's escape and death. In Italy her story, like that of Walter Reder, had disappeared from the headlines. To a whole new generation of Italians, the Kappler affair, along with the wartime horrors of Via Rasella and the Ardeatine Caves, were consigned to history. Then, just over a decade after Kappler's death, his legacy once again loomed large over Rome.

Anneliese Kappler had long felt that her husband's life, and in particular his wartime role in Italy, had been misrepresented in the press. She wanted to offer an alternative view of the man to whom she had been married for nearly six years. To this end she began to chronicle how their relationship had developed and to detail the kind of man she had found him to be. Her aim was to show that there was another side to the man whom the media had labeled as a ruthless killer. Anneliese was determined to show that Kappler had been made a scapegoat for the actions of others. She wanted to convey her belief that he was a caring, thoughtful man whose real personality had never been revealed.

In 1988 Anneliese Kappler published a memoir of her life with the former head of the Gestapo in Rome, and because the book related her role in his controversial escape from the city, it was entitled *Ich Hole Dich Heim* ("I Will Bring You Home"). She argued that her late husband had opposed the deportation of Jews from Rome and had done much to help Jews during the Nazi occupation. Keen to promote her version of events, she informed the Italian media that she would travel to Italy in late October to publicize her book. Her planned visit drew instant criticism from politicians and representatives of those who had died in the Ardeatine Caves. Tullia Zevi, who represented many Jews throughout Italy, said that "the killings in the caves still burn here" and described the book as "indecent."

Italy's minister of Justice, Giuliano Vassalli, also spoke out against Anneliese's promotional trip and then sent a telegram to her urging her to stay home out of respect for those who had been killed in Italy by the Nazis. Vassalli knew what he was talking about because as a member of the Resistance he had had personal experience of the Nazis' behavior during their occupation of Rome. He had been imprisoned and undergone brutal torture at the hands of Herbert Kappler's men.

Vassalli had been arrested after the Ardeatine Massacre, and as a leading figure in the Resistance, he was viewed by the Gestapo as a prize catch. As an opponent of the Nazis, he had expected to be executed, a fate that had then recently befallen his cousin. But in early June 1944, shortly before the Allies liberated Rome, he was spared death. He was taken from his cell in Via Tasso and greeted by Kappler. The German had not come to supervise more torture or further interrogation, but to impart good news. "You can thank the Holy Father that you are not being sent to the wall," he told Vassalli. He then handed the prisoner over to Father Pfeiffer, whom the Pope often sent as an emissary in attempts to secure the release of prisoners. Before the Resistance commander left Via Tasso, Kappler turned to him and said, "Don't ever let me see you again."

Since Vassalli's personal involvement in the Kappler story stretched back over forty years, his comments about Anneliese Kappler in 1988 were accorded great respect. As the story of her planned visit gathered momentum, Italy's minister of the Interior, Antonio Gava, upped the stakes by stating that if Herbert Kappler's widow tried to enter Italy she would be turned back. Such was the clamor against her visit that the authorities were urged to officially regard her as an "undesirable." Just as Anneliese Kappler's flight from Italy with her husband had sparked a political outcry, so too did her planned return.

By now her chances of visiting the country to promote her book seemed very slim. However, she had a point to make to the man who first told her not to travel to Rome. She claimed that Giuliano Vassalli's request that she should stay in West Germany was odd, for Italy's minister of Justice owed his life to her late husband. "My husband saved Vassalli's life as a personal favor to Pope Pius XII, when he was arrested as a Resistance fighter."

However, others would recall the events of June 1944 very differently and suggested that Anneliese Kappler was rewriting history. Giorgio Angelozzi Gariboldi, a lawyer and friend of Vassalli, says it was another Nazi officer rather than Herbert Kappler who had secured his freedom. The author Robert Katz states that the Pope used Father Pfeiffer to secure Vassalli's freedom. In his account the Pope's liaison officer personally asked General Karl Wolff, who as the head of the SS in Italy had greater authority than Kappler, to intervene. Wolff promised Father Pfeiffer that he would do what he could and then, true to his word, instructed Kappler to release the Resistance commander. To the friends and family of Giuliano Vassalli, this was the true version of events. It was Wolff who had saved the life of Giuliano Vassalli, not Herbert Kappler.

In October 1988, just days before she was due to travel to Italy, Anneliese Kappler cancelled her trip. Given the widespread opposition she had little option, but determined to save face, she suggested to reporters that she would make the journey in the future. The latest chapter in the Kappler affair seemed to have ended.

Two and a half years later, in May 1991, Walter Reder, who had been imprisoned alongside Kappler in Gaeta, died in Austria. Like Kappler, he had desperately wanted to be allowed to spend his last days at home. Unlike his former colleague, he had spent his dying days as truly a free man, having been officially repatriated to his native country. The seventy-five-year-old, who had been ill for some time, died in a hospital in Vienna. Naturally his death made headlines and resurrected the memories of the massacre he had sanctioned in Marzabotto back in 1944. The media reported that the last Nazi war criminal to leave Italy was dead.

Nature was now dealing with those who had occupied and terrorized the country during the German occupation. Many of the leading Nazi figures were either dead or in the twilight years of their lives. Some, like Kappler and Reder, had been through the legal process and been imprisoned, while others had evaded justice entirely. They had simply disappeared. Some had slipped away quietly during the Allied liberation, while others had been officially helped to leave the country and forge new lives elsewhere.

One notable escapee was Herbert Kappler's deputy, Captain Erich Priebke. Like Kappler, Priebke had been arrested by Allied forces in May 1945, days after Italy was officially liberated. He was a good catch for the Allies, and his role in the Ardeatine Massacre meant that he was of interest to those investigators who were beginning to prepare cases alleging war crimes. However, interrogators were slow to interview him, and it wasn't until August 1946 that he was questioned on his role in the killings. Priebke admitted his involvement and was then taken to a POW camp in Rimini. His confinement was very short, for after obtaining a pair of wirecutters, he managed to escape and reach Vipiteno, where his wife, Alice, lived with their children. But rather than stay with his family, he was given shelter by a local priest; his family came to visit him. The former Gestapo officer knew he could not stay in Italy in the long term and began preparations to find a new home a long way from Europe. He would be helped by the "Rat Line" organization, the secret Catholic operation run by priests who were Nazi sympathizers. With their help Red Cross passports were obtained for the Priebke family in the suggestive name of "Pape," the French word for "pope."

In September 1948 Priebke's new identity was complete when he was baptized as a Catholic. Like Kappler, he had changed his religion, but Priebke's conversion smacked more of pragmatism than spiritual conversion. A month later a new life beckoned for the family, and with the help of a friendly monsignor, they secured places on a cargo ship that was to sail from Genoa to Buenos Aires.

As Priebke started his new life in Argentina, his former colleague Kappler was adjusting to imprisonment in Italy as a war criminal. The pair remained in touch and soon letters from South America started to appear in Kappler's mailbox. His mail was censored before he received it, but clearly little attention was paid by the prison authorities to who exactly was writing to him. Priebke was a wanted man in Italy and warrants for his arrest had been issued. But no one had figured out that the friendly correspondence from a man called Erich just happened to be from the same Erich who was being sought for his role in the Ardeatine Massacre.

Throughout Kappler's nearly thirty years in prison, Priebke was a regular correspondent, keeping him up to date on how he was adapting to his new life in Argentina. In the late 1940s Kappler knew that the Priebke family was well, and in July 1956 Kappler wrote to a friend and explained how his old colleague was getting along: "The Priebkes are well and undisturbed down there. They earn well and they even had a long holiday."

The Priebkes had made their new life in Bariloche, a pretty town tucked into the Andes 850 miles southwest of Buenos Aires. When Priebke first arrived in the mountain resort, he had little money and had at first been a dishwasher before progressing to waiter in a local restaurant. Eventually he got enough cash to open a delicatessen. Living under his own name, Priebke and his family were accepted as part of the community. He made no attempt to hide his nationality and was a member of a German-Argentine cultural association. Using his German passport, the popular businessman traveled widely, visiting New York and Paris and even making a brazen trip to Rome. To many in Bariloche he was simply a German businessman who was an active member of the community and loved music and travel. There was no reason why anyone in the town should connect him with the former SS captain of the same name.

In 1994, however, Erich Priebke's past came back to haunt him as he was about to get into his car in Bariloche. A television reporter appeared with a camera on his shoulder and sidled up to him. Holding a microphone and speaking in English, the journalist identified himself as Sam Donaldson from American television and asked if they could talk for a moment. Priebke agreed, and within minutes his secret life was shattered and the hard-working owner of Bariloche's Vienna Delicatessen was revealed to be a former SS captain who had been on the run for nearly five decades. In his interview for the ABC television network, Priebke described his role in the Ardeatine Massacre and said he had simply obeyed orders from the man in command of Rome's Gestapo, Lieutenant Colonel Herbert Kappler.

Sam Donaldson's journalistic scoop would trigger a series of events that began with Priebke's arrest and ultimately would lead to the former Gestapo officer's extradition to Italy.

In 1996 Erich Priebke finally faced a court in Rome, accused of war crimes committed more than half a century earlier. His arrival in Italy naturally reawakened memories of 1944 and of Herbert Kappler. Although some of the relatives of the victims were now dead, their grandchildren and great-grandchildren helped to keep alive the memory of those who had died in the Ardeatine Caves. Many of the families attended the hearing, and some carried banners and posters, one of which read, "Priebke is 83, the 335 of the Ardeatine Caves will never be." One relative spoke for many when he said, "Let's make sure we don't lose this one too."

History was repeating itself. Those who had protested against Herbert Kappler during his war-crimes trial nearly half a century before had now been replaced by younger voices who were demanding tough action against his deputy. Kappler had been dead for eight years, but his name and reputation still hung over Rome. Priebke's legal arguments would mirror those of his comrade: He would argue that he was simply following orders and that he had no choice but to take part in the killings.

As their forebears had done at Kappler's trial, the victims' families wanted to see and hear the evidence in person. Many managed to get into the hearing, and they crowded into the seats set aside for the public in the narrow courtroom. The room was hot and often seemed airless, causing some of those present to faint.

The three judges of the military tribunal found Erich Priebke guilty. However, to the consternation of relatives the judges ruled that he had been following orders, and as his case fell under a statute of limitations, the octogenarian was controversially released. The sight of Priebke walking free angered the relatives and provoked demonstrations. Protesters laid siege to the courtroom, which led to clashes with the carabinieri. Some of the relatives barricaded themselves inside the court building and refused to leave. Family members screamed in protest and many were in tears. Others sat in silence, stunned at what they had witnessed. To many it seemed that their relatives had been killed again and that, half a century later, another injustice had been imposed on their families.

However, the legal battle resumed. Priebke was rearrested and within months the Supreme Court annulled the original decision. Priebke's defense that he was simply obeying orders was rejected. The military tribunal declared the killings in the Ardeatine Caves to be war crimes, and Priebke was sentenced to life imprisonment. The sentence was later reduced to fifteen years under house arrest.

At the time of this writing, Erich Priebke, born in 1913, is alive and lives in Rome's Boccea district. He rarely leaves his apartment, spending much of his time reading, listening to music, and watching television. The price of his past is that he is kept under constant police guard.

CHAPTER 20

Rome Revisited

"Did Monsignor O'Flaherty pass information on to the Germans?"
—QUESTION POSED BY A JOURNALIST

ON A JULY DAY IN 2000, HUGH O'FLAHERTY, THE MONSIGNOR'S nephew, was relaxing and trying to enjoy the summer despite the traditional Irish rain. Life for the sixty-two-year-old had changed dramatically in the past year since he had resigned as a Supreme Court judge, one of the most powerful positions in Ireland's judicial system.

Sitting at home he was handed the telephone and told that a reporter wished to speak to him. Even though he had retired and was rarely in the headlines, the phone call from a tabloid journalist was hardly surprising. During his years in the public eye, Hugh O'Flaherty had grown used to dealing with the media. Like his namesake, he had a reputation for being courteous and helpful. He was relaxed in the company of reporters and understood the pressure of deadlines, having worked on the *Irish Press* newspaper before he entered the legal profession. He and the journalist exchanged pleasantries and then it became clear the caller wasn't interested in him but in the activities of his uncle. The question was as short as it was shocking: Did Monsignor O'Flaherty pass information on to the Germans?

The line of questioning had emerged from Washington, where wartime documents contained in the archives of the Central Intelligence Agency had just been released to the public. Messages sent between Rome and Berlin during the Nazi occupation were monitored by Allied intelligence, and one report sent by Herbert Kappler specifically mentioned Monsignor Hugh O'Flaherty. Kappler had sent the report to Berlin from his office in Rome in the evening of October 19, 1943. The cable read:

> *The representative of the American Red Cross at the Vatican, the Irishman Monsignor O'Flaherty, who is a friend of the envoy Osborne, told a reliable informant here during a discussion today among other things that in addition to 4 to 5 Italian divisions, there were now also 2 American divisions in Sardinia. As a landing by the Anglo-Americans in the Balkans was not desired by the Russians the former (he said) were obliged to make progress in Italy their objective. O'Flaherty declared that there was a probability of an imminent landing from Sardinia between Civitavecchia and Leghorn. OBS and BDS informed Kappler.*

What did all this mean? Was this message really proof that, rather than assisting the Allies, the Irish priest had been secretly betraying them? Hugh O'Flaherty simply could not accept that his uncle would have handed over Allied secrets, and he was dismissive of any suggestion that the Germans had received information from him. He was forthright with the journalist and told him that the story simply did not stack up. He explained, "I could not make any sense of these claims," and asked, "How would he be privy to where the Allies were going to land?"

Inevitably the suggestion that a war hero could have been a traitor appealed to the press, and the story was covered by a number of newspapers in Britain, Ireland, and Italy. Under the headline "Saviour or Nazi Stooge?" *The Times* suggested that O'Flaherty may have been an informer. The journalist who wrote the story wondered whether the monsignor had given the information unwittingly and speculated that he may have tried to mislead the Germans.

The accusation that O'Flaherty had passed secrets on to the Germans during the war clearly ignited public interest. Following the press coverage a series of letters appeared in national newspapers in support of him, suggesting that there was little evidence to claim he had betrayed the Allied cause.

So what is the truth behind Kappler's message to Berlin? Was O'Flaherty really betraying crucial information or is there another explanation? The first point to highlight is that there is no documentation to suggest that O'Flaherty was in any way sympathetic to the Nazi regime. In fact, all the evidence points the other way. His work with Allied prisoners and the Escape Line, his private and public comments, and his personal attempts to rescue Jews and escapees all make perfectly clear where his loyalties lay. The timing of Kappler's message is also worth considering.

Mid-October 1943 was a dangerous time in Rome. The Nazi occupation was in its second month, and some days before the message about O'Flaherty was sent, they had rounded up hundreds of Jews across the city and deported them. O'Flaherty was acutely aware of the horror and pain this caused, and indeed it was such actions that spurred him to rescue Jews and to begin providing safe hiding places for Allied escapees. He told his Escape Line colleague Sam Derry that after the Nazis began to round up Jews, he was motivated to act. "You know the sort of thing that happened after that, it got worse and worse, and I knew then which side I had to believe."

Since it seems fair to conclude that O'Flaherty was in no way inclined to assist the Nazis, how do we interpret Kappler's message? A number of conclusions can be reached. It is possible that Hugh O'Flaherty was unaware he was talking to a Nazi informer and felt relaxed enough to discuss the very subject that everybody was talking about. O'Flaherty's information about troop movements was not detailed. It was most probably an educated guess that, in reality, proved to be incorrect—for the Allies had already landed in Sicily and would invade the mainland at Anzio and Salerno, not Civitavecchia. In any case, as his nephew points out, there could be no reason why O'Flaherty would have knowledge of the landing plans of the Allies. The monsignor's trusting nature meant that he probably had a conversation with the informer that, with hindsight, he perhaps should not have had. We know that his relaxed manner with others, including strangers, was legendary, and he had a reputation for trusting everyone and often saying too much. We also know from Sam Derry that there were occasions when the monsignor's openness and innocent friendliness could have compromised the security of the escape operation.

Hugh O'Flaherty's encounter with the unnamed Nazi informer in October 1943 may also have been exaggerated. By quoting the monsignor, who was a well-known Vatican figure and of course on the Gestapo's wanted list, the man would have made his report look quite impressive to Herbert Kappler. In turn the ambitious Kappler, who had recently been promoted, was keen to show officials in Berlin that he had spies who were able to provide him with access to the Allies' battle plans.

Had O'Flaherty routinely acted as an informer for the Nazis, it would be reasonable to expect to find more documentary proof to back up this claim. In the large volume of previously classified documents now available to the public, there should surely be more messages between Rome and Berlin quoting the monsignor. Instead what we do know is that Kappler and O'Flaherty became rivals in wartime Rome, with the Gestapo chief repeatedly trying to arrest the priest and even planning to have him murdered. Had O'Flaherty been a useful source of information, why would Kappler have attempted to kidnap him and plot to kill him?

As we know, Kappler was obsessed with the activities of the Irishman and suspected him of supplying more than simple refuge and support to the Allied cause. Consider an Allied intelligence document that was referred to earlier in this book. The report was drawn up in July 1944 after the liberation of Rome, when Kappler was still at large, operating in northern Italy. The note, which is in the National Archives in London and was kept secret for decades, gives some insight into Kappler's thinking. Titled "An Appreciation of Kappler," it states: "During the last few months he was firmly convinced that the Vatican was his chief enemy and that the British Intelligence Service was centered there in the person of Monsignor O'Flaherty, the Red Cross delegate in charge of Prisoners of War. He suspected the genial and garrulous O'Flaherty of having a V man [informer] inside the SD [Gestapo]."

It seems that, far from O'Flaherty being sympathetic to the Nazis and passing information on to Rome's occupiers, Kappler believed the opposite to be true. He was insistent that the monsignor was in fact the eyes and ears of the British intelligence service inside the Vatican. Moreover, he was convinced that a spy ring was operating behind the walls of the Holy See and O'Flaherty was the chief organizer. So was O'Flaherty involved in more than just welfare work for Jews and Allied escapees? Was he, as Kappler alleges, working for British intelligence?

There is no doubt that during his time in the Escape Line, O'Flaherty would have had information that would have been of interest to British intelligence officers. Living in the security of the Vatican and, early on at least, free to travel all over the city, he would have been in an ideal position to provide information on life in Rome during the Nazi occupation.

Even before the German tanks rolled onto the streets of Rome in September 1943, rumors had been circulating among local Fascists about the activities of the Irishman. In the early part of 1943, O'Flaherty's visits to Allied prisoners of war at a camp near Brindisi had infuriated the Fascists, who suspected him of passing on military information to the Allies.

However, it is abundantly clear from an analysis of memoirs and diaries that the monsignor's chief concern during the Nazi occupation was to provide a safe haven for those in danger, rather than spend his time collating intelligence. Besides, O'Flaherty's skills as a communicator and an organizer undoubtedly made him more suited to practical work than subterfuge.

It is true that, in being involved with the Escape Line, Hugh O'Flaherty was putting at great risk his relationship with his employer, the Catholic Church. But that risk would have been even greater if he had been using his position inside the Vatican to organize a spy ring, as Kappler believed.

When the singer Veronica Dunne was studying music in Rome after the war, she dined every week with the monsignor, and they used their regular meetings to catch up on the latest news from Rome and from Ireland. During one lunch she was in O'Flaherty's quarters as the meal was being prepared, and she spotted a strange-looking gadget sitting to one side. She later recalled: "I noticed a large black box with earphones and a microphone in a corner. I quizzed the monsignor as to their purpose. He told me that he had used them during the German occupation to contact British intelligence." The transmitter was used by O'Flaherty and others to pass on messages to a branch of British intelligence known as the Special Operations Executive (SOE). Many of these messages were about prisoners, and the transmitter was used in conjunction with the Vatican radio service to inform families back in the United Kingdom that their loved ones were safe and well.

Long after the war Herbert Kappler remained convinced that O'Flaherty had worked for the Allies in more than simply a welfare role. Even though they had become friends by this time, he still insisted that his one-time rival had been involved in espionage. In 1972, nine years after O'Flaherty's death, Kappler would repeat the accusation that the monsignor had set up a spying operation inside the Vatican. By then the former Nazi had spent twenty-seven years in custody. It seemed time had done little to diminish his beliefs, and even though his old adversary was dead, Kappler clearly felt he had scores to settle.

O'Flaherty's strange relationship with Kappler during and after the Second World War has been a central theme of this book. But what provides an important context to this narrative is his position within the Catholic Church, and in particular his dealings with the upper echelons of the Vatican. The Church has long been criticized for its actions, or, as some argue, inaction, during the war. The arguments about whether Pope Pius XII should have both said more and done more during the Nazi occupation are well documented. What is also clear is that O'Flaherty's work with the Escape Line was well known within the Holy See and, while it was not officially sanctioned, it was tolerated.

One key figure during this time was Monsignor Giovanni Montini, who worked as a deputy at the Secretariat of State and would later become Pope Paul VI. His close friend Sir D'Arcy Osborne described him as "a man with vision, courage and a nice dry wit." Montini's role in the O'Flaherty story is important and explains why the Escape Line was able to function behind the walls of the Vatican. Montini was sympathetic to the plight of prisoners of war and had shown some concern toward Italian and Allied servicemen who were held in camps across the country. When two British naval officers turned up at the Vatican seeking refuge, he had personally intervened and arranged accommodations for them in the Vatican gendarmerie's barracks.

Through his friendship with D'Arcy Osborne, Montini knew the full details of the Escape Line, and as Montini had the ear of Pope Pius XII, he also knew what was happening on Vatican territory. When the Germans protested about the Escape Line operation, it was Montini whom the German ambassador, Baron Ernst von Weizsäcker, went to see. Montini passed the German's concerns on to O'Flaherty and warned him that everyone was aware of his work with the Escape Line. However, no moves were made to close down the operation, though O'Flaherty was instructed by his superiors to remove Derry from his lodgings and the British major went to stay at the British legation.

No attempt was ever made by the Vatican authorities to expel Osborne, whom the Germans correctly suspected of being involved in the Escape Line. Such a move would have incurred the wrath of the British government and caused diplomatic tension between the Holy See and London. In addition, the Pope was keen to keep

Rome and the Vatican safe from the Allied bombing raids, so he may have decided to avoid alienating the British.

Monsignor Montini, who was no stranger to giving refuge to escapees, may well have argued that the Escape Line was above politics and was not about taking sides but simply about keeping people safe. Certainly that was the argument that would have been articulated by Osborne. So, despite intense diplomatic pressure from the Germans, Pope Pius XII and Monsignor Montini turned a blind eye to the Allied escape operation, and it was allowed to continue its work.

Hugh O'Flaherty's role in the Escape Line did not only bring personal risks, but his involvement also probably affected his post-war career in the Church. Like all large institutions, the Catholic Church had its share of internal politics and personality clashes. There is no doubt that O'Flaherty antagonized those who felt his wartime role had been exaggerated and were probably a little jealous of the media attention he started to attract in the years following the war. When he was made a Domestic Prelate by Pope Pius XII in 1953, he was pleased, but he knew that within the Vatican he still had a number of enemies. He would later allude to his lack of career progress when he told writer J. P. Gallagher, "I have lost too much promotion."

Even today some within Vatican circles feel that O'Flaherty's wartime role has been overstated and he has been given a status he does not deserve. One senior cleric who knew him and was prepared to talk about him but wished to remain anonymous said, "He seriously compromised the Vatican and, remember, in all this he remained a monsignor. That should tell you everything." That statement tells us that, more than half a century later, some views have not changed. It reeks of jealousy and suggests that O'Flaherty was not capable of promotion. The truth is very different. As we have seen, toward the end of his life discussions began about his taking up the important post of Papal Nuncio to Tanzania, but ill health brought his career in Rome to a crashing halt.

Just as he gained enemies inside the Church, O'Flaherty attracted critics among his Irish colleagues in Rome. Within the Irish government, too, there were some who clearly disapproved of the monsignor's activities. Michael MacWhite, who was an Irish envoy to the Italian government, wrote to Dublin in 1942 and described O'Flaherty as being like a "traveling postman," wondered how he had obtained a Vatican passport, and suggested that he had abused this privilege. He said that Montini had reprimanded O'Flaherty, who was now under police observation and could end up in a concentration camp. MacWhite added that such a period of detention "might develop in him a sense of proportion and responsibility." Was MacWhite envious of O'Flaherty's growing status? Perhaps he was also concerned that the monsignor's assistance directed toward Allied soldiers compromised Ireland's wartime neutrality.

In his native land there has been little official recognition of O'Flaherty's life and work. Successive Irish governments have often ignored those who fought alongside or assisted the British during the First and Second World Wars. For years Irish men and women who wore the uniform of the "Crown" were seen as an embarrassment and were written out of Ireland's story. For political reasons there was an ambivalent attitude toward them. That "official amnesia" has now disappeared, and in the past decade much has been done to recover the memory of the thousands of Irish citizens who fought in the two world wars. Similarly, in recent years Hugh O'Flaherty's contribution has been brought to public attention through an annual memorial event in Killarney backed by his family and supporters. A book written by Brian Fleming has been published in Ireland, and an Irish-language television documentary about the monsignor's wartime activities was produced by his great-niece Catherine O'Flaherty. There is also a proposal to erect a statue of the priest in County Kerry.

Hugh O'Flaherty's story is slowly becoming part of Ireland's wartime narrative. Ironically, as a man who was genuinely modest, he would be embarrassed by the attention his life is now receiving. Motivated by his faith, not by fame, he did not seek acknowledgement of his efforts. He simply had a desire to help his fellow man.

In Germany the memory of O'Flaherty's one-time adversary, Herbert Kappler, has been handled very differently. It is his family who has kept his name and his story alive through a book written by his widow, Anneliese, and by the occasional interviews she gives to the media. For the most part Kappler's role in the war is treated like that of the many thousands who wore the German uniform. To many in Germany Kappler's life simply belongs to the past, to a period in their history that must never be repeated. Accordingly there will be no statue or commemorative plaque to his life or official recognition of his role in the Second World War.

In Italy Kappler will be remembered by many as the man who planned and plotted terror during the Nazi occupation of Rome. To the victims' families he will forever be the man who led the Ardeatine Massacre and, eventually, the prisoner who, instead of serving his sentence in Italy, managed to escape to his native country. To the wider world Herbert Kappler became known through two films: *Massacre in Rome* in 1973 and, ten years later, *The Scarlet and the Black*. On screen he was portrayed as a typical fanatical Nazi, but that is only part of the story.

Kappler was a complex figure. He followed orders, yet on key occasions he questioned them. When the arrest and deportation of Jews was demanded by his superiors in Berlin, he proposed an alternative plan. He sought to delay the arrests and instead collected gold from the Jewish community and said that he did not have enough manpower to carry out the operation. When his superiors in Berlin insisted that the deportation proceed, he abandoned his alternative plan and complied. Was his original opposition to what he was being ordered to do motivated simply by practicalities or did he genuinely believe that it was wrong?

Anneliese Kappler has argued that her late husband did make attempts to halt the deportation of the Jews, but we know that ultimately he obeyed his orders. His role in the Ardeatine Massacre is well documented, and he has never sought to deny his involvement in drawing up the death list and ordering, as well as participating in, the shootings.

The degree of detail Kappler provided in his defense was a notable feature of his war-crimes trial. He was regarded as one of the best witnesses to the killings, and ironically his openness led the court to sentence him to life imprisonment. During his time in prison in Italy, Kappler spent much time analyzing his role on March 24, 1944, as the letters he wrote and the interviews he gave testify. Like many other war criminals, he would use the standard defense that he was simply a soldier following orders.

However, Kappler took steps that were different from the standard behavior of jailed Nazis. His decision to write to Monsignor O'Flaherty and invite him to visit him in prison was the rekindling of an old relationship. Kappler clearly enjoyed the priest's company, but it was more than a simple desire to spend some time with an old foe. Kappler wanted to convert to Catholicism, and he accepted

O'Flaherty's advice to delay the conversion until his trial was over, lest it be interpreted as opportunistic. As we know, when Kappler eventually became a Catholic, the baptism was carried out by the monsignor. Cynics suggest that Kappler's conversion and his desire to be allowed to visit the Ardeatine Caves to pray for the dead were an attempt to secure early release. O'Flaherty was careful not to enter into the debate over whether Kappler should be released early.

What is clear is that Kappler's faith would become a constant part of his life. During the last days he was in Rome, he was regularly visited by the hospital chaplain, and before he died in Soltau he spent time with a local priest and, according to Anneliese, he acknowledged that he would soon need to seek God's mercy.

Would O'Flaherty have welcomed Kappler into the Church if he had doubted his sincerity? The Irishman was renowned for his ability to see good in all people, even those who had committed terrible acts of violence and murder. Sam Derry would recall the monsignor speaking about two agents who had betrayed the Allies: "They did wrong, but there is good in every man." Yet O'Flaherty was not gullible and did not simply accept everything at face value. Friends remember him rigorously questioning those who wished to embrace Catholicism. It seems most likely that he and Kappler would have had lengthy conversations about the German's desire to become a Catholic. O'Flaherty would also have been well aware of how Kappler's conversion would have been interpreted by the outside world. It would remain secret for some time, and when it finally became public O'Flaherty characteristically downplayed it.

What separated Hugh O'Flaherty and Herbert Kappler were the value they attached to life and the moral code they used in their day-to-day dealings. During the Nazi occupation of Rome, the lives of the priest and the head of the city's Gestapo could not have been more at odds. They were two men from contrasting backgrounds thrown together by fate. The cleric hid prisoners, and the SS officer tried to find them. The monsignor tried to save lives, while the Gestapo chief destroyed them. O'Flaherty's instinct was to trust people; Kappler's was to be suspicious of them. They saw life through very different lenses.

Nearly seventy years later, Rome still bears the visible scars of Herbert Kappler's reign. The Ardeatine Caves are a national memorial to the 335 people who were butchered there in 1944, and every week fresh flowers are laid at the tombs.

In Via Rasella, where German troops were killed by the Resistance, the bullet holes are still visible. The cells in Via Tasso, where the Gestapo once brutalized prisoners, have been preserved as part of a museum that tells the story of the Nazi occupation. On the walls you can still read the scratched names and drawings made by inmates who were tortured there by their interrogators. Outside, instead of the sound of screams, the street is filled at certain times of day with the joyous noise of children playing in a nearby schoolyard.

Most of the safe houses that Hugh O'Flaherty used are still standing. They are now occupied by people blissfully unaware of the role their homes played in the fight against Fascism.

St. Peter's Square no longer has the white line around it that the Nazis painted to mark their territory. But the steps, the fountains, and the tall columns are still there in the shadow of the Basilica. This holy place with its imposing architecture draws pilgrims, tourists, and historians every day of the year. And it was in these calm, classical surroundings that two men, one Irish, the other German, once played a deadly game of hide and seek.

Acknowledgments

I FIRST CAME ACROSS THE STORY OF HERBERT KAPPLER AND HUGH O'Flaherty when I was researching my previous book in 2006. The two men and their unique relationship fascinated me, and in 2008 I began a journey that would span five countries.

Over time I became aware of the work of other writers who had examined parts of this narrative before. I was assisted by the works of Robert Katz, Raleigh Trevelyan, Owen Chadwick, and J. P. Gallagher. I also understood more about wartime Rome by reading the memoirs of Sam Derry, John Furman, and William Simpson. However, I felt there was room for a book that examined the lives of Kappler and O'Flaherty before, during, and after the war. I also wanted to bring the story up to date with recently released archive material.

Without the help of many people in the United Kingdom and Ireland, Italy, Germany, and the United States, this story would not have been written.

In Ireland the O'Flaherty family showed me great kindness. Hugh and Kay O'Flaherty and their daughter Catherine O'Flaherty were always available to answer questions and help me secure interviews. They warmly welcomed me on my visits to Dublin and Killarney, and Hugh kindly read a first draft of the manuscript.

In County Kerry the Dineen family, particularly Pearl and Cormac, were most accommodating and provided me with hospitality and transport. I was also assisted by Danny O'Connor, Dr. Veronica Dunne, Sister Elizabeth Matson, and the late Fred O'Donovan, who sadly died before this book was published. I also spent an enjoyable day with Monsignor Eamonn Marron and Monsignor John Hanley.

In the United States Jeremy Bigwood conducted research at the National Archives in Washington, DC, and in California David Alvarez offered advice and guidance. Riccardo Valsecchi went hunting documents and files in Berlin and was most helpful. In Rome I was assisted by Elisabeth Giansiracusa, Luca Attanasio, Pierangelo Maurizio, Veronica Scarisbrick, Ambrogio Viviani, Martin Fagan, Franco Bucarelli, Monsignor Bergin, Monsignor Charlie Burns, and Father Hayden. The British ambassador to the Holy See, Francis Campbell, a native of Northern Ireland, was also keen to support this book.

In London the staff at the National Archives were always courteous, particularly William Spencer, who often pointed me in the right direction. Kevin Fane-Hervey, whose father was a most colorful part of the Rome Escape Line, was an enthusiastic supporter of this project, as was his daughter Rebecca. North Down Borough Council kindly supported me, and in 2009 I was awarded the Kilfedder Arts Bursary, which allowed me the space and the time to write in the picturesque surroundings of the Tyrone Guthrie Center in County Monaghan.

My colleagues at BBC Northern Ireland and BBC Westminster have been very supportive, and my friends in the Political Unit were most gracious when my writing took me away during busy times. Mark Carruthers kindly read an early draft of this book and made helpful suggestions, as did Philip Orr, who also conducted research in Dublin. My fellow journalists David Sharrock and Mark Hennessy helped in discovering some old newspaper reports.

I was blessed to have a trio of translators, Julie Beckett, Jenny Kirkwood, and Anja Oliver, who often studied obscure documents at short notice. My friends on Gray's Hill always encouraged me, and I am grateful for their kindness. My agents Paul, and Susan Feldstein, have been good friends and have always offered wise counsel. I enjoyed working with them and all the staff at Harper-Collins, particularly Iain MacGregor, Richard Dawes, and Louise Stanley, who first commissioned this book and granted me the time to finish it.

My family and friends seemed to accept my fascination with Herbert Kappler and Hugh O'Flaherty with great understanding. My parents, to whom I owe so much, and my brothers, Matthew and Geoff, and sister, Kate, were very supportive. I hope my children, Grace, Jack, and Gabriel, forgive me for sitting in front of a keyboard when I should have been spending time with them. Without my wife, Katrin, this book would not have been completed. She makes it all worthwhile.

Notes and Sources

This book is based on material gathered from archives, personal interviews, newspapers, magazines, and books. In the autumn of 2009 I traveled to Rome to visit places central to the story. I also went to Dublin and County Kerry, to interview friends and relatives of Monsignor Hugh O'Flaherty, and to Cahersiveen, where he is buried. In March 2010 I visited the National Archives and Records Administration in Washington, DC, to study the Kappler Decodes held by the CIA. In addition I examined material at the National Archives in London. Philip Orr carried out further research in Dublin, at the National Archives and the Jesuit Archives at Mungret College. In the United States Jeremy Bigwood conducted research at the National Archives in Washington, DC, and in Berlin Riccardo Valsecchi assisted in hunting for documents and files. In Rome I was assisted by Elisabeth Giansiracusa.

The sources of material quoted from books, newspapers, magazines, archives, and interviews are given below.

PROLOGUE
News reports in August 1977 originally suggested that Herbert Kappler had escaped from his prison hospital hidden inside a large suitcase. This version added much drama to the story but was never proved. In an interview with the Italian journalist Franco Bucarelli,

Anneliese Kappler said her husband had in fact escaped by walking out of the hospital building and then getting into a car.

"Please do not disturb me before 10 a.m." *Economist,* August 20, 1977.

a bottle of good German wine. Guido Gerosa, *Il caso Kappler: dalle Ardeatine a Soltau* (Sonzogno, 1977), 14.

"Yes, everything is fine." Translated from Anneliese Kappler's memoir *Ich Hole Dich Heim* (self-published, 1990), Chapter 13, 339.

CHAPTER 1: APPOINTMENT TO KILL

One March morning. J. P. Gallagher, *Scarlet Pimpernel of the Vatican* (Souvenir Press, 1967), 11. Sadly Gallagher's book does not contain source notes. However, O'Flaherty did tell friends and family that Kappler had tried to kidnap him.

"To Herbert from his Himmler." David Alvarez and Robert Graham, *Nothing Sacred: Nazi Espionage Against the Vatican, 1939–1945* (Cass, 1997), 72.

"Seize him, hustle him down the steps … Understood?" J. P. Gallagher, *Scarlet Pimpernel of the Vatican,* 12.

"most magnificent scrounger I have ever come across." Ibid., 32.

"So long as they don't use guns … it not?" Ibid., 13. In Gallagher's account the Swiss Guards handed Kappler's men over to a group of anti-fascists, who beat them up. Since the Germans would have been armed and would have had backup, this part of the story needs clarification.

CHAPTER 2: DESTINATION ITALY

a series of extramarital affairs. Reported in Herbert Kappler file, National Archives, London, WO 204/12798.

product of the Lebensborn. Robert Katz, *Massacre in Rome* (Jonathan Cape, 1967), 35.

Born into a middle-class family. Herbert Kappler file, National Archives, London, WO 204/12798.

In September 1934 he married. Herbert Kappler File Archives, Berlin.

Kappler's travels continued. Herbert Kappler file, National Archives, London, WO 204/12798.

he wanted to be a priest. Author's interview with Hugh O'Flaherty, nephew of Monsignor O'Flaherty.

"Catholicity and Nationality." Jesuit Archives, Dublin.

"unchristian productions of African savages." Ibid.

He also became proficient in Latin. Author's interview with Hugh O'Flaherty, nephew of Monsignor O'Flaherty.

"to render you immune against the worst forms of Anglicization." Jesuit Archives, Dublin.

a pledge to refrain from drinking. Author's interview with Pearl Dineen.

"The USA stands for the world's peace." Jesuit Archives, Dublin.

"Chris Lucy has been shot." J. P. Gallagher, *Scarlet Pimpernel of the Vatican* (Souvenir Press, 1967), 16.

"One day we will sink the whole British Navy." Quoted, with no source given, in ibid., 17.

"We will take a look at you in the Barracks." Daniel Madden, *Operation Escape: The Adventure of Father O'Flaherty* (Hawthorn Books, 1962), 52.

"gone off to Limerick for the day." Jesuit Archives, Dublin.

"some had exciting experiences, arrests, escapes, etc." Ibid.

CHAPTER 3: ROME IS HOME

On a fairway at Rome Golf Club. O'Flaherty family letters.

"Why don't you hold the club like any other human being?" Daniel Madden, *Operation Escape: The Adventure of Father O'Flaherty* (Hawthorn Books, 1962), 152.

"For the correct grip in hurling ... the left." Ibid., 153.

"nothing like golf for knocking ... your mind." Sam Derry, *The Rome Escape Line* (George G. Harrap, 1960), 153.

"The links are far from the city ... is robbed." O'Flaherty family letters.

"trying to sink a long putt using a live eel as a putter." Owen Chadwick, *Britain and the Vatican during the Second World War* (Cambridge University Press, 1986), 130.

the skills of Herbert Kappler. Herbert Kappler file, National Archives, London, WO 204/12798.

"Behind a table sat a man ... my arm." *Daily Telegraph*, January 23, 1970.

"I'll have you burned alive ... understand?" Ibid.

he glanced at the morning paper. Captain S. Payne Best, *The Venlo Incident* (Hutchinson & Co., 1949), 15.

A little girl was playing ball. Ibid., 17.

"Our number is up, Best." Ibid.

"If anything should become known ... forfeit." Owen Chadwick, *Britain and the Vatican during the Second World War*, 91.

"I believe that daily reports . . . dull reading." Ibid., 168.

He accompanied the Papal Nuncio. Ryan Report into the Rome Escape Line, National Archives, London, WO 204/1012.

"I don't think there is anything to choose between Britain and Germany." J. P. Gallagher, *Scarlet Pimpernel of the Vatican* (Souvenir Press, 1967), 61.

CHAPTER 4: SECRETS AND SPIES

Albert Penny nonchalantly pedaled. Owen Chadwick, *Britain and the Vatican during the Second World War* (Cambridge University Press, 1986), 171.

"I take my hat off to him." Ibid.

"It all makes me, against my will, very anti-Vatican and anti-Italian." Ibid., 172.

"a prisoner in a concentration camp." Ibid., 171.

Kurtna had first been recruited. Herbert Kappler file, National Archives, London, WO 204/12798.

Kurtna's personal journey. Notes provided by David Alvarez.

He met Dr. Ferdinand Bock. David Alvarez and Robert Graham, *Nothing Sacred: Nazi Espionage Against the Vatican, 1939–1945* (Cass, 1997), 121.

an academic called Engelfried. Herbert Kappler file, National Archives, London, WO 204/12798, and Kappler Decodes, OSS Records, Record Group 226, entry 122, Box 1, 16 October 1943, National Archives, Washington, DC.

One such individual was Charles Bewley. Herbert Kappler file, National Archives, London, WO 204/12798.

"As a student of affairs . . . pitfalls." *New York Times*, June 9, 1929.

Helmut Loos, who became. Herbert Kappler file, National Archives, London, WO 204/12798.

Chapter 5: The End of Mussolini

"worried sick." Owen Chadwick, *Britain and the Vatican during the Second World War* (Cambridge University Press, 1986), 242.

Shortly before 5:30 p.m. Robert Katz, *Fatal Silence: The Pope, the Resistance and the German Occupation of Rome* (Cassell, 2003), 15.

Pope Pius's clothes were marked with blood. John Cornwell, *Hitler's Pope: The Secret History of Pius XII* (Penguin, 1999), 298.

Gino Rosati. Ryan Report into the Rome Escape Line, National Archives, London, WO 204/1012.

"I will help you personally . . . Vatican State." J. P. Gallagher, *Scarlet Pimpernel of the Vatican* (Souvenir Press, 1967), 33.

"At this moment you are the most hated . . . protected." Christopher Hibbert, *Benito Mussolini* (The Reprint Society, 1962), 233.

"Then it is over." Ibid., 234.

was highly rated by Himmler. Wilhelm Hoettl, *The Secret Front* (Weidenfeld & Nicolson, 1953), 228.

"Once again it would have been heroic . . . doing so." Greg Annussek, *Hitler's Raid to Save Mussolini* (Da Capo Press, 2005), 91.

"the strength of German bayonets." Robert Katz, *Massacre in Rome* (Jonathan Cape, 1967), 35.

Chapter 6: Operation Escape

"You do not have to do it." J. P. Gallagher, *Scarlet Pimpernel of the Vatican* (Souvenir Press, 1967), 37.

Byrnes, John Munroe Sym. Ryan Report into the Rome Escape Line, National Archives, London, WO 204/1012.

Sneddon, a New Zealander. Ibid.

"Do you think the Vatican impresses me . . . swine." John Cornwell, *Hitler's Pope: The Secret History of Pius XII* (Penguin, 1999), 313.

"I wish I could put down all the facts . . . diary." Owen Chadwick, *Britain and the Vatican during the Second World War* (Cambridge University Press, 1986), 266.

ambulance from Villa Savoia. Robert Katz, *Fatal Silence: The Pope, the Resistance and the German Occupation of Rome* (Cassell, 2003), 21.

port of Gaeta. Christopher Hibbert, *Benito Mussolini* (The Reprint Society, 1962), 245.

August 1943. Herbert Kappler file, National Archives, London, WO 204/12798.

"Security preparations around the Gran Sasso complete." Greg Annussek, *Hitler's Raid to Save Mussolini* (Da Capo Press, 2005), 178.

At nine o'clock in the evening on September 5. Kappler Decodes, OSS Records, Record Group 226, entry 122, Box 1, 5 September 1943, National Archives, Washington, DC.

"I knew my friend Adolf Hitler . . . me." Greg Annussek, *Hitler's Raid to Save Mussolini*, 228.

Shortly after six o'clock. Kappler Decodes, OSS Records, Record Group 226, entry 122, Box 1, 12 September 1943, National Archives, Washington, DC.

"Today, you have carried out a mission . . . Sturmbannführer." Greg Annussek, *Hitler's Raid to Save Mussolini*, 235.

CHAPTER 7: OCCUPATION

Hungry and poorly dressed. Ryan Report into the Rome Escape Line, National Archives, London, WO 204/1012, and Owen Chadwick, *Britain and the Vatican during the Second World War* (Cambridge University Press, 1986), 292.

"Look, Monsignor, this thing . . . hardly begun!" J. P. Gallagher, *Scarlet Pimpernel of the Vatican* (Souvenir Press, 1967), 35.

"It is worth taking a good . . . in Italy." Owen Chadwick, *Britain and the Vatican during the Second World War,* 295.

"Even in my own palazzo . . . spies now." Pamphili's support is confirmed in the Ryan Report into the Rome Escape Line, National Archives, London, and the story appears in J. P. Gallagher, *Scarlet Pimpernel of the Vatican,* 41.

First the caller congratulated. Robert Katz, *Fatal Silence: The Pope, the Resistance and the German Occupation of Rome* (Cassell, 2003), 61.

"exclusively from intelligence sources controlled by me." Kappler Decodes, OSS Records, Record Group 226, entry 122, Box 1, 4 October 1943, National Archives, Washington, DC.

Then there were the practicalities. Robert Katz, *Fatal Silence: The Pope, the Resistance and the German Occupation of Rome,* 62.

"We Germans regard you only as Jews, and thus our enemy." Ibid., 69.

Twice Foa and Almansi appealed. Ibid., 75.

The package was marked. Ibid., 76.

He contacted Kappler. Kappler Decodes, OSS Records, Record Group 226, entry 122, Box 1, 11 October 1943, National Archives, Washington, DC.

The Pope seemed genuinely surprised. Robert Katz, *Fatal Silence: The Pope, the Resistance and the German Occupation of Rome*, 103.

"It is painful for the Holy Father . . . descent." Susan Zuccotti, *Under His Very Windows: The Vatican and the Holocaust in Italy* (Yale Nota Bene, 2002), 159.

"I am thinking of the consequences . . . provoke." Ibid., 159.

"action against the Jews . . . the office." Kappler Decodes, OSS Records, Record Group 226, entry 122, Box 1, 16 October 1943, National Archives, Washington, DC.

"these gentle people [are] being treated like beasts." J. P. Gallagher, *Scarlet Pimpernel of the Vatican*, 63.

One day a couple approached him. Ibid., 62.

CHAPTER 8: TARGET O'FLAHERTY

In the morning sunshine. This story was verified by Dr. Veronica Dunne.

"I am afraid Colonel Kappler . . . Via Tasso." J. P. Gallagher, *Scarlet Pimpernel of the Vatican* (Souvenir Press, 1967), 57.

By mid-October. Ryan Report into the Rome Escape Line, National Archives, London, WO 204/1012.

"Our first Irish Guardsman." J. P. Gallagher, *Scarlet Pimpernel of the Vatican*, 46.

"In places like this . . . officer." Ibid., 52.

"The men here are . . . up here." Unpublished diary stored at the Arizona Aerospace Foundation, Tucson, Arizona, USA.

"Had afternoon tea . . . other room." Ibid.

"Father . . . into the Vatican." Sam Derry, *The Rome Escape Line* (George G. Harrap, 1960), 28.

"Let us see what happens . . . with him." J. P. Gallagher, *Scarlet Pimpernel of the Vatican*, 69.

"I have been sent here . . . all right?" Sam Derry, *The Rome Escape Line*, 32.

"Now my boy . . . coat back." Ibid., 36.

"Take your time . . . the way." Ibid., 37.

"Now that you know . . . command." Ibid., 47.

Even as the British major spoke. Owen Chadwick, *Britain and the Vatican during the Second World War* (Cambridge University Press, 1986), 297.

CHAPTER 9: CLOSING THE NET

At exactly seven o'clock. J. P. Gallagher, *Scarlet Pimpernel of the Vatican* (Souvenir Press, 1967), 91.

"How many of you live here?" Ibid.

"those who find themselves . . . change lodging." Susan Zuccotti, *Under His Very Windows: The Vatican and the Holocaust in Italy* (Yale Nota Bene, 2002), 222.

"clear out that gang of swine." John Cornwell, *Hitler's Pope: The Secret History of Pius XII* (Penguin, 1999), 313.

"if a skilful person . . . agree." Kappler Decodes, OSS Records, Record Group 226, entry 122, Box 1, 1 October 1943, National Archives, Washington, DC.

"a gross misunderstanding." " a joke." Ibid.

"You must still . . . will be." Sam Derry, *The Rome Escape Line* (George G. Harrap, 1960), 55.

Monsignor O'Flaherty was predictably christened "Golf." The code names are detailed in the Ryan Report into the Rome Escape Line, National Archives, London, WO 204/1012.

"It's a hell of a surprise to see you here." Sam Derry, *The Rome Escape Line*, 71.

an Italian called. Raleigh Trevelyan, *Rome '44: The Battle for the Eternal City* (Book Club Associates, 1981), 109.

Derry, as instructed. Sam Derry, *The Rome Escape Line*, 64.

"Where do we go from here?" Ibid., 65.

Two days before Christmas. William Simpson, *A Vatican Lifeline '44* (Leo Cooper, 1995), 75.

Keeping with tradition. J. P. Gallagher, *Scarlet Pimpernel of the Vatican*, 104.

"For a time I had wrestled . . . charity." Aidan O'Hara, *I'll Live till I Die* (Drumlin Publications, 1997), 115.

in the monsignor's small room, the Kiernans were joined. Ibid., 124.

On December 28. David Alvarez and Robert Graham, *Nothing Sacred: Nazi Espionage Against the Vatican, 1939–1945* (Cass, 1997), 107.

The plan was to build a chapel. This story is verified in the Kappler Decodes, OSS Records, Record Group 226, entry 122, Box 1, 14 and 15 October, National Archives, Washington, DC.

In the second week of December. Notes provided to author by David Alvarez. See also David Alvarez and Robert Graham, *Nothing Sacred: Nazi Espionage Against the Vatican, 1939–1945,* 106.

Basilius Sadathierascvili. He is referred to in a number of Kappler Decodes, OSS Documents, National Archives, Washington, DC.

Using money. David Alvarez and Robert Graham, *Nothing Sacred: Nazi Espionage Against the Vatican, 1939–1945,* 104.

In November there would be a new arrival. Ibid., 128.

CHAPTER 10: RAIDS AND ARRESTS

The New Year. The Ryan Report into the Rome Escape Line, National Archives, London, WO 204/1012, confirms that the Germans knew about the Escape Line.

"It has gone on . . . have said." Sam Derry, *The Rome Escape Line* (George G. Harrap, 1960), 108.

"Your Excellency is too considerate . . . sometimes." J. P. Gallagher, *Scarlet Pimpernel of the Vatican* (Souvenir Press, 1967), 117.

There was more bad news. Sam Derry, *The Rome Escape Line,* 109.

Some were beaten with spiked mallets. Raleigh Trevelyan, *Rome '44: The Battle for the Eternal City* (Book Club Associates, 1981), 21.

A specially constructed soundproofed room. Herbert Kappler file, National Archives, London, WO 204/12798.

A leader of the Italian underground. William Simpson, *A Vatican Lifeline '44* (Leo Cooper, 1995), 89.

Gardner and Wilson. Sam Derry, *The Rome Escape Line,* 100.

The German went to leave. John Furman, *Be Not Fearful* (Anthony Blond, 1959), 124.

Bill Simpson, who was on his way back. William Simpson, *A Vatican Lifeline '44*, 91–2.

"Just let them try it." Ibid., 92.

Across the city. Sam Derry, *The Rome Escape Line*, 120.

Despite the threat. J. P. Gallagher, *Scarlet Pimpernel of the Vatican*, 123.

Charming and gregarious. Major Fane-Hervey Obituary, *The Times*, February 13, 2003.

Fane-Hervey and Simpson were relaxing. This story was verified by Kevin Fane-Hervey.

"This communist Mattei . . . methods." Robert Katz, *Fatal Silence: The Pope, the Resistance and the German Occupation of Rome* (Cassell, 2003), 170.

all non-clerics should be dismissed. Susan Zuccotti, *Under His Very Windows: The Vatican and the Holocaust in Italy* (Yale Nota Bene, 2002), 225.

"When will the blessed English come?" William Simpson, *A Vatican Lifeline '44*, 102.

"Back in Rome . . . John." Sam Derry, *The Rome Escape Line*, 130.

"In the name of God . . . us all." John Furman, *Be Not Fearful*, 175.

"piece of gross stupidity." Owen Chadwick, *Britain and the Vatican during the Second World War* (Cambridge University Press, 1986), 281.

Father Michael Tarchnisvili. David Alvarez and Robert Graham, *Nothing Sacred: Nazi Espionage Against the Vatican, 1939–1945* (Cass, 1997), 109.

The undercover college plan was in tatters. Ibid., 110.

On March 15. J. P. Gallagher, *Scarlet Pimpernel of the Vatican*, 145.

Brother Robert Pace. The Ryan Report into the Rome Escape Line, National Archives, London, WO 204/1012.

"All right, I understand . . . forgive him." J. P. Gallagher, *Scarlet Pimpernel of the Vatican*, 146.

"The English have never understood . . . certain generosity." Branko Bokun, *Spy in the Vatican* (Vita Books, 1973), 187.

CHAPTER 11: RESISTANCE AND REVENGE

It was one of the brightest. Robert Katz, *Massacre in Rome* (Jonathan Cape, 1967), 62. In a number of books Robert Katz has pieced together one of the most vivid and detailed accounts of this event.

By a quarter to two. Robert Katz, *Fatal Silence: The Pope, the Resistance and the German Occupation of Rome* (Cassell, 2003), 220.

One of the first. Robert Katz, *Massacre in Rome*, 75.

"drawing room soldier . . . anybody else." Raleigh Trevelyan, *Rome '44: The Battle for the Eternal City* (Book Club Associates, 1981), 13.

"The scene was beyond . . . very intense." Herbert Kappler, war-crimes trial testimony, 1948.

"They are all to be shot." Robert Katz, *Fatal Silence: The Pope, the Resistance and the German Occupation of Rome*, 228.

"I thought I would examine . . . bombardments." Alessandro Portelli, *The Order Has Been Carried Out* (Palgrave Macmillan, 2003), 140.

"make the world tremble . . . fifty Italians." Robert Katz, *Fatal Silence: The Pope, the Resistance and the German Occupation of Rome*, 229.

Derry dispatched a series of messengers. Sam Derry, *The Rome Escape Line* (George G. Harrap, 1960), 173.

313

Sitting at his desk. Robert Katz, *Massacre in Rome,* 104.

"We were told . . . killed." Robert Katz, *Fatal Silence: The Pope, the Resistance and the German Occupation of Rome,* 234.

"I can only promise . . . three times." Ibid.

"otherwise who knows what will happen." Robert Katz, *Massacre in Rome,* 113.

"Then give us some Jews." Robert Katz, *Fatal Silence: The Pope, the Resistance and the German Occupation of Rome,* 240.

He rattled off a series of excuses. Raleigh Trevelyan, *Rome '44: The Battle for the Eternal City,* 221.

"It is up to you, Kappler." Ibid.

"Three hundred and twenty people will have to be killed." Robert Katz, *Fatal Silence: The Pope, the Resistance and the German Occupation of Rome,* 244.

"He said that this . . . at the end." Alessandro Portelli, *The Order Has Been Carried Out* (Palgrave Macmillan, 2003), 152.

"He is in Kappler's hands then?" Raleigh Trevelyan, *Rome '44: The Battle for the Eternal City,* 220.

"It is possible that . . . a bloodbath." Robert Katz, *Fatal Silence: The Pope, the Resistance and the German Occupation of Rome,* 232.

"Excellent! I am . . . inform them." Ibid.

"the countermeasures are not . . . executed." Ibid., 241.

"I calculated the number of minutes . . . one shot." Herbert Kappler, war-crimes trial testimony, 1948.

CHAPTER 12: MASSACRE

ripped out his toenails. Raleigh Trevelyan, *Rome '44: The Battle for the Eternal City* (Book Club Associates, 1981), 222.

"Father, bless us!" Robert Katz, *Fatal Silence: The Pope, the Resistance and the German Occupation of Rome* (Cassell, 2003), 250.

"This was an unusual sight . . . out names." Raleigh Trevelyan, *Rome '44: The Battle for the Eternal City*, 223.

"lay heavily in the air." Ibid., 224.

"When the chaplain makes contact . . . have him." Herbert Kappler, war-crimes trial testimony, 1948, and Alessandro Portelli, *The Order Has Been Carried Out* (Palgrave Macmillan, 2003), 181.

"a minute per death." Herbert Kappler, war-crimes trial testimony, 1948.

"I raised my gun . . . to shoot." Lieutenant Amonn's statement in National Archives, London, WO 310/137, and Raleigh Trevelyan, *Rome '44: The Battle for the Eternal City*, 224.

"What shall I . . . saw everything?" Alessandro Portelli, *The Order Has Been Carried Out*, 179.

"The reprisal has been . . . get drunk." Robert Katz, *Fatal Silence: The Pope, the Resistance and the German Occupation of Rome*, 253.

"true executioner." "flaming deep livid eyes." Raleigh Trevelyan, *Rome '44: The Battle for the Eternal City*, 226.

"the people of Rome . . . favored treatment." Robert Katz, *Massacre in Rome* (Jonathan Cape, 1967), 154.

"When I told him . . . believe it." Raleigh Trevelyan, *Rome '44: The Battle for the Eternal City*, 227.

"On the afternoon of 23 March 1944 . . . been executed." *Il Messaggero*, March 25, 1944.

"In the face of such . . . escaped arrest." *Osservatore Romano*, March 25, 1944.

"have the inconvenience eliminated." Robert Katz, *Massacre in Rome*, 178.

One visitor recalled. Author's interview with Dr. Veronica Dunne.

CHAPTER 13: CLAMPDOWN

"How would you like to . . . come out?" Sam Derry, *The Rome Escape Line* (George G. Harrap, 1960), 177.

"That bastard Perfetti . . . the Boche." National Archives, London, Ryan Report into the Rome Escape Line, WO 204/1012.

O'Flynn was an alias. William Simpson, *A Vatican Lifeline '44* (Leo Cooper, 1995), 163.

"Listen, I am not English . . . and you." Ibid., 170.

In late April it became clear. National Archives, London, Ryan Report into the Rome Escape Line, WO 204/1012.

Allied escapees were often seen lunching. Ibid.

"Tell us all or you die tonight." J. P. Gallagher, *Scarlet Pimpernel of the Vatican* (Souvenir Press, 1967), 158.

"He wants to make a bargain . . . to Germany." Sam Derry, *The Rome Escape Line*, 215.

"Tell Koch I agree . . . mother." Ibid.

Then one day as John Furman. J. P. Gallagher, *Scarlet Pimpernel of the Vatican*, 169.

"Rome is yours! . . . the enemy." Raleigh Trevelyan, *Rome '44: The Battle for the Eternal City* (Book Club Associates, 1981), 311.

he could thank the pope. Robert Katz, *Fatal Silence: The Pope, the Resistance and the German Occupation of Rome* (Cassell, 2003), 314.

"Don't ever let me see you again." Ibid.

"When will you arrive?" Sam Derry, *The Rome Escape Line*, 218.

Its number included Captain John Armstrong. Personal File of John Armstrong, National Archives, London, HS9/9/3.

CHAPTER 14: LIBERATION

On the top floor of the British legation. Sam Derry, *The Rome Escape Line* (George G. Harrap, 1960), 222.

"This is a great day for the Fifth Army ... victory possible." General Clark, quoted in press reports in June 1944.

"Say, sister ... arse beside me." Aidan O'Hara, *I'll Live till I Die* (Drumlin Publications, 1997), 135.

"Why were you so long in coming?" Dominick Graham and Shelford Bidwell, *Tug of War: The Battle for Italy 1943–1945* (Pen and Sword Military Classics, 1986), 342.

A Scottish piper made his way. *Time*, August 22, 1955.

"We do have some ... gentlemen." J. P. Gallagher, *Scarlet Pimpernel of the Vatican* (Souvenir Press, 1967), 173.

"typical Nazi ... SD (German Police)." Herbert Kappler file, National Archives, London, WO 204/12798.

"Aim well!" Robert Katz, *Fatal Silence: The Pope, the Resistance and the German Occupation of Rome* (Cassell, 2003), 331.

"They did wrong but there is good in every man." *Reader's Digest*, November 1975.

"Surely the Italian government ... a scandal." Richard Lamb, *War in Italy 1943–1945: A Brutal Story* (Da Capo Press, 1993), 276.

One day as the monsignor and the British ambassador. J. P. Gallagher, *Scarlet Pimpernel of the Vatican*, 180.

"Now do you see . . . on it." Author's interview with Dr. Veronica Dunne.

"There is something I want to show you." Ibid.

"the overpowering smell of flowers . . . his face." Ibid.

CHAPTER 15: CONVICTION AND CONVERSION

"The blood of my husband claims justice!" *Time,* December 9, 1946.

"He took a great liking . . . in English." Author's interview with Dr. Veronica Dunne.

"At some stage Kappler . . . a mouse." Author's interview with Hugh O'Flaherty, nephew of Monsignor O'Flaherty.

"You are not going to be executed." Daniel Madden, *Operation Escape: The Adventure of Father O'Flaherty* (Hawthorn Books, 1962), 179.

"I'd like to tear out . . . my brother." Alessandro Portelli, *The Order Has Been Carried Out* (Palgrave Macmillan, 2003), 258.

shouts of "Schweinehund." *Time,* August 2, 1948.

"As a German soldier . . . a soldier." Alessandro Portelli, *The Order Has Been Carried Out,* 259.

"I was very happy . . . little house." Translated from Pierangelo Maurizio, *Lettere dal carcere 1948–1950* (1997), 15.

"Tell me, how did . . . the Forte." Ibid., 18.

"Our Christian doctrine . . . help me." Ibid., 19.

"I assure you . . . a soul." Ibid.

"I lived under his care . . . to me." Sam Derry, *The Rome Escape Line* (George G. Harrap, 1960), 90.

"Why? Aren't you doing fine? Why change?" Author's interview with Hugh O'Flaherty, nephew of Monsignor O'Flaherty.

"holding hands around . . . 'Silent Night, Holy Night.'" Translated from Pierangelo Maurizio, *Lettere dal carcere 1948–1950,* 44.

"You can serenely . . . or acquitted." Ibid., 23.

"It has been a dark year . . . your heart." Ibid., 45.

"You know well that . . . human dignity." Ibid., 50.

"Now I will say . . . spoke of it." Ibid., 108.

"Today then, after Mass . . . Giuseppe." Ibid., 121.

The book was a great success. *New York Times,* April 2, 1950.

"You think politics is bad. Religious politics is worse." Author's interview with Dr. Veronica Dunne.

"Why, that is not news . . . time ago." Daniel Madden, *Operation Escape: The Adventure of Father O'Flaherty,* 177.

"He came in with heart problems . . . people escape." Author's interview with Sister Elizabeth Matson.

"He was going downhill . . . falling apart." Ibid.

CHAPTER 16: KERRY CALLING

"a one-handed golfer." Author's interview with Hugh O'Flaherty, nephew of Monsignor O'Flaherty.

"The doctors say . . . main thing." *Sunday Express,* circa 1962.

"Who is that new priest . . . is terrific!" Daniel Madden, *Operation Escape: The Adventure of Father O'Flaherty* (Hawthorn Books, 1962), 186.

"I believe all our wanderings . . . at home." *Sunday Express,* circa 1962.

"I think, to be honest . . . all emotional." Author's interview with Pearl Dineen.

"He was always very nervous . . . the time." Author's interview with Danny O'Connor.

"I try hard to answer everybody . . . go unanswered." *Sunday Express*, circa 1962.

"He was a shattered man . . . was shattered." Author's interview with Dr. Veronica Dunne.

"We chatted and he told . . . in Ireland." Author's interview with Fred O'Donovan.

"He was chatty . . . the RAF." Ibid.

"Eamonn rang me . . . Sam Derry." Ibid.

"Eamonn was upset . . . the producers." Ibid.

"I remember the BBC . . . big program." Author's interview with Danny O'Connor.

"He would . . . very quiet." Ibid.

"The BBC kept coming back . . . he agreed." Author's interview with Hugh O'Flaherty, nephew of Monsignor O'Flaherty.

"Hello, Sam, it seems . . . in Rome." BBC TV program *This Is Your Life*, February 1963.

"These were dark . . . right man." Ibid.

"You are getting a few surprises tonight." Ibid.

"We have time enough . . . O'Flaherty CBE." Ibid.

"Suddenly the monsignor appeared . . . for joy." *Reader's Digest*, November 1975.

"He didn't come near me, so I kept in the background." Author's interview with Fred O'Donovan.

"**Everybody thought it was magnificent . . . Major Derry.**" Ibid.

"**He was chuffed . . . several parties.**'" Author's interview with Hugh O'Flaherty, nephew of Monsignor O'Flaherty.

"**He was embarrassed . . . were grateful.**" Author's interview with Dr. Veronica Dunne.

"**He was just quiet and peaceful . . . all night.**" Author's interview with Danny O'Connor.

"**personal friend.**" *Irish Independent,* October 1963.

CHAPTER 17: DEAR HERBERT

"**There have not been any prisoners . . . years ago.**" Translated from Anneliese Kappler, *Ich Hole Dich Heim* (self-published, 1990), 4.

"**I could send parcels . . . to the front.**" Ibid.

"**He answered all my questions . . . grandmother's recipe.**" Ibid.

"**When I watch them . . . the woods.**" Ibid.

"**I followed an order . . . my situation.**" Translated from Guido Gerosa, *Il caso Kappler: dalle Ardeatine a Soltau* (Sonzogno, 1977), 135.

"**Now do not write . . . martyr's halo.**" Alessandro Portelli, *The Order Has Been Carried Out* (Palgrave Macmillan, 2003), 266.

"**The first thing I noticed . . . felt natural.**" Translated from Anneliese Kappler, *Ich Hole Dich Heim,* 25.

"**I did not want you to fall . . . last Wednesday.**" Ibid., 33.

One good vantage point was the Villa Irlanda. Author's interview with Monsignor Eamonn Marron.

"**I went into the room . . . taken out.**" Author's interview with Franco Bucarelli.

"his military pension." *Irish Times,* April 20, 1972.

"they withdrew a little earlier." *New York Times,* May 14, 1973.

"I knew that if I had refused . . . someone else." Interview given to Italian state broadcaster RAI, *The Times,* February 11, 1974.

"If I might have . . . would have met." Ibid.

"pardon of the dead." Ibid.

"if discipline required . . . front gate." Author's interview with Monsignor John Hanley.

"Holy Father, I beseech . . . dies in Italy." Translated from Anneliese Kappler, *Ich Hole Dich Heim,* 254.

"He had the look of a shattered man." *New York Times,* November 15, 1976.

"Why can't I die in my own country . . . in prison?" Kappler said this in December 1976 and it was reported in *Time* on August 29, 1977.

Anneliese asked Herbert if he trusted her . . . Germany. Anneliese Kappler, *Ich Hole Dich Heim,* 318.

CHAPTER 18: THE GREAT ESCAPE

"Yes, tonight, if it is all quiet." Translated from Anneliese Kappler, *Ich Hole Dich Heim* (self-published, 1990), 332.

"Tomorrow night you will be sleeping in your own bed!" Translated from ibid., 333.

"Please do not disturb me before 10 a.m." *Economist,* August 20, 1977.

Anneliese drove at great speed . . . would end?" Anneliese Kappler, *Ich Hole Dich Heim,* 343.

"Austria . . . yes." Translated from ibid., 345.

"Just look at the meadows . . . so beautiful." Ibid.

"Am I really free now?" Ibid., 349.

At around eleven o'clock the headquarters. *The Times*, August 16, 1977.

"I was inundated by people . . . the building." Author's interview with Monsignor Eamonn Marron.

"This is a strange kind of flight . . . be help." *New York Times*, August 17, 1977.

"She must have been . . . too incredible." Ibid.

"The Italians will judge . . . this case." Ibid.

"violating orders." *Irish Times*, August 17, 1977.

"Bravo, Mrs Kappler." Associated Press report, August 16, 1977.

"a new homecoming." Translated from Anneliese Kappler, *Ich Hole Dich Heim*, 366.

She made sure he ate organic vegetables. *Guardian*, November 24, 1977.

"I wrapped the colonel up . . . going fast." Anneliese Kappler's interview with Franco Bucarelli.

"the escape was entirely . . . my son." Ibid.

"right under my hands any day, any hour." *Newsweek*, January 30, 1978.

"this will only happen over my dead body." Ibid.

"very, very wretched." Ibid.

"Soon I will appear before God . . . his mercy." Anneliese Kappler's interview with Franco Bucarelli.

Chapter 19: Good-bye

"be a just judge ... united us." Associated Press report, February 13, 1978.

"countless comrades of the Greater German Wehrmacht armed forces." Associated Press report, February 13, 1978, and *The Times*, February 14, 1978.

"You Herbert Kappler acted ... have done." Associated Press report, February 13, 1978.

"Have you no shame? ... business here!" Translated from Anneliese Kappler, *Ich Hole Dich Heim* (self-published, 1990), 388.

"My only comrade." Associated Press report, February 13, 1978.

"Your sacrifice, our obligation." Ibid.

"These people weren't known ... to this." Ibid.

"It was definitely ... hidden way." Interview with Ambrogio Viviani for this book.

"I only have the desire ... in silence." United Press International report, December 28, 1984.

"nothing is further ... those martyrs." Ibid.

"the killings in the caves still burn here." *New York Times*, October 23, 1988.

"Don't ever let me see you again." Robert Katz, *Fatal Silence: The Pope, the Resistance and the German Occupation of Rome* (Cassell, 2003), 314.

"My husband saved Vassalli's life ... Resistance fighter." *Guardian*, October 19, 1988.

"The Priebkes are well ... long holiday." Ibid., 143.

"Priebke is 83, the 335 of the Ardeatine Caves will never be."
Alessandro Portelli, *The Order Has Been Carried Out* (Palgrave Macmillan, 2003), 270.

"Let's make sure we don't lose this one too." Ibid., 267.

CHAPTER 20: ROME REVISITED

On a July day in 2000. Author's interview with Hugh O'Flaherty, nephew of Monsignor O'Flaherty.

"The representative of the American . . . Kappler." Kappler Decodes, OSS Records, Record Group 226, entry 122, Box 1, 19 October 1943, National Archives, Washington, DC.

"I could not make any sense of these claims . . . to land?" *Daily Mirror,* July 4, 2000.

"You know the sort of thing . . . to believe." Sam Derry, *The Rome Escape Line* (George G. Harrap, 1960), 56.

"During the last few months . . . inside the SD." Herbert Kappler file, National Archives, London, WO 204/12798.

"I noticed a large black box . . . British intelligence." Online article by Dr. Veronica Dunne and conversation with the author.

"a man with vision, courage and a nice dry wit." Raleigh Trevelyan, *Rome '44: The Battle for the Eternal City* (Book Club Associates, 1981), 24.

"I have lost too much promotion." J. P. Gallagher, *Scarlet Pimpernel of the Vatican* (Souvenir Press, 1967), 183.

"He seriously compromised the Vatican . . . you everything." Author's conversation with unidentified cleric.

"traveling postman." Brian Fleming, *The Vatican Pimpernel: The Wartime Exploits of Monsignor Hugh O'Flaherty* (The Collins Press, 2008), 23.

"might develop in him a sense of proportion and responsibility." Ibid.

SELECT BIBLIOGRAPHY

David Alvarez and Robert Graham, *Nothing Sacred: Nazi Espionage Against the Vatican, 1939–1945* (Cass, 1997).

Greg Annussek, *Hitler's Raid to Save Mussolini* (Da Capo Press, 2005).

Captain S. Payne Best, *The Venlo Incident* (Hutchinson & Co., 1949).

Branko Bokun, *Spy in the Vatican* (Vita Books, 1973).

Richard Brietman, Norman Goda, Timothy Naftali, and Robert Wolfe, *U.S. Intelligence and the Nazis* (Cambridge University Press, 2005).

Owen Chadwick, *Britain and the Vatican during the Second World War* (Cambridge University Press, 1986).

John Cornwell, *Hitler's Pope: The Secret History of Pius XII* (Penguin, 1999).

Sam Derry, *The Rome Escape Line* (George G. Harrap, 1960).

Brian Fleming, *The Vatican Pimpernel: The Wartime Exploits of Monsignor Hugh O'Flaherty* (The Collins Press, 2008).

Eric Frattini, *The Entity* (JR Books, 2010).

John Furman, *Be Not Fearful* (Anthony Blond, 1959).

J. P. Gallagher, *Scarlet Pimpernel of the Vatican* (Souvenir Press, 1967).

Guido Gerosa, *Il caso Kappler: dalle Ardeatine a Soltau* (Sonzogno, 1977).

Dominick Graham and Shelford Bidwell, *Tug of War: The Battle for Italy 1943–1945* (Pen and Sword Military Classics, 1986).

Christopher Hibbert, *Benito Mussolini* (The Reprint Society, 1962).

Wilhelm Hoettl, *The Secret Front* (Weidenfeld & Nicolson, 1953).

Anneliese Kappler, *Ich Hole Dich Heim* (self-published, 1990).

Robert Katz, *Fatal Silence: The Pope, the Resistance and the German Occupation of Rome* (Cassell, 2003).

Robert Katz, *Massacre in Rome* (Jonathan Cape, 1967).

Richard Lamb, *War in Italy 1943–1945: A Brutal Story* (Da Capo Press, 1993).

Daniel Madden, *Operation Escape: The Adventure of Father O'Flaherty* (Hawthorn Books, 1962).

Pierangelo Maurizio, *Lettere dal carcere 1948–1950* (1997).

Aidan O'Hara, *I'll Live till I Die* (Drumlin Publications, 1997).

Alessandro Portelli, *The Order Has Been Carried Out* (Palgrave Macmillan, 2003).

Ryan Report into the Rome Escape Line, National Archives, London.

Jane Scrivener, *Inside Rome with the Germans* (The Macmillan Company, 1945).

William Simpson, *A Vatican Lifeline '44* (Leo Cooper, 1995).

Raleigh Trevelyan, *Rome '44: The Battle for the Eternal City* (Book Club Associates, 1981).

Joshua Zimmerman, *Jews in Italy under Fascist and Nazi Rule 1922–1945* (Cambridge University Press, 2005).

Susan Zuccotti, *Under His Very Windows: The Vatican and the Holocaust in Italy* (Yale Nota Bene, 2002).

NEWSPAPERS AND PERIODICALS
Daily Mirror
Daily Telegraph
Guardian
Sunday Express
The Times
Irish Independent
Irish Times
New York Times
Economist
Newsweek
Reader's Digest
Time
Avanti
Il Messaggero
Osservatore Romano

FILMS AND TELEVISION PROGRAMS
Massacre in Rome, Compagnie Cinematografica Champion, 1973.
The Scarlet and the Black, Artisan, 1983.
This Is Your Life, BBC Television, February 1963.
The Pimpernel of the Vatican, Igloo Films and TG4, 2008.

Index